Indian water in the new
West /

DATE DUE

GAYLORD   PRINTED IN U.S.A.

INDIAN WATER IN THE NEW WEST

INDIAN
WATER
IN THE NEW WEST

THOMAS R. McGUIRE

WILLIAM B. LORD

MARY G. WALLACE

E D I T O R S

THE UNIVERSITY OF ARIZONA PRESS
TUCSON & LONDON

The University of Arizona Press
Copyright © 1993
Arizona Board of Regents
All Rights Reserved

♾ This book is printed on acid-free, archival-quality paper.
Manufactured in the United States of America

98 97 96 95 94 93   6 5 4 3 2 1

Library of Congress Cataloging-in-Publication Data
Indian water in the new West / Thomas R. McGuire, William B.
Lord, and Mary G. Wallace, editors.
     p.   cm.
   Includes index.
   ISBN 0-8165-1392-9 (acid-free paper)
    1. Indians of North America—West (U.S.)—Water
rights. 2. Indians of North America—West (U.S.)—
Claims. 3. Water-supply—West (U.S.) I. McGuire,
Thomas R. II. Lord, William B. III. Wallace, Mary
G., 1959–   .
KF8210.N37I55   1993
346.7304'32—dc20
[347.306432]   93-15609
                                                CIP

British Library Cataloguing-in-Publication Data
A catalogue record for this book is available from the British Library.

CONTENTS

PART V   REFLECTIONS

ACKNOWLEDGMENTS

The issues addressed in this collection were originally aired at a symposium, Indian Water Rights and Water Resources Management, which was held in Missoula, Montana, in June of 1989. The symposium was a joint effort of the American Water Resources Association and the Northern Lights Research and Education Institute. It was cosponsored by the U.S. Bureau of Indian Affairs, the Montana Forest and Range Experiment Station, the Salt River Project, the South Florida Water Management District, the U.S. Forest Service, the U.S. Geological Survey, the University of Arizona Water Resources Research Center, and the University of Montana. We appreciate the support of these organizations.

We wish, as well, to thank the U.S. Geological Survey for supporting the research project that led the three of us to collaborate on the symposium and on this volume, and to thank Hanna J. Cortner of the Water Resources Research Center, University of Arizona, which allowed one of us (MGW) the time to see it to fruition.

Finally, for their countless hours in front of one or another type of electronic machine, the editors would like to thank Magdalena Abalos, formerly with the Bureau of Applied Research in Anthropology, and the late Walter J. Allen of the Department of Anthropology, University of Arizona.

INDIAN WATER IN THE NEW WEST

INTRODUCTION:
NOTES ON CONTEXT AND FINALITY

Thomas R. McGuire

Against the emerging consensus reported here—among practitioners and observers of Indian water rights negotiations—I want to sketch a dissent. My intent is not to impugn these authors and their efforts but to put into relief the time and place in which these efforts are being made. What we face, and what these authors address, without quite saying so, is a Hobson's choice in the new, postliberal West. What these authors do with honesty and, I think, a great deal of success, is suggest how best to face this choice. It is the choice itself which I find troublesome.

The choice was most eloquently defined by a young councilwoman from the San Xavier District of the Tohono O'odham reservation near Tucson, Arizona. Addressing engineers and planners from the U.S. Bureau of Reclamation, she alluded to a curse that was to last seven generations should the bones of her ancestors be disturbed by leveling the desert for a new 9,000-acre farm. But the alternative, as she well knew, was worse. Eying the newly confirmed water supply for the district in 1983, a developer broached the idea of leasing 18,000 acres from the Indians for ninety years to house 100,000 newcomers to the Sunbelt city.

The water supply for the new farm, or the new city, was assured by the Southern Arizona Water Rights Settlement Act of 1982, an event that typifies, and indeed in many ways initiated, the historical moment that the authors herein are addressing and defining. The settlement act terminated a suit against 17,000 claimants to water in the Tucson basin. It fulfilled the Indians' rights to water under the *Winters* doctrine, the historic U.S. Supreme Court ruling that reserved water for reservations. It invoked federal and local aid to transport this supply through the aqueducts of the Central Arizona Project. Characteristically, too, the settlement act guaranteed that non-Indian water users would no longer face uncertainty over their access to water.

There is no doubt that these were all commendable outcomes, and those who have crafted subsequent water settlements have replicated, or at least striven for, similar principles. Briefly, these principles acknowledge *history,* that is, the valid claim of the Indians to water when reservations were established for them. They acknowledge *interests,* which are the competing claims by local water users as well as the legitimate fiscal responsibilities of the federal government. They embody, fundamentally, the *process* of negotiating a consensus. Finally, and inevitably, they imply issues of *use.* In the now-familiar discourse over water settlements, the Indians are about to get "wet water."

While we have used these elements to partition this collective assessment of the state of the art, it is really the conjunction of history, interests, process, and use that deeply troubled the councilwoman from San Xavier. She was, I would suspect, gratified that the settlement might fulfill the historical promise of a viable homeland, that the interests of the Tohono O'odham were being successfully advanced against the competing interests of non-Indians, that the process of negotiation had truncated a prolonged suit, and, finally, that water would come. Her concern (again, this is my suspicion) was precisely with that finality.

The choices are specific to the context: to build a new farm, to mine minerals, to industrialize, to preserve a stream for fish, to lease water to off-reservation users. But they share this finality. Indians are now making or ratifying choices— choices on quantity and use—and are thus committing their future generations. Some choices are more reversible than others; some allow options for these future generations. But few at San Xavier believed that 9,000 acres of desert land, once subjugated, would ever return to a pristine state. Few believed that 100,000 non-Indians would abandon their homes when the ninety-year lease expired. Nonetheless, few Indians are willing or able to avoid, postpone, or forgo these choices altogether. This is the crux of the issue.

The pressure for finality comes in part from refinements in the *Winters* doctrine. There was virtual unanimity throughout the non-Indian West that an open-ended, unquantified claim on water was untenable. The Supreme Court agreed in 1963, but in the process, it created a quantification standard—the amount of water needed to inundate all practicably irrigable acres of a reservation—that gave little solace to the expanding region. Thirty years later, the quantification standard remains intact, albeit by the slimmest of margins in the Supreme Court in 1989, which was, indeed, an "equally divided Court."[1] But the forum for determining Indian water rights has changed. The Supreme Court's *San Carlos* decision in 1983, which deflected general stream adjudications into the judicial forums of the various states, raised the expectations of westerners that such courts would respond to their desires and demands. Ultimately, though, the import of *San Carlos* lay not in the presumed beneficence of one judicial forum or another but in the fact that it assured a forum. General stream adjudications could be brought against tribes and the government—whether they liked it or not. Thus, by the 1980s, the judicial mechanisms were in place to finalize Indian claims to water. Negotiation became, for many, an attractive alternative.

But judicial refinements to *Winters* and the growing demands on a scarce resource account only in part for the finality contained in recent settlements and adjudications in the West. These resolutions are also, I would argue, embodiments of what legal scholar Bryant Garth identifies as the "post-liberal agenda" that took shape in the 1980s, an agenda of "reduced government spending, fewer social programs, containment of the rights explosion, and the creation of a more harmonious, spiritual social order where 'less is more.'"[2]

In the West—the new West—there is an economic ideology that fits comfortably with this political agenda. In the wake of the aborted Sagebrush Rebellion, which would simply have substituted one level of bureaucracy for another, a compelling move toward privatization of resources has taken place. Most directly, this is manifested in the growth recently of water markets, predicated on a notion of a well-defined property right. Efficient use of resources will result, the argument goes, if those resources are exclusively owned and transferable: water will flow from low-valued uses to high-valued ones, from farms to cities. And the transactions need take place with little interference from a postliberal government.

Water in the West remains inherently poorly defined as long as *Winters* rights are outstanding and undetermined. For this contemporary western political economy to function, such rights must be clarified and finalized. These rights, following the directive of *Arizona v. California,* no doubt would have been quantified eventually. But the postliberal agenda of the 1980s brought such processes to the fore.

Virtually all of the writers here acknowledge the obvious irony: the extension of this new economic philosophy slows, even stops, at the borders of Indian Country. Well-defined property rights are, by definition, transferable, but the transferability of Indian water has haunted all of the settlements examined in this collection. The issue is volatile and as yet unresolved. The reason is clear: there is widespread fear that Indians will become the water brokers of the West, extracting rents for their unused entitlements from those now using that water. If so, the federal government in this postliberal era is beginning to argue, so be it. The rents thus extracted could be used in lieu of direct federal funding to underwrite social and economic programs on the reservations. The revenues could be used, in short, to foster the intent of *Winters:* to create economically viable tribal homelands.

3

There is logic in this concept, but again it returns us to the conundrum of finality. Does this presage a new phase of termination, the end to federal supervision and support of the reservation system? Perhaps it does, but as yet we cannot tell. Perhaps, many argue, it *should*. Indians have become competent to manage their own affairs, to use and (perhaps) to market their water entitlements. The problem has been, in many cases, that they have not owned "their own affairs." Timber has been cut by outsiders, minerals mined by outsiders, land cultivated by outsiders. There is hope, now that Indians are coming to own water through these settlements, compacts, and adjudications, that this situation will change.

The participants and observers of these processes reach few firm conclusions here. This is necessarily so. Although substantial progress has been made and a number of settlements have been negotiated and signed and are now being implemented, we are still in the early stages of this new era. What this collection seeks to do, simply, is to report accurately on the events and lessons of these early years of conflict and resolution in the new West. There is a consensus here that these conflicts need resolution and compromise. Over the results to date, and the prospects for the future, there is less unanimity. Some of the writers here are optimistic, some skeptical, and some more cautiously analytical. There is at the present, I think, an equally divided court.

NOTES

1. The subsequent fate of this decision is traced by Katherine Collins in "Water: Fear of Supreme Court Leads Tribes to Accept an Adverse Decision," *High Country News* 24 (19), October 19, 1992. Although the standard of practicably irrigable acreage was not abrogated by recent actions of Wyoming courts, tribal control over some of the award has been diminished.

2. Bryant Garth, "The Movement Toward Procedural Informalism in North America and Western Europe: A Critical Survey," in *The Politics of Informal Justice*, vol. 2, ed. Richard Abel (New York: Academic Press, 1982), p. 196.

PART I   HISTORY

1

INDIAN WATER RIGHTS CONFLICTS IN PERSPECTIVE

David H. Getches

The *Winters* doctrine of reserved water rights has been viewed by western states and their non-Indian water users with fear and loathing. Commentators have referred to it ominously as a "cloud" on western water rights and in other disparaging terms.[1] Its application is seen as a threat to the survival of established non-Indian economies and communities.[2] The doctrine was created to resolve a dispute arising on the Fort Belknap Indian Reservation in north-central Montana.[3] Shortly after the doctrine turned eighty years old, the United States Supreme Court narrowly upheld its application in a water rights dispute involving the Wind River Indian Reservation in Wyoming.[4]

Indian tribes cling tenaciously to the Supreme Court's noble pronouncements of their water rights as if these incantations were enough to irrigate dry reservation lands. In reality, the impacts of eighty years of "prior and paramount" Indian water rights have been modest. The story of the aftermath of the famous, vigorously contested *Winters* case, and its reaffirmation in several other reserved rights cases of this century, does not justify the strong sentiments evoked by the doctrine. Neither the hopeful expectations of the Indians nor the grave fears of the non-Indians have been realized.

The Indians' hopes may nevertheless be legitimate. The Colorado River Indian Tribes secured their rights in the Supreme Court's 1963 decision in *Arizona v. California*.[5] It has taken a long time, but they are finally enjoying the fruits of their victory. Large-scale farming operations on the tribes' reservation, which straddles the Colorado River, are now profitable, and the value of the tribes' water rights is supporting the issuance of bonds for a new water and sewer system.

The non-Indians' fears are not insubstantial either. In 1988, as drought parched much of Wyoming, the state supreme court's decision in the Wind River case gave the tribes of that reservation a legal basis for altering a long-standing regime for using the waters of the Wind River. The prior rights of the tribes to use a large quantity of water resulted in limits on non-Indian irrigators' water diversions so that a fishery could be maintained through the distress of a dry year. The limits were few and their duration short. But the non-Indians tasted what the decision could portend.

For a law as old and notorious as the Indian reserved rights doctrine, one would anticipate serial stories of dashed non-Indian expectations and of satisfied tribal ambitions for wealth and security. But those stories are few; Indian reserved rights are still not being fully utilized. Most of this century has passed without the tribes' being able to enjoy the benefits of the doctrine and thus without unduly upsetting the established uses of non-Indians or even preventing new uses. Realizing the full potential of the doctrine is increasingly difficult; today, non-Indian water uses, which are laying claim to most of the West's water, have been firmly cemented by the passage of time.

The reserved rights doctrine has had a mercurial history. It lay dormant for about half a century, after which it went through a rather agonized period of clarification, first being strengthened, then being limited in a number of ways. The most significant limitation, however, was not the result of principled considerations of equity or law but rather was the consequence of massive water development for the benefit of non-Indians, made possible by large federal subsidies. Nevertheless, the states, the tribes, and the United States have options open to them to make the application of the tribes' reserved rights workable and fair, while still consistent with emerging notions of wise and efficient water use.

The Origin of Reserved Water Rights

Until the last quarter of the nineteenth century, the expanse of unoccupied western land seemed limitless. But as settlers moved west to fulfill the destiny of the United States, it became obvious that the Indians were in the way. Treaties were negotiated with the idea of confining tribes to a defined area where they could have their independence. There they would hunt, gather, and fish. They would run their own affairs. But outside the tribes' defined territories, non-Indians could settle, states could grow, and the laws of the non-Indians would apply to all.

The hunger of non-Indians for more and more land was hard to satisfy, and so successive treaties were often sought a few years apart. The government explained to the Indians that the pressures of settlement—the lust for land and the greed for gold—were so great that it could not protect the tribes' large land areas from intrusions by non-Indians. If the Indians would agree to be confined to small land areas, the United States would promise to protect their borders from non-Indian intruders and would promise not to seek any further land cessions. Rarely were either of these promises long kept.[6]

The United States also promised tribes who had ranged over vast areas in search of their subsistence that the government would assist them with the necessities of life so that they could survive in new endeavors on their diminished lands. This usually meant giving them tools and training so that they could make a living from farming and giving them rations to make up for the fact that their lands were frequently too limited in scope or fertility to produce sufficient commodities for their survival.

The fate of the Fort Belknap Reservation is typical of the historical pattern in some respects, not so in others. By an 1855 treaty, Indians of several tribes agreed with the United States that they would limit the territory used by them to most of what is now north-central Montana.[7] Many of the tribes lived by traditional pursuits of hunting and gathering that took them throughout the vast territory. Running through their territory or bordering it were numerous substantial rivers, including about 450 miles of the Missouri River. In 1874, Congress designated boundaries for the Great Blackfeet Indian Reservation, constituting less than half of the 1855 territory.[8] The reservation was for the use of the Gros Ventre, Piegan, Blood, Blackfeet, and River Crow Indians. It was bordered by a long stretch of the Missouri River, bisected by the Milk River (a major tributary of the Missouri), and crossed by a number of other tributaries. When pressures for non-Indian settlement in the area mounted, the United States sought out several of the tribal groups within the 1874 reservation, again asking them to cede additional territory in return for their security on smaller reservations.

In 1888, the tribes signed an agreement ceding all their lands except for three reservations (Fort Belknap, Fort Peck, and Blackfeet). The Gros Ventre and Assiniboine secured rights to occupy the Fort Belknap Indian Reservation.[9] It was a tiny fraction of the area ceded. The 1888 agreement described the northern boundary of the reservation as the center of the Milk River. Only one other tributary stream of any significance was included in the new reservation.

Immediately after the 1888 agreement was signed, settlers began moving into the area relinquished by the tribes. They eventually acquired titles under the homestead and desert land laws of the United States. The settlers had been encouraged by the United States to occupy the area and to establish farms. Consistent with the Desert Land Act, settlers began appropriating water from the Milk River and its tributaries according to the laws of the territory of Montana (and state laws after Montana achieved statehood in 1889).

The Indians struggled to eke out an existence in an arid and hostile environment. The settlers established communities on the north side of the Milk River and created various ditch and irrigation companies. The United States held out hope for a federally supported reclamation project to assist their irrigation efforts.

About the same time that settlers began irrigating and producing crops, Indians began diverting small amounts of water. The history of the Fort Belknap Reservation is different from others in one important respect. The United States acted soon after the reservation was established to develop water in order to assist the tribes in making their homeland livable. The United States through the Indian Irrigation Office planned and began an irrigation project for the Fort Belknap Reservation. By 1898, the Indians were diverting water with a canal constructed under this project. Seeing the tribes' diversion, the settlers built upstream dams and reservoirs to ensure that they would not be left with insufficient water.

After the homesteaders began their upstream diversions, the Department of the Interior decided to take legal action to protect water needed for the Indian project. At first, the Department of Justice believed, based on information received from the Indian agent, that the Indian irrigation project had begun using water before any settlers had. This enabled the government to proceed against the settlers, invoking the prior appropriation doctrine. As it turned out, the government's legal claim was not limited to prior appropriation grounds, nor could it have been.

A maverick U.S. attorney for the state of Montana took up the tribes' cause. He was not content to wrap their claim in the language of established legal entitlements and argued on several innovative theories that it would be wrong to deprive them of water needed for their reservation. It was fortunate that he pleaded these novel grounds because it turned out that the settlers had actually begun taking some water before the Indians. Though the U.S. attorney was pressured by his superiors in Washington to retreat from the bold, unpopular claims that did not rest solely on prior appropriation, he persisted. He persuaded the United States District Court for the District of Montana to grant an injunction against the settlers, preventing their interference with water needed for the tribes' irrigation project.[10]

The local judge's decision was affirmed by the Ninth Circuit Court of Appeals and then by the United States Supreme Court.[11] The U.S. attorney's advocacy for Indian rights and the clear victories he secured in three courts seems surprising. This was an era that venerated the pioneer spirit of individual settlers conquering the West. The United States induced the settlers to move into inhospitable territory to try their hand at farming. Many gave up their homes in the East, uprooted their families, and exhausted their savings in efforts to start a new life in the rugged lands of Montana. It could not have been easy for the courts to reject their claims to water. The difficulty was compounded by a contemporary western infatuation with a new idea for water allocation that was taking hold in state after state—prior appropriation.

The miner's ethic taught that the first person to stake a claim to minerals on the public land and to begin working a deposit would have the right to those minerals. The same principle of "first in time, first in right" was extended to water on the public land and later even to private land.[12] Congress was slow to give any indication of how it wanted to parcel out waters on the public lands. Finally, it dealt obliquely with the subject in three statutes enacted between 1862 and 1877.[13] The federal government essentially deferred to the laws of the western states and, where there were no laws, to local customs of the miners. Thus, to favor the tribes in *Winters* meant ruling against the prior user who had the better rights according to the emerging western doctrine.

So the decision in *Winters* was surely difficult politically, but it must not have been entirely out of line with prevailing notions of justice. What would cause a government attorney to proceed against the will of his superiors, bucking the political tide, and to beseech a circuit court covering several western states (and, ultimately, the Supreme Court) to uphold a novel theory? It must have been clear that the tribes' position was fundamentally and morally "right" and ought to be vindicated.

To put the case in perspective, it helps to look at the milieu in which it was decided. Remember that the prior appropriation doctrine, now so familiar and well-established throughout the West, was relatively new. At the time *Winters* was decided, details of the prior appropriation doctrine were still being crafted by courts and legislatures. Furthermore, although the records are unclear, the "priority" of the senior settlers appears to have been by only four days.

The manifest unfairness of a finding for the settlers—a finding that the Indians retained no water rights for their diminished lands—would have created a race for the use of waters from tribal lands. The federal government was in the process of fulfilling its promise to help the Indians develop ways to survive primarily through agricultural pursuits. To deny access to water needed for those purposes would have read into the agreement a hidden condition that would have undermined the Indians' chances of succeeding.

The cruel irony of such a result was recognized by the Supreme Court in the *Winters* decision when it said: "It would be extreme to believe that . . . Congress destroyed the reservation [by letting others appropriate the water] and took from the Indians the consideration of their grant, leaving them a barren waste—took from them the means of continuing their old habits, yet did not leave them the power to change to new ones."[14]

The Supreme Court could have interpreted the agreement's silence as to water rights to mean that the tribes had given up the water on their lands. Instead, it found that the agreement's silence implied that the tribes had retained a right to use water to fulfill the purposes of the agreement.[15] The issue did not detain the Court for long. The opinion was short—only a few pages. The Court held that creating the reservation had had the effect of reserving water rights to the tribes.

There may have been a practical as well as a moral motive for the Court's decision. To have decided otherwise would have pleased a handful of settlers, but it also could have been so unfair to the tribes as to erode the underpinnings of federal public land policy. All the land in the West came from the Indians. The security of non-Indian occupancy of that land and the viability of schemes to open more Indian lands to non-Indian settlement could be thrown into question if the consideration for Indian land cessions failed. This might have been argued if the Fort Belknap agreement and other similar agreements were read to deny the tribes the water needed to make the arrangements workable and just. If tribes that had been promised viable homelands on the vestiges of their former territory were actually condemned to places where survival was impossible, they might have left those lands to reoccupy their traditional areas. Thwarting them would have meant more bloodshed than the nation could tolerate.

Although the outcome in *Winters* may have been fundamentally just, it did not seem fair at the time from the perspective of the settlers. The outcome might theoretically have been equitable, but it fit awkwardly at best with the prior appropriation doctrine that underlay all other water rights on the river. Though reserved rights were designed to follow the hierarchy that determines which rights to water are superior to others in the prior appropriation system, they depart in an important way: the priority date for reserved rights is not the date Indians started *using* particular quantities of water but the date that the reservation was established.

The fact that the reserved right is not based on use causes several potential problems for appropriators. Besides going against the grain of a system that commits rights to resources based on productive efforts, it creates uncertainty. Those who have grown dependent on using water could have their expectations disappointed when a tribe with reserved rights later decides to use its water. To make matters worse, the amount of water that the tribes are entitled to use is uncertain. Thus, an appropriator who begins using water after an Indian reservation is established cannot dependably estimate how much will be available in the stream if and when the tribe begins taking its water. Until the reserved right has been "quantified," non-Indian neighbors must guess at the level of impact.

The reserved rights doctrine holds that the tribes did not give up the water needed to make their reservation "valuable or adequate" both "as an Indian reservation and for a permanent home and abiding place."[16] This potentially means that the tribes could later use all the available water. Subsequent decisions, however, have tied specific quantities of tribally reserved waters to particular uses needed to fulfill the broad purposes of an Indian reservation. Uses such as agricultural irrigation, fishing and hunting, and power generation have been recognized by the courts.[17] The Supreme Court has not been called upon to decide whether quantities of water based on these uses constitute the outer limits of rights that could be claimed.[18] Instead, the cases focus on uses that the tribes and the United States had clearly intended to promote when the reservation was established (usually farming), and this has resulted in standards that produce entitlements to enormous quantities of water. Once a tribe's reserved water rights are quantified according to their needs for a particular purpose (e.g., agricultural irrigation), the tribe can apply the water to any other beneficial use.[19] Because quantifications have been based on specific, high water-demand uses, most tribes have few practical limitations on their ability to use water for almost any purpose.

Evolution of the Reserved Rights Doctrine

Since the 1908 *Winters* decision, the evolution of the Indian reserved water rights doctrine can be characterized by two major stages. The first was a period of neglect that persisted for over 50 years after the decision was handed down. The second, a period of increased legal activity, began with the decision in *Arizona v. California.*

The Period of Neglect: 1908 to 1963

Winters was decided in an era of intensive water development in the West. A few years before, the 1902 Reclamation Act established the reclamation program to aid the settlement of the arid West by yeoman farmers.[20] In the years following *Winters,* dam and canal construction achieved its apex. Almost no major watershed in the West was left untouched. Indian tribes had prior rights under the reserved rights doctrine to significant quantities of the same water demanded by reclamation projects, but the delivery and storage systems built by the U.S. Bureau of Reclamation were for the benefit of non-Indians.

Indians' needs were often neglected while their non-Indian neighbors received generous subsidies to develop water. The National Water Commission, in its 1973 report to the president and Congress, assessed the situation during this period as follows:

> Following *Winters,* . . . the United States was pursuing a policy of encouraging the settlement of the West and the creation of family-sized farms on its arid lands. In retrospect, it can be seen that this policy was pursued with little or no regard for Indian water rights and the *Winters* doctrine. With the encouragement, or at least the cooperation, of the Secretary of the Interior—the very office entrusted with the protection of all Indian rights—many large irrigation projects were constructed on streams that flowed through or bordered Indian Reservations, sometimes above and

more often below the Reservations. With few exceptions the projects were planned and built by the Federal Government without any attempt to define, let alone protect, prior rights that Indian tribes might have had in the waters used for the projects. . . . In the history of the United States Government's treatment of Indian tribes, its failure to protect Indian water rights for use on the Reservations it set aside for them is one of the sorrier chapters.[21]

Two developments contributed to ending the period of neglect of Indian reserved water rights. Neither had to do with a concern for the tribes' welfare. Both were connected with efforts to confront uncertainty in entitlements to use increasingly scarce water resources in the West, an issue that unavoidably encountered the existence of inchoate Indian rights.

Allocation of the Waters of the Colorado River / The quantities of reserved rights held by the United States and the Indian tribes of the Colorado River became an issue in an original action (a lawsuit that began in the United States Supreme Court) initiated by the state of Arizona against California and Nevada. Efforts to achieve an interstate apportionment of waters in the river among the states of the Colorado basin had been proceeding on a number of fronts since the early 1920s and culminated in this epic litigation that was filed in 1956.[22]

Consent to Adjudicate Federal Water Rights in State Courts / In 1952, Congress passed a law allowing the United States to be joined as a defendant in state court adjudications of all the water rights in a stream system to determine the extent of federal rights relative to the rights of all others.[23] The law, known as the McCarran Amendment, waived the government's immunity from suit where "the United States is the owner of . . . water rights." The waiver was later held by the Supreme Court to apply to Indian reserved rights as well as to all federal water rights.

The result of the Colorado River apportionment was a reaffirmation of the *Winters* decision and the announcement of a standard for quantification of Indian reserved rights when a reservation is established primarily for agricultural purposes. Thus, the Court looked at the circumstances of the five Indian reservations along the main stem of the Colorado River to determine what was necessary to make them adequate "permanent homes and abiding places" for the tribes in question. There was copious evidence that the United States and the Indians intended the dry desert lands to be put into agriculture. This required irrigation water. The Supreme Court appointed a special master to hear evidence in the case, and he recommended a formula for determining the amount of water necessary to achieve the agricultural purposes of the reservations. The first step is to identify all the practicably irrigable acreage (PIA), next to determine how much water is required to irrigate an acre in that vicinity, then to calculate the quantity of water to which the tribes were entitled by multiplying the two figures. The Court also extended the reserved rights doctrine to imply a reservation of rights for federal lands set aside for specific purposes as well as for Indian reservations set aside as tribal homelands.[24]

The Period of Readjustment: 1963 to 1989

Beginning with the decision in *Arizona v. California,* legal activity related to Indian reserved water rights increased dramatically. This period was marked by a series of lawsuits concerning the proper court to adjudicate Indian reserved rights. The McCarran Amendment described above was the basis for attempts by a number of states to join the United States in basinwide adjudications of federal and Indian rights. The United States and Indian tribes vigorously resisted the inclusion of reserved rights under the terms of the McCarran Amendment. First, they argued that the amendment applied only to water rights acquired under state law or by other methods. Second, they argued that even if the statute did apply to reserved rights, it did not apply to Indian reserved water rights. The argument was that Indian rights are essentially privately owned property rights that the United States holds in trust for the tribes, not water rights "owned" by the United States. Finally, the government and the tribes argued that even if the McCarran Amendment applied to Indian water rights in some states (such as Colorado) whose constitutions and statehood enabling acts do not disclaim jurisdiction over Indian lands, it could not apply to Indian water rights in other states (such as Montana and Arizona) with express disclaimers of jurisdiction over Indian lands.

The Supreme Court accepted none of these arguments. The Court made it abundantly clear that the quantities of water to which Indians are entitled under the reserved rights doctrine are to be decided in state courts.[25] In reply to expressions of concern by the United States and the tribes about the fairness and competence of state forums to decide federal and Indian rights, the Supreme Court reiterated a pledge to act as the final arbiter of reserved rights determinations.

Since the first decision in the line of cases establishing state court jurisdiction, dozens of cases seeking quantification of Indian and federal reserved rights have been initiated by states. In fact, however, the dire predictions of disregard of Indian rights and inherent bias have not been realized. Only one Indian reserved water rights case has been fully litigated in the state courts. The Big Horn case decided in 1989 applied the reserved rights doctrine to find the Wind River tribes entitled to nearly half a million acre-feet of water.[26] Reserved rights to water for federal lands, as well as Indian lands, are being adjudicated and quantified in state courts throughout the West. In these cases, the federal government is winning on some points and losing on others. For instance, the United States won the right to present claims in Colorado state courts for rights to sufficient flows in national forest streams to flush out and scour stream channels.[27] This decision came after

15

the Supreme Court looked restrictively at national forest purposes in *United States v. New Mexico* and found that the United States had not reserved in-stream flows for recreation or fish and wildlife.[28] Federal attorneys then sought to present evidence that they needed water to maintain the stream channels for water flows. If the state courts were inherently biased against reserved rights claims, the earlier Supreme Court decision could have provided an excuse for the Colorado court to rule against the government on all in-stream flow claims in the national forest.

Perhaps proponents of reserved water rights have fared as well in state courts as they would have in federal court. The greatest setbacks have been in the United States Supreme Court. Without abandoning the doctrine itself, the Court (upon whom Indians ultimately depend to safeguard their rights) has, with few exceptions, acted to narrow and limit the assertion of reserved rights in every decision since *Arizona v. California* in 1963. Thus, the Court's promise to oversee quantification cases has been of doubtful value to tribes or the government in practice.

The decision in *United States v. New Mexico* narrowed the scope of federal reserved rights when it said the purpose of national forests could not justify protecting stream flows for wildlife or livestock. Perhaps the worst setbacks for Indian reserved rights, however, were in two cases involving tribal attempts to reopen or expand upon court decisions quantifying their rights. In one case, the Court rejected an attempt by the Pyramid Lake Paiute Tribe to litigate its claim for water rights to satisfy the purpose of setting aside the reservation as a fishery.[29] The tribe showed that decades earlier the United States (plagued by a major conflict of interest because of its obligations to protect and promote development of water for the Newlands Reclamation Project, which benefits primarily non-Indians) had not adequately represented the tribe's competing claim to water rights. The government claimed only a small amount of water for the tribe to irrigate its lands. The people were not farmers, but fishermen, yet no water was claimed to keep the lake viable as a fishery. Years later, the Supreme Court denied the tribe an opportunity to protect its own water rights. Though the fishery purposes of the reservation were not in doubt, the Court invoked the strong interest of achieving finality in western water rights determinations and said that the earlier decision could not be revisited.

Similarly, in an attempted reopening of *Arizona v. California,* the five Colorado River tribes were denied the opportunity to present evidence on various irrigable lands that had been omitted from the government's claim because of neglect or mistakes by federal attorneys, or because the reservation boundaries had not been finally determined at the time the 1963 decision was handed down. The Court again expressed its concern with assuring certainty and finality in water rights determinations and denied the tribes virtually any opportunity to expand the quantity of water rights to which they were entitled.[30]

The upshot of these cases is that tribes are bound by quantifications notwithstanding the inadequacy or incompetence of the legal representation of the United States or the existence of a clear federal conflict of interests. In the future, tribes would be best advised not to rely entirely upon representation of the United States but to participate fully in the litigation through independent counsel.

Tribes feared a retreat from the principles of reserved rights when the United States Supreme Court accepted Wyoming's petition to review the Big Horn decision (*Wyoming v. United States*). The state, recognizing the huge quantity of water awarded to the tribes by the state courts, challenged the practicably irrigable acreage standard for quantifying rights for agricultural purposes. The Wyoming Supreme Court decision, however, was affirmed by a deadlocked United States Supreme Court.

Both sides claimed the state court had erred. The tribes complained that they were denied the right to water for energy development purposes and that the court ambiguously indicated that they had no right to groundwater. The tribes also objected to being held to a standard of irrigation efficiency in future water development more rigorous than the standard applicable to non-Indians. Wyoming petitioned for *certiorari,* attempting to get the Court to find that the application of the practicably irrigable acreage standard was unfair and improper under the circumstances of the case. The Court agreed to hear the case only on the state's petition challenging the PIA standard but would not hear the tribes' arguments that the decision contained some elements unfavorable to them. The eight members of the Court hearing the case were split equally.

The decision in *Wyoming v. United States* affirmed, though narrowly, the state court quantification of Indian reserved water rights and reaffirmed the general principles of reserved rights traceable to *Winters* and *Arizona v. California*. As such, the Court refused to disrupt the many years of reliance on those principles and the established method for applying them. The basic doctrine and its corollary—the quantification standard where agricultural purposes are involved—appear to be here to stay. For the Court to have decided otherwise would have been a radical departure that would have upset past and pending efforts to resolve quantity issues through negotiation as well as through litigation. Since the first session of Congress following the decision in *Winters,* Congress has had many opportunities to abrogate, limit, or modify the *Winters* doctrine. It has not taken any of those opportunities. Repeated proposals to alter the doctrine have not been able to garner sufficient political support.[31] This court-made doctrine, then, seems sealed by congressional acquiescence.

During the period of readjustment, the Supreme Court reaffirmed the reserved rights doctrine while making it less attractive to tribes. Since the decision of *Arizona v. California* in 1963, the Court has tempered the application of the reserved rights doctrine to restrict quantities of water available to the federal government. Tribes have been denied the ability to reexamine flawed adjudications of the past. And the Court has left the determination of Indian water rights to the state courts. But the cornerstones of the doctrine remain fundamentally intact.

The Big Horn case gave the Supreme Court an opportunity to rethink the rudiments of reserved rights. The present Court is one of the most politically oriented panels to occupy the office in this century. It is also the most western of any Court in the period, with four members coming from prior appropriation states. If any court were to respond to the cries of western states that the PIA standard is too generous and that the reserved rights doctrine needs to be curbed, the Big Horn case would have presented the opportunity. Nevertheless, the Court could not muster the five votes needed for a reversal. It did not bend to the enormous pressures and resentments that were reflected in *amicus curiae* briefs and publicity.

The greatest erosion of Indian rights under *Winters* was not at the hands of the Court during the period of readjustment. Nor has Congress expressly abrogated those rights. Instead, the doctrine was sapped of much of its value to Indians by a water development scheme cast during the period of neglect that allocated to non-Indians the very water to which Indians are entitled. This is best illustrated by the irrigation system on the Fort Belknap Reservation, where the *Winters* case arose. This project, which started operating around the turn of the century, is still only half complete, and the portion of the project that is complete has fallen into disrepair. If use of water by the tribes on the Fort Belknap Reservation presents no immediate threat to non-Indians drawing on the Milk River, it is because the tribes still lack adequate means to develop their water more than eighty years after their rights to do so were heralded in the Supreme Court's decision.

Today the Milk River is heavily appropriated, being allocated by a treaty between the United States and Canada and used by several water projects that have been developed in the area. One project resulted in construction of a dam upstream of the reservation. The tribes agreed to the project in return for a fractional interest in the stored water. But between 1983 and 1985 a severe drought led the Bureau of Reclamation and the Bureau of Indian Affairs to decide not to release any water and to close the Fort Belknap irrigation project. The tribes believed that this decision ignored their senior reserved right, and they sued.[32] The suit was dismissed after late summer rains made releases of water possible.

The Future: A Period of Fulfillment?

Indian tribes are becoming acutely aware that the application of court-made doctrine is not enough to meet their water needs. The power of formidable paper rights is significant in getting the attention of other water users and states, but it falls short of delivering wet water.

Most western states have initiated litigation that enables them to join the United

States to represent and adjudicate Indian water rights. The cost of these adjudications, however, is enormous for everyone involved. Furthermore, once a number is put on Indian water rights in a quantification proceeding, uncertainties linger over whether or when water will be developed. This has caused states and non-Indian water users to gravitate to the negotiating table.

These practical concerns of states converge with a growing willingness among western state officials to deal with tribes as sovereign entities. The credibility of Indian tribes as governments has been enhanced by major legal developments parallel to the battles over the meaning of reserved rights since *Arizona v. California*. Tribes and states have spent decades in often-bitter confrontations over which sovereign has jurisdiction over activities on reservations. The result has been a series of strong judicial pronouncements upholding tribal governmental status to convince states that tribes do indeed have powers of self-government over their members and territory.[33]

As the basic principles of Indian reserved rights have become solidly ensconced in the law, and as tribal governments have been received with greater respect by states, tribes have gained greater faith in the negotiation process. It is largely through negotiation, I believe, that they will be able to determine what the doctrine means in practice. It is now reasonable to expect the parties in the Big Horn case to negotiate what the decision means to them and how it will apply in practice. Many years and millions of dollars spent on litigation have provided certainty only about the quantities of water that are at stake, not when, where, and by whom water will actually be used and who will administer the rights.[34]

Litigation is a starting point for sharpening the issues and articulating the positions of the parties. Negotiation is a more promising vehicle for reaching a meaningful, practical resolution that provides the Indians with deliverable water and non-Indians with genuine certainty. Indeed, nearly all of the successful Indian water rights settlements in the past few years began with litigation. Yet a genuine resolution of approximately fifty pending lawsuits will ultimately depend on negotiations.

The Big Horn litigation can have substantial value to the tribes in reserved rights cases. The Supreme Court's reluctance to meddle with the quantification standard should mark the end of quibbling over the basic doctrine. The Court has said, albeit shrouded in the ambiguity of a decision without opinion on an equally divided vote, that *Winters* and its progeny are the law. The Court is unlikely to revisit those basic questions; therefore, parties are well advised to proceed to find practical solutions.

Solutions to the actual and anticipated problems of water users, Indian and non-Indian alike, can be worked out and can be made compatible with state water allocation systems. Practical arrangements, designed by mutual agreement, can realize the benefits of Indian rights without major dislocations of non-Indian

19

water users. Whether the future marks a period of fulfillment of Indian reserved water rights—fulfillment consistent with today's federal policy of Indian self-determination and without sacrificing fairness toward non-Indians whose rights have been affected—depends on the level of federal commitment and participation.

The United States has a well-recognized trustee relationship with Indian tribes. Indians legitimately look to the federal government for protection and assertion of their rights.[35] The federal government, however, has not always been a reliable participant in negotiated settlements of Indian reserved water rights cases. Although the Departments of the Interior and Justice typically encourage negotiated resolutions of these disputes, they do not have a consistent policy to guide their participation. Their role does not resemble that of a fiduciary whose paramount interest is in furthering Indian rights and well-being. Moreover, non-Indian parties are understandably perplexed by the lack of clear indications of the federal position. Often, federal representatives participating in negotiations have limited authority, and sometimes their directions are contrary to the directions of representatives of other federal agencies who are in the same negotiations.

A federal commitment of funds is often a necessary ingredient in settlement negotiations because the development of storage or delivery facilities is needed to produce wet water for both Indians and non-Indians. The Office of Management and Budget generally resists large expenditures for these purposes. The Reagan and Bush administrations took the position that their obligation to protect Indian water rights was limited to pursuing litigation. Thus, they estimated the financial exposure in litigation and used that estimate to limit the sums that they would spend for actual water development. This is effectively a disclaimer of the federal government's responsibility for the economic, social, cultural, and political implications of prolonged denial of effective access to tribal resources and for protecting the future of reservations as tribal homelands. Furthermore, it denies any moral or political responsibility for having created an inequitable situation in which tribal rights are denied, on one hand, and non-Indian uses are threatened by disruption, on the other.

It is especially appropriate that the United States supports the tribes' ability to use and develop their own water. The announced federal Indian policy is one of promoting self-determination. The United States and, increasingly, the states are recognizing that tribes are sovereign entities as they were before the founding of the nation. The federal policy of Indian self-determination includes components of economic self-sufficiency and rights of self-government. The policy can only have meaning if tribes have the ability to use their own natural resources productively.

The United States should articulate the components of a federal policy for Indian water rights settlements. Some components of an ad hoc policy can be gleaned from the recent experiences of tribes and their non-Indian neighbors in a number of states. Since 1982, Congress has approved fourteen settlement agreements to resolve the reserved water rights claims of Indian tribes.[36] Four elements were common to each of those settlement packages:

1. A federal investment in water development facilities or acquisition of water to enable tribes to put their water to use without impairing established non-Indian uses
2. Significant nonfederal cost sharing—state and local contributions toward the costs of project construction and other elements of the settlement
3. Creation of substantial Indian trust funds from federal and nonfederal moneys that may be used by the tribes to develop their water and for other purposes
4. Limited off-reservation water marketing, allowing tribes to gain economic benefits from their water resources and non-Indians to use water that would otherwise be unavailable if tribes put it all to use on the reservations

These elements did not result from a deliberate federal policy, but without further explanation by the executive branch or Congress, they furnish a framework for parties seeking to direct future negotiations toward a politically feasible outcome.

Recent settlements approved by Congress achieved the goals of successful negotiated dispute resolution. They gave the parties more certainty. They left everyone in a better position than the parties could have expected if the tribes' litigation had succeeded. The outcome in each case was generally considered to be fair. Success was only possible, however, because Congress was willing to contribute funds that exceeded the estimated cost of litigation (though, in most cases, not by much). This contribution recognized a trust relationship broader than a duty to engage in defense of legal rights in litigation. It also reflected a policy of equity toward non-Indian water users.

The government's role in the process of reaching recent settlements of Indian reserved water rights and the manner in which Congress dealt with some of the settlement packages can be criticized. First, the settlements were accomplished only after overcoming stiff opposition at a number of levels within the federal establishment to construction financing, acquisition of water rights, and Indian trust funds. Obviously, the parties to such negotiations are not entitled to a blank check. Yet they are entitled to know the principles that will guide the federal government in determining the level of its financial commitment.

Second, some in Congress took a crabbed approach to Indian water marketing. There is no principled reason to deny Indians the same right to market water enjoyed by other water users in prior appropriation states. States impose reasonable limitations, designed to avoid injury to other water users, on everyone's right to change the place or purpose of water uses. Presumably the same restraints would apply to Indian water rights. In addition, the United States may have an interest in ensuring satisfaction of international obligations regarding a water source and in preserving the integrity of interstate compacts. But beyond such basic protections, it is difficult to imagine the reason for a federal policy that would limit leases, exchanges, and other arrangements for off-reservation use of Indian water rights. To do so is a backhanded way of curtailing the quantity of water rights to which tribes are entitled under the reserved rights doctrine.

It is reasonable to expect several more Indian water settlement agreements to be negotiated in the near future. The process allows for optimal solutions to difficult problems. Consider the recent agreement among the Pyramid Lake Paiute Tribe, the state of Nevada, the Sierra Pacific Power Company, and local governmental agencies.[37] Under the agreement, non-Indian water users are to receive the right to 39,500 acre-feet of water to cover shortages in times of drought. The tribes are guaranteed a steady flow of water into Pyramid Lake to protect their historic fishery. Endangered species of fish jeopardized by low lake levels in the past will be protected. The United States will buy water to supplement flows and to improve fish habitat. Non-Indian water users in a three-county area must adopt conservation measures, including the installation of water meters. This agreement is remarkable, considering that eighty years of litigation failed to produce a result satisfactory to the many interests that had a stake in the conflict. Though the legal battles generated more than a dozen reported federal cases and two Supreme Court decisions, they did not solve water problems for the tribe or its neighbors. The Pyramid Lake settlement is a paradigm for Indian water settlements, showing that Indian hopes staked on the *Winters* decision can be vindicated without harsh consequences for non-Indians.

Conclusions

Whether tribes and states can succeed in efforts to negotiate Indian reserved water rights depends heavily on the federal commitment to the process. If the government articulates a policy of settlement compatible with its well-established policy of self-determination, success is possible. The policy should include, at a minimum, statements concerning the level of financial commitment of the federal government, how equity for non-Indians will be achieved, standards for ensuring efficient use of water, and principles concerning water marketing. The federal government should also support the negotiation process through adequate technical assistance to the tribes. Finally, Congress itself must fulfill commitments arrived at through the negotiation process. It should avoid second-guessing and politicizing an agreement that is delivered to it by Indians and their non-Indian neighbors.

The neglect of Indian water rights that characterized the half-century after *Winters* will not be repeated. The reality and strength of Indian reserved water rights was entrenched during the period of readjustment that began with *Arizona v. California* and culminated in *Wyoming v. United States*. At the same time, tribes gained new strength as governments. Federal policy, more than any other factor, will decide whether or not the future marks a period of fulfillment of those Indian reserved rights and whether that fulfillment occurs in a way that is fair to Indians, to non-Indians, or to both. Tribal governments are apt to insist on no less.

NOTES

1. See Michael S. Laird, "The *Winters* Cloud over the Rockies: Indian Water Rights and the Development of Western Energy Resources," *American Indian Law Review* 7 (1979): 155; Charles Corker (in "A Real Live Problem or Two for the Waning Energies of Frank J. Trelease," *Denver Law Review* 54 [1977]: 499) calls the doctrine a "rhetorical, chimerical phantasmagoria . . . a perversion and a prevarication."

2. Paul L. Bloom, "Law of the River: A Critique of an Extraordinary Legal System," in *New Courses for the Colorado River,* ed. Gary D. Weatherford and F. Lee Brown (Albuquerque: University of New Mexico Press, 1986), pp. 139–54.

3. *Winters v. United States,* 207 U.S. 564 (1908).

4. *Wyoming v. United States,* 492 U.S. 406 (1989).

5. 373 U.S. 546 (1963).

6. See Felix S. Cohen, *Handbook of Federal Indian Law* (Charlottesville, Va.: Michie Bobbs-Merrill, 1982), pp. 62–107; see also Charles F. Wilkinson and John M. Volkman, "Judicial Review of Indian Treaty Abrogation: 'As Long as the Water Flows or Grass Grows Upon the Earth'—How Long a Time Is That?," *California Law Review* 63 (1975): 601, 611.

7. Treaty with the Blackfeet, Oct. 17, 1855, 11 Stat. 657.

8. 18 Stat. 28 (1874).

9. 25 Stat. 113 (1888).

10. For the history of the Fort Belknap Reservation and the background of the *Winters* case, see Norris Hundley, "The 'Winters' Decision and Indian Water Rights: A Mystery Re-Examined," *Western Historical Quarterly* 13, no. 1 (1982): 17–42. See also Daniel McCool, *Command of the Waters* (Berkeley: University of California Press, 1987), pp. 36–49. The foregoing account is based on these sources and the statement of the case in *Winters v. United States.*

11. 148 F. 684 (9th Cir. 1906).

12. See *Irwin v. Phillips,* 5 Cal. 140 (1855); *Coffin v. Left Hand Ditch Co.,* 6 Colo. 443 (1882).

13. Mining Act of July 26, 1866, 14 Stat. 251, 43 U.S.C. § 661; Amendment to Mining Act, Act of July 9, 1870, 6 Stat. 217, 43 U.S.C. § 661; Desert Land Act of 1877, Act of March 3, 1877, 19 Stat. 377, 43 U.S.C. § 321.

14. 207 U.S. at 577 (1908).

15. Just three years before the *Winters* decision, the Court had decided another case in which it based an Indian right to fish on an implication that fishing was necessary to carry out the purposes of a treaty. The tribes in that case ceded their territory but kept a right to fish in the ceded area outside their remaining territory. Non-Indians began fishing with equipment that monopolized old Indian fishing sites, and they prevented Indians from crossing private lands to get to the river. The United States sued on behalf of the Indians. Justice McKenna, who later wrote the *Winters* decision, held that although the treaty was silent on the Indians' continuing interest in the ceded lands, the circumstances and purposes of the treaty required that the Indians have an easement in those lands. Because the Indians were promised a continuing right to fish at their usual and accustomed places in the ceded area, "no other conclusion would give effect to the treaty." *United States v. Winans*, 198 U.S. 371 (1905).

16. 207 U.S. at 576 (1908); Statement of the Case, 207 U.S. at 565 (1908).

17. E.g., *Arizona v. California*, 373 U.S. 546 (1963) (irrigation); *United States v. Adair*, 723 F.2d 1410 (9th Cir. 1983), cert. denied, 467 U.S. 1252 (1984) (hunting and fishing and agriculture); *United States v. Walker River Irrigation Dist.*, 104 F.2d 334 (9th Cir. 1939) (power generation).

18. The reserved rights doctrine also has been applied to reservations of federal public lands for specific government purposes: *Arizona v. California*, 373 U.S. 546 (1963) (wildlife refuge, recreation area); *Cappaert v. United States*, 426 U.S. 128 (1976) (national monument); *United States v. New Mexico*, 438 U.S. 696 (1978) (national forest); and *Sierra Club v. Block*, 622 F.Supp. 842 (D.Colo. 1985), vacated on procedural grounds, *Sierra Club v. Yeutter*, 911 F.2d 1405 (10th Cir. 1990) (wilderness areas). In the case of such special-purpose reservations the courts have read the implied reservation of water rights narrowly, as extending to "only that amount of water necessary to fulfill the purpose of the reservation, no more" (*Cappaert v. United States*, supra at 141). In *United States v. New Mexico*, supra, the Court distinguished between the original or "primary" purposes of national forests, being timber production and watershed maintenance, and other added purposes such as recreation, fish and wildlife, and grazing. It found that the quantity of reserved water rights claimed by the United States should be limited to the original "primary" purposes. While perhaps these distinctions are appropriate where a federal reservation is set aside for particular statutorily defined purposes, the "primary purpose" analysis should have little bearing on rights to water on Indian reservations. Although all parties to Indian treaties and agreements may have intended certain identifiable water uses, it would be straining that intent to consider such uses to be limitations on Indian rights. It is inconsistent with the *Winters* doctrine to read into treaties and agreements an inherent limit that would narrow the tribes' capacity to fulfill the broad, overriding purpose of making the reservation a permanent home and

abiding place. Thus, the Supreme Court has not indulged a distinction between primary and secondary purposes in any case dealing with an Indian reservation, and it would be inappropriate for the Court to do so. Cf. *United States v. Adair* (referring to a "dual primary" purpose of hunting and fishing and agriculture).

19. *Arizona v. California,* 439 U.S. 419, 422 (1979).

20. Reclamation Act of 1902, 32 Stat. 388, as amended, 43 U.S.C. §§ 371 et seq.

21. United States National Water Commission, *Water Policies for the Future: Final Report to the President and to the Congress of the United States by the National Water Commission* (Washington, D.C.: Government Printing Office, 1973), pp. 474–75. Until the case of *Arizona v. California* was decided, the Supreme Court cited *Winters* twice, only once in a water case. See *United States v. Powers,* 305 U.S. 527, 532 (1938).

22. See David H. Getches, "Competing Demands for the Colorado River," *Colorado Law Review* 56 (1985): 413.

23. 43 U.S.C. § 666.

24. *Arizona v. California,* note 19 above.

25. *United States v. District Court in and for Eagle County,* 401 U.S. 520 (1971); *Colorado River Water Conservation Dist. v. United States,* 424 U.S. 800 (1976); *Arizona v. San Carlos Apache Tribe,* 463 U.S. 545 (1983).

26. *In re Rights to Use Water in Big Horn River,* 753 P.2d 76 (Wyo. 1988).

27. *United States v. Jesse,* 744 P.2d 491 (1987).

28. *United States v. New Mexico.*

29. *Nevada v. United States,* 463 U.S. 110 (1983).

30. *Arizona v. California,* 460 U.S. 605 (1983). The tribes were permitted to expand the extent of the practicably irrigable acreage on which their quantification of water rights was based only where the boundaries of such lands had been *judicially* determined after the case was decided.

31. Between 1955 and 1979, over fifty bills designed to modify or abolish federal reserved water rights were introduced in Congress. See Note, "Indian Reserved Water Rights: The Winters of Our Discontent," *Yale Law Journal* 88 (1979): 1703–4.

32. *Gros Ventre and Assiniboine Tribes of Fort Belknap Indian Community v. Hodel,* No. CV-85-213-GF (D.Mont. Aug. 25, 1985).

33. See Charles F. Wilkinson, *American Indians, Time and the Law* (New Haven, Conn.: Yale University Press, 1987).

34. Following the Supreme Court decision, the tribes and the state continued to dispute issues such as whether the tribes could use their water for in-stream flows to protect a fishery in the river and whether the state engineer could administer water rights on the reservation. After a state supreme court rejected the tribal position on these issues in an incomprehensible set of opinions (five opinions for the court of five justices, 835 P.2d 273 [Wyo. 1992]), the tribes decided not to pursue it to the U.S. Supreme Court. Negotiations are likely.

35. E.g., *United States v. Sioux Nation of Indians*, 448 U.S. 371 (1980); *Joint Tribal Council of Passamaquoddy Tribe v. Morton*, 528 F.2d 370 (1st Cir. 1975); *Pyramid Lake Paiute Tribe v. Morton*, 354 F. Supp. 252 (D.D.C. 1973).

36. See Table 2.1, this volume.

37. Truckee-Carson–Pyramid Lake Water Rights Settlement Act, 104 Stat. 3289, November 16, 1990. See also David Yardas, "Water Transfers, Paper Rights, and the Truckee-Carson Settlement," chapter 14, this volume.

2

CONFLICTING FEDERAL ROLES IN INDIAN WATER CLAIMS NEGOTIATIONS

Benjamin Simon and Harvey Doerksen

In recent years Indian water claims have begun to attract increasing attention as states recognize the significance of tribes' *Winters* rights. The threat of potential litigation to quantify these claims creates a significant degree of uncertainty about water use and development and also raises the possibility that satisfying Indian water claims may involve reallocations of existing water supplies, with consequent social dislocations.

Although to a certain extent both Indians and non-Indians resent federal intervention in water resource decisions, they also frequently call on the federal government to protect their rights. The federal government's trust responsibility toward Indian tribes and the fact that many federally constructed projects may be affected by Indian claims make it virtually inevitable that the federal government will play an important role in settling Indian water claims. In addition, federal approval is thought to be required for off-reservation leasing of water—a potentially important means of resolving water claims.

Negotiation, rather than litigation, has assisted in the settlement of a number of recent cases. However, negotiations are often complicated by the multiple roles played by the federal government. These multiple roles make it difficult for the federal government to negotiate effectively. How the Department of the Interior organizes its negotiation efforts may also affect negotiations. To understand the process of settling water claims through negotiations, it is crucial to recognize these conflicting roles of the federal government.

Importance of Indian Water Claims to the Federal Government

Indian water claims are important to the federal government for several reasons: (1) the potential settlement costs are large; (2) settlement of claims can represent alternative means through which the federal government can assist in the economic development of tribes through the establishment of funds or infrastructure improvements; (3) uncertainty about water rights can impede economic development; and (4) the government has legal responsibilities to protect tribes, honor existing water contracts, and protect fish and wildlife resources. To a certain extent, the federal government is likely to shoulder development costs either through programmatic expenditures or through settlement costs. Before the 1990s eight claims were settled, which resulted in a total cost to the federal government of approximately $750 million.

As shown in Table 2.1, there is a great deal of variety in both the costs of settlements and the quantities of water awarded. No settlement identified in Table 2.1 was settled solely through a negotiated effort; most resulted from negotiations that had been preceded by litigation and were then followed by implementing legislation.

Because federally constructed facilities are usually involved, the government has an important role in settling Indian water claims. All of the cases identified in Table 2.1 involve some use of federally constructed facilities to either store or transport water awarded in settlement. Typically, the operation and management of a Bureau of Reclamation project may be a key point in resolving a water claim, or a federally constructed project may be proposed as a solution to the dispute. For example, the Colorado Ute settlement is predicated on the construction of Reclamation's Animas–La Plata Project; the Arizona settlements rely extensively on Reclamation's Central Arizona Project.

Virtually all of the settlements have also involved substantial federal financing. This is at least a partial result of the weak bargaining position in which the government finds itself as a result of internal conflicts. Lacking the fortitude to assume a strong bargaining position, to threaten to break off negotiations and resume litigation if necessary, or to marshal its forces in Congress, the federal government becomes the source of funds but may not greatly influence the outcome of the negotiations.

Why Negotiate to Settle Water Claims?

Settlement of resource disputes through litigation can be an expensive and time-consuming process.[1] Historically, litigation has provided the primary means for settling Indian water claims. The costs of the litigation approach have been borne by both Indian interests and the federal government. Negotiations potentially offer

TABLE 2.1. Summary of Enacted Western Indian Water Claims Settlements

Settlement	Year of Settlement	Quantity of Water (acre-feet)	Estimated Total Federal Cost (millions of $)
San Carlos	1992	150,000	38.4
Jicarilla Apache	1992	32,000	6.0
Northern Cheyenne	1992	91,300	56.5
Fort Hall	1990	130,000	22.0
Fallon–Pyramid Lake	1990	10,590	108.0
Fort McDowell	1990	36,400	66.0
San Luis Rey	1988	16,000	32.0
Salt River Pima-Maricopa	1988	122,000	60.0
Colorado Ute	1988	119,300	184.0
Fort Peck	1985	1,000,000	0
Tohono O'odham	1982	66,000	143.0
Ak-Chin	1978, 1984	85,000	93.0
Utah Ute	1965, 1992	—	198.5
Navajo	1962	508,000	602.0

SOURCES: Ak-Chin Settlement Act; Ak-Chin Indian Community Water Rights Act; Colorado Ute Indian Water Rights Settlement Act of 1988; Fallon Paiute Shoshone Tribal Settlement Act; Truckee-Carson–Pyramid Lake Water Settlement; Fort Peck–Montana Compact, A Water Rights Settlement Negotiated by the Montana Reserved Water Rights Compact Commission and the Assiniboine and Sioux Tribes; Salt River Pima-Maricopa Indian Community Water Rights Settlement Act of 1988; San Luis Rey Indian Water Rights Settlement Act; Southern Arizona Water Rights Settlement Act of 1982; Ute Deferral Agreement, contract of September 20, 1965, between the Bureau of Reclamation, Bureau of Indian Affairs, Ute Tribe, and the Central Utah Water Conservancy District; Reclamation Projects Authorization and Adjustment Act of 1992; Fort Hall Indian Water Rights Settlement Act; Jicarilla Apache Tribe Water Rights Settlement Act; Northern Cheyenne Indian Reserved Rights Settlement Act of 1992.

Indian and non-Indian entities more timely clarification of water rights in an nonadversarial setting and give all parties greater control over the eventual outcome. However, negotiations are not a panacea. Unless basic conditions are set forth concerning the power differentials between the negotiating entities, the existence of a power base from which to negotiate, and the entities' abilities to understand and advocate their own interests, negotiations may not be an effective mechanism for the resolution of disputes.[2]

Costly delays in reaching settlement through litigation, and the attendant impact of continuing water right uncertainties, prompted the Reagan administration to launch an initiative in 1982 to negotiate rather than litigate Indian water claims.[3] Negotiations were seen as a way to give the executive branch a voice in the settlements, as well as water transfers and Indian economic development.

Federal Role in Negotiated Settlements

Although it is convenient to think of the federal government as a single entity with which to bargain or negotiate, this is far from the actual case. The federal government is not a monolith but is composed of many different bureaucratic entities whose roles, as well as goals and objectives, often conflict.

Negotiating with a federal agency that has a single goal or a small number of related nonconflicting goals may be easier because the internal agency conflicts may be less intense. However, opposing organizational missions and potential property exchanges that may adversely affect the agency's constituents act to exacerbate internal tensions as each organization strives to protect its constituents, making concerted federal actions difficult.

The primary responsibility for negotiating water claims typically rests with the Department of the Interior, primarily because Interior's programs and activities directly affect the parties to water claims. Interior's lead role may be altered depending on the status of any existing litigation (potential Department of Justice involvement) or the involvement of other federal agencies such as the Army Corps of Engineers. The secretary of the interior, acting through various bureaus, has legal obligations to protect Indian rights to water, to fulfill existing water contracts to which it is party, and to protect certain fish and wildlife resources. Although these obligations are not mutually exclusive, disagreements between the Interior bureaus charged with their implementation are frequent because the enhancement of one activity may come at the expense of another.

Under the Interior umbrella the bureaus with an important stake in Indian water claims settlements are the Bureau of Reclamation, the Bureau of Indian Affairs, and the Fish and Wildlife Service. These bureaus do not have common goals or congressional directives, are accustomed to setting their own agendas and objectives, and are not of equal relative strength. Entering into a negotiation with nonfederal entities requires these bureaus to relinquish some control over the federal goals, objectives, and outcome.

The balance of power among these agencies within the Department of the Interior is well established. The Bureau of Reclamation has traditionally been the most powerful of these three agencies, and Reclamation's constituents have been known to exercise considerable sway over departmental decision makers. When a consensus position must be reached, the balance of power may be shifted toward the Bureau of Reclamation. For example, in the negotiations surrounding the Colorado Ute settlement, the strength of the Bureau of Reclamation (and its constituents) precluded any solution that did not involve construction of the Animas–La Plata Project. For settlements involving other major Reclamation facilities that were under construction, such as the Ak-Chin and Tohono O'odham cases, the overriding local concerns were to allow completion of the project and to protect existing non-Indian water users.

Federal agencies outside of the Department of the Interior also play an important role in shaping any water negotiation. For example, the Office of Management and Budget, which is concerned primarily with the costs of federal programs and with ensuring that the president's program is followed, exercises considerable influence in decisions concerning potential settlements. Other federal agencies such as the Environmental Protection Agency or the Army Corps of Engineers may also be involved. For example, if additional development in the Colorado River basin is required to settle claims, the Environmental Protection Agency may be involved because water quality is likely to be an important consideration.

Consequence of Conflicting Roles

Lack of a Single Voice

Of the several consequences of the federal government's conflicting roles, the most significant is the internal disagreements that make it difficult for the government to negotiate with a single voice as it attempts to reach decisions that balance the interests of the Interior bureaus that are involved, as well as those of the taxpayers. The federal government, consequently, is constrained to the role of financing the settlement but may not actively participate in shaping the outcome.

Lack of Federal Goals

The opposing organizational missions of the Interior bureaus involved in negotiating water claims settlements make it difficult to establish goals for water claims negotiations in general and for any one negotiation in particular. Is the goal to minimize federal costs, to protect non-Indian water users, to construct a facility that has been previously proposed, to provide the tribes with a resource that can be used to develop their reservations, or all of these? Lack of a clear conception of what the federal government wants to attain from a negotiation effort can hamper even the most able departmental negotiators.

Existence of Guiding Principles

In the Department of the Interior's efforts to settle Indian water claims, one common thread is that cases have been handled on a case-by-case, ad hoc basis.

31

Nevertheless, the individual cases identified in Table 2.1 have become powerful precedents and substitute for general principles. The most significant precedents have been the provision of federal financing, the protection of existing non-Indian water users, and only limited use of water transfers. Nonfederal entities are likely to insist that future settlements embody these precedents.

Since 1985, the Department of the Interior has had lengthy discussions concerning the development of a set of general principles for settling Indian water claims. Some of the principles for settlement that have been emphasized include resolving all claims, structuring settlements to promote economic efficiency, and sharing costs based on proportionate shares of benefits. These principles, while quite general, establish a starting point for departmental negotiators. What remains uncertain is the degree to which any principles will be used for guidance and the amount of discretion that will be left to individual negotiators.

Bargaining Strength

The conflicting missions of the Interior bureaus that are involved in a negotiation effort can limit how strongly the government can negotiate. The bargaining strength of a particular negotiator usually is no greater than the ability of the sponsoring organization to follow through. Thus, it may be difficult to achieve a position that reflects the views of all the Interior bureaus in an equitable and balanced manner. Lacking a strong consensus position, the federal government might adopt a weaker position that is more closely aligned with a particular bureau or a position that simply defends itself against adverse outcomes but does not set forth any strong demands for preferred outcomes.

Lack of bargaining strength can also lead to a loss of control over the agenda of the negotiations. Unable to influence the agenda, federal negotiators are put in a reactive, rather than a proactive, mode.

In addition, because Interior bureaus with very different missions are involved, it may be difficult for federal negotiators to make commitments, to propose new approaches, or even to break off negotiations. Given the lack of federal bargaining strength, it is possible that Indians and non-Indians will coalesce, leaving the federal government to fund the outcome (e.g., construction of water projects or capitalization of development funds).

Federal negotiators can also be weakened by the existence of legislation that mandates performance or by previous decisions that have resulted in a federal liability. The severe penalties for nondelivery of water that were enacted in the Ak-Chin and Tohono O'odham settlements weakened the ability of the government to consider alternative proposals, but the penalties probably provided the federal government with the incentive to act in a more expeditious manner. The existence of a federally constructed canal across the San Luis Rey reservation designed to serve non-Indians also weakened the government's bargaining position.

Finally, because internal agreement can be difficult for federal negotiators, nonfederal entities may be left with the perception that the government is being unresponsive, when in actuality it is responding to its own internal constituents.

Organizational Factors Affecting Negotiations

Level of Individual Appointed as Negotiator

Early in the 1980s, when the Department of the Interior was beginning its negotiation efforts, negotiations were organized in a way that gave them high visibility in the department and ensured high-level policy support. Initially, an individual in the Office of the Secretary was appointed with direct responsibility for the Ak-Chin and Tohono O'odham settlements. This individual had easy access to departmental decision makers (including the secretary), had full authority to negotiate for the department, and could quickly resolve conflicts between bureaus. This is one of the most important reasons that these particular cases were resolved. The success (at least in terms of relatively quick enactment and a broad base of local and state support) of the Tohono O'odham and Ak-Chin settlements was largely attributable to the high-level support provided by the department for the negotiation process and for working with Congress to ensure enactment.

Policy Guidance by Committee

Between 1984 and 1987 the undersecretary's Water Working Group provided general policy guidance for teams of departmental negotiators. The group also served as a forum to provide information to decision makers about potential settlements. Although the teams were responsible for conducting negotiations, they did not have easy access to policy makers, nor were they directly responsible to the secretary for resolution of the problems being addressed. With direct responsibility removed from a single individual, negotiations proceeded more slowly, and directions from policy makers were less clear.

The Water Working Group was disbanded in 1987, reducing the direction and guidance for departmental negotiators. As a result, after 1987 settlements were discussed on a more ad hoc basis, and several settlements—such as Salt River and San Luis Rey—were enacted by Congress with minimal involvement by the Department of the Interior.

Mitigating Factors

While many of the above factors argue against the federal government being an effective negotiator, there are a number of mitigating factors. The most important of these are the physical and hydrologic conditions present in a particular case under negotiation. If the supply of water is not a constraint (as in the Fort Peck case) and downstream water users do not appear to be affected, the conflicts between the federal negotiating entities may be considerably lessened because the threat to existing water rights may be less severe. The conflicts between the other negotiating entities are also likely to be less severe. In situations where water supplies are limited—for example, in Arizona—conflicts between different federal entities may be intensified as each jockeys in response to constituent pressure.

Another mitigating factor relates to federal financing of settlements. If no federal outlays are required (as in the Seminole and Fort Peck settlements), the conflict between Interior bureaus and between Interior and other agencies may be lessened. Although property exchanges between Indian and non-Indian parties may still be an issue, it may be easier for the federal parties to reach a consensus position.

Lessons from Past Negotiation Efforts

Negotiations are not a panacea. To obtain effective settlements, the government needs to take full advantage of all available mechanisms (including litigation) for settling Indian water claims. But there are cases that are well suited to negotiations. Much of the success of the negotiation process depends on the effectiveness of the federal government, a major player in all Indian water rights negotiations.

Several lessons can be learned from past negotiation efforts about the ability of the federal government to negotiate effectively and with relative unanimity. Effective negotiations require solid organization with high-level support from political leaders. If high-level support is lacking, federal negotiators are at a decided disadvantage in any negotiation. But even if all of the ideal conditions are present, the federal government can be expected to appear indecisive at times because it is subject to strong internal cross-currents of conflict.

NOTES

1. Lawrence S. Bacow and Michael Wheeler, *Environmental Dispute Resolution* (New York: Plenum Press, 1984).

2. John R. Ehrmann, Patricia A. Bidol, James E. Crowfoot, and Michael T. Lesnick, "Interest-Based Bargaining and Environmental Policy Decisionmaking: The Potential of Non-Traditional Conflict Management Approaches," *Technical Report of the Research Project on Consensus Building and Potential Applications to Emerging Environmental Issues in Michigan* (Ann Arbor: University of Michigan, School of Natural Resources, Environmental Conflict Project, 1984).

3. "President Reagan's Veto of Water-Rights Measure Left Standing by Congress," *Congressional Quarterly,* June 12, 1982, p. 1404.

3

SOLUTIONS OR SYMBOLS? AN INDIAN PERSPECTIVE ON WATER SETTLEMENTS

Austin Nuñez and Mary G. Wallace

I want to emphasize the moral and ethical considerations here. I think too often they get forgotten as we discuss the policies and the procedures and the legalities of all of this. We need to ask ourself what's right and what's wrong and what's best for the Native people.

Ada Deer, Menominee Tribe[1]

Indian water rights represent a new and often competing demand for water in the West. These rights are a largely unquantified block of water that must be woven into the framework of western water law. However, in many areas of the West, water is fully appropriated, raising the specter of displacing non-Indian water users to meet Indian needs. One way to avoid this reallocation of water and to fulfill the claims of an Indian tribe is to negotiate a settlement among the water users in an area. This approach is being pursued as an alternative to litigation throughout the West.

By 1992, thirteen negotiated settlements had been passed by Congress, affecting tribes from Arizona, Florida, California, Colorado, Idaho, Montana, New Mexico, Nevada, and Utah. Moreover, twenty-three separate negotiations are now underway across the West.[2]

A key question facing Indian tribes across the West is whether to participate in the crafting of these settlements or whether to litigate in court. Indian water rights settlements are undeniably a means of satisfying Indian water rights claims. Each Indian reservation in this country is unique, however. From physical characteristics such as topography to cultural differences, these reservations and the indigenous people who reside on them have very different needs for, and views of, water. Nevertheless, some general observations can be drawn about the essential elements of Indian water rights and what should be considered by tribes in pursuing negotiated settlements.

In reviewing the nature of Indian water rights, it becomes apparent that there exist four dimensions of an Indian water right—quantity, management, economic aspects, and spiritual qualities. These may be examined more closely through a case study of the San Xavier Reservation of the Tohono O'odham Nation (formerly the Papago Reservation) and the Southern Arizona Water Rights Settlement Act (SAWRSA), the negotiated settlement of San Xavier's water claims.[3] Significant issues have arisen during the implementation of the settlement act, including continued groundwater pumping in the Tucson area, a proposed farm on San Xavier, and allottee water rights. Some conclusions about these issues extend to Indian water rights settlements in general.

Winters Rights

The Indian tribes and the federal government hold a type of water right—the federal reserved right—that is different from water rights held under state law. The cornerstone of Indian reserved rights is the *Winters* doctrine.[4] First established in 1908 in *Winters v. United States* and later expanded in a series of cases, the United States Supreme Court held that when land was withdrawn and reserved from the public domain, such as for an Indian reservation, enough water to fulfill the purposes of the reservation was implicitly reserved.[5] The right is given a priority date of the time the reservation was established, and unlike state water rights, the right is not measured by the criterion of beneficial use and cannot be lost through nonuse.

Indian water rights remained essentially unquantified until *Arizona v. California* in 1963.[6] In this landmark case, the Supreme Court awarded five Indian tribes along the Colorado River 761,562 acre-feet of water. The standard for quantification used by the Court was the practicably irrigable acreage (PIA) standard. Under this standard, Indian tribes are to be awarded enough water to irrigate all the practicably irrigable acreage on the reservation, a substantial amount of water for many reservations in the West. To date, the PIA standard has been the only standard for quantification used.

Arizona v. California put parameters on the *Winters* doctrine, and since this case, pressure has mounted across the West to quantify Indian water rights. The long-standing rule governing non-Indian water use and water allocation in the West is the doctrine of prior appropriation. Under this rule, "first in time is first in right." *Arizona v. California* put Indian water rights squarely within the prevailing framework of western water law not only by quantifying Indian water rights, but also by holding that these rights must be met from the affected states' water supply. Because most Indian rights are senior once quantified, junior non-Indian water users will have to forgo water uses during times of shortage.

In the years following this decision, it became clear that Indians were legally entitled to large blocks of water in the West, rights that heretofore had been unexercised. Some estimates of the amount of water to which they were entitled ranged as high as 30 million acre-feet of water for the tribes in Arizona alone.[7] Because of the magnitude and seniority of these rights, interest began to wax in methods of quantifying these rights—most commonly in the general adjudications of water rights. Every western state has established either an administrative or a judicial proceeding to manage conflicts over water. However, it was not until 1983 that Indian and federal rights could be brought into state court systems to be quantified. The decision of the U.S. Supreme Court in *Arizona v. San Carlos Apache Tribe* in 1983 to allow these rights to be adjudicated in state courts encouraged the filing of suits to initiate general stream adjudications throughout the West.[8]

Many of the parties involved in disputes over Indian water rights issues, however, began to doubt the efficiency, equity, and practicality of resolving these disputes through the courts.[9] The complexity of Indian water rights conflicts, particularly the many competing parties that must be involved, is often the best argument for negotiations. In court, the judge is limited to discussions concerning the quantity and the priority of a water right. There can be no discussion of water marketing, water conservation, deferred water uses, funding, improved water management, or the development of new supplies of water.

The primary factor encouraging negotiations, however, is that the adjudications often cannot provide the alternative sources of water that will be required to settle Indian claims without significant injury to non-Indian water users. In basins that are fully appropriated, every acre-foot of water awarded to the Indians will require an acre-foot cutback on non-Indian water use. In negotiated settlements, however, the parties pursue other sources of water (usually federally funded water), which lessens the impact on non-Indian water users.

An incentive for the Indian tribes to negotiate stems from the fact that many tribes lack the capital to develop an award of water and cannot generally obtain conventional financing. Moreover, historically, federal funding has been inadequate for Indian water development projects.[10] Negotiated settlements can provide funds—in large measure supplied by the federal government—to develop water resources on a reservation.

The Spiritual Nature of Indian Water Rights

Indian water rights are different from state water rights and other federal water rights in another respect—the underlying spiritual nature of the relationship between Indian people and water and other natural resources. Indian people have revered water as one of the most sacred elements provided by the Creator.[11] Many

Indian tribes across the country perform prayers, songs, and dances to provide water for their communities, especially during times of planting and harvest.

The values and beliefs that underlie Indian water differ markedly from the values and beliefs that underlie western water law. In the West, water is a commodity to be used for economic and personal gain. Water is viewed primarily as a means for providing a supply of products, whether it be hay, copper, or energy production. The prior appropriation doctrine is designed to maximize water use. In the West, many still view water freely flowing in a stream as "wasted water." Under this system of water appropriation, entire ecological systems—grasslands, wetlands, forests, and the habitat associated with flowing rivers—have been sacrificed to meet the demands of human consumption.

As Vine Deloria, Jr., a noted Indian writer, observes, this type of legal doctrine "understands water only as a representation of property in the legal sense. . . . [I]t completely eliminates the intuitive sense of life and emotional content that makes water important as an element of universal life and reduces it to a quantifiable income-producing entity." [12] This legalistic and economic view "has no place for natural features and entities themselves. . . . [A]ir, water, and land, are conceived in a legal sense as if they had no existence apart from the human legal rights that have been attached to them." [13]

For many Indian people, the whole notion of "ownership" of water, land, and other natural resources is foreign. As one Tohono O'odham noted, "Nobody ever thought about water in that way—owning water." [14] Water and all other natural elements belong to the Creator. Under this philosophy, the indigenous people of this continent are the stewards of Earth, with attendant responsibilities. Under this philosophy, water is not simply a commodity. Instead, "Water is precious. It is a special gift." [15]

In recent years, however, "non-Indians have finally come to recognize that many Indian ideas were ecologically and scientifically sound." [16] Whether it is the maintenance of fish runs, the management of forests, or water management, Indians are slowly being included in natural resource management activities. A growing concern for the environment among many Americans, including the protection of resources for future generations, complements the spiritual dimension of Indian resources.

Dimensions of an Indian Water Right

Indian water rights settlements have been hailed as a way to improve Indian and non-Indian economies, to improve the management of water resources in an area, and to improve intergovernmental relations between tribes and other entities.[17] However, the primary purpose of a settlement is to fulfill the *Winters* rights claims of an Indian reservation, with a corollary purpose of promoting self-sufficiency and economic health in Indian Country. In this section, we would like to propose that Indian water rights have four dimensions: (1) quantity, (2) management, (3) economic aspects, and (4) spiritual qualities.

The first dimension is the quantity of water. A key objective facing Indian tribes when confronting negotiations is to secure a reliable supply of "wet water" to fulfill the *Winters* rights of the reservations.[18] The desired characteristics of this supply of water are that it be reliable (meaning free from interruptions in supply, including drought) and that the water be of appropriate quality. Ideally, groundwater resources are free of contaminants, and there is a steady level in the water table, with no significant overdrafting of the groundwater reserves. Similarly, surface water supplies should be of adequate quality for the purposes required by the tribe, a factor that should include provisions for treatment, if needed, and also with some protection built in for variations in supply. Reservoirs, improved dam management, and water exchanges can provide this protection.

The second dimension is management of water on the reservation. In most cases, tribes are seeking control over the use and development of the natural resources on a reservation, including water. This administrative and regulatory authority includes jurisdiction over all water use on the reservation.[19] Management activities of the tribes may include permits for water use, the regulation of diversions, and water quality activities.[20] Essential to assuming this management authority are the collection and interpretation of data about water resources on the reservation and the development of an on-reservation management institution. In addition, tribes can work to secure a role in decision making in water decisions in an area. Increasingly, water is being managed on a watershed basis, requiring partnerships among tribal, state, and local entities to improve resource management. These management practices can be instituted in a "nonthreatening manner" by sharing data on water resources and by establishing boards with joint membership of tribal and state interests.[21]

A third dimension is economic. Indian tribes want the ability to put the water to a productive use consistent with that tribe's culture. Many Indians believe that their future as a people lies in their ability to attain economic security into the next century, and most Indian tribes do not see the federal government as a valuable trustee or partner to assist in attaining this economic security.[22] A chief consideration is that the tribal rights to use water should be no more restrictive than the rights non-Indians enjoy, which include leasing water off-reservation, if that is the preference of a particular Indian tribe. In sum, flexibility is an essential element that can be built into a settlement so that there are no constraints on change in water use. Moreover, funding to foster water use and development on the reservation is essential.

A fourth dimension is spiritual. On many Indian reservations, economic development, to be successful, "should not be conceived as economic development, but as community development." [23] In that sense, water use may generate more benefits for the community if consistent with the tribal culture. A concern for future generations of indigenous people and the relationship between Indian people and the Creator are often important elements of tribal culture and an Indian community. Further, many Indians argue that survival of a viable tribal culture for the Indian will depend on the relationship between Indian people and the land, which is affected by economic development.

Indian people face hard choices in deciding whether to negotiate water rights claims. It is a decidedly different arena than the court system. Other issues, often political, can affect the negotiations. An "open playing field" is essential, where groundwork is often laid to build the institutional relationships needed to improve water management in an area. However, experience shows that this is not always the case. As the following sections show, settlements can sometimes be driven by other water management issues.

The San Xavier Reservation

The San Xavier Reservation is located in southeastern Arizona and is part of the Tohono O'odham Nation. San Xavier is one of the largest Indian reservations in the United States, encompassing more than 2.8 million acres. In 1982, the water rights claims of the San Xavier Reservation and part of the Schuk Toak District of the Tohono O'odham Nation were settled through a negotiated settlement.

The San Xavier Reservation was established in 1874. Historically, it had been a viable homeland for the indigenous people of the village of Wa:k (San Xavier) because of a stable and secure water supply—the surface water and groundwater of the Santa Cruz River. Both groundwater and surface water were readily available to the Tohono O'odham at San Xavier. In 1697, a Spanish officer described the area: "Here at San Agustin the river was running with some volume and the stretch from here to Bac (San Xavier) was the most populous and the most fertile spot in the whole valley." [24] In 1874, the year the San Xavier Reservation was established by executive order, the Santa Cruz River had a general surface flow for most of the year.[25]

Ancestors of the people of San Xavier have lived in the area since time immemorial. Irrigation use by the Indians was reported by Father Kino in the late 1600s and also by non-Indian explorers as early as 1732.[26] In the 1880s, the people of the reservation were "industrious, self-sufficient, independent, trustworthy, and peaceful . . . who raised their own food, built their own homes, raised their own cattle." [27] Elders on the reservation recall days when numerous crops including cotton, peaches, corn, squash, and other vegetables were grown on the reservation.

In addition, wildlife was abundant. Wolves, quail, and pronghorn antelope inhabited a large 1,000-acre mesquite bosque near San Xavier.[28] In 1849, a company of explorers "threaded its way through a large mesquite bosque to reach an abundant flow of water in the Santa Cruz River" and noted that "there was a good grass cover on the adjacent floodplain, and two pronghorn were shot near the mission."[29] During this period, the groundwater reserves underlying the reservation were full, with groundwater available "to members of the Tribe living at a distance from the Santa Cruz River by means of shallow hand dug wells."[30]

However, after the reservation was established in 1874, non-Indian water use increased, at first gradually and then quite dramatically with the advent of engine-driven pumps. Groundwater withdrawals began in earnest in the 1940s to meet the needs of agricultural, mining, and municipal and industrial users. In addition, much of this pumpage has been concentrated around the San Xavier Reservation. As one author notes, "Mining Arizona's underground waters became the principal means of meeting the new and growing demands upon the Tucson Basin."[31]

At the same time, little was done on the part of the federal government to protect or sustain a water supply for the San Xavier Reservation. In 1917, in contrast to the surrounding non-Indian water users, the federal government "quit the pumps" on San Xavier because of costs and developed a gravity supply system. This system of underground piping collapsed in 1929, leaving the Tohono O'odham with no water to irrigate.[32] By 1931, the farmers on the San Xavier Reservation had only one-fifth of the previous water supply provided by the pumps and could irrigate only 100 to 300 acres of the 2,000 that otherwise could have been cultivated.[33]

A severe shortage of water has continued ever since.[34] By the mid 1950s, many tribal members began to work off the reservation, either picking cotton or working in the mines because of the lack of a viable economy on the reservation.[35] In 1992, the people at San Xavier are among the poorest in the Tucson area, with no water supply and few economic enterprises, standing in contrast to the reservation at the turn of the century and in stark contrast to neighboring non-Indian lands.

Southern Arizona Water Rights Settlement Act

In 1975, the federal government, on behalf of the tribe and the allottees on San Xavier, filed a water rights suit against Tucson, the mining companies, and agricultural interests. The allottees are a group of individual Tohono O'odham who hold allotments of land on San Xavier. The water rights claims of the San Xavier Reservation and the allottees were particularly significant for water users in the Tucson area. These water rights claims were generally senior to most (if not all) water users in the Tucson area, could not be lost through nonuse, and represented a large block of water rights that had never been exercised. Until these rights

41

were quantified, few water users in the Tucson area could be certain of their rights, including the right to continue pumping groundwater.

Negotiations among local water users toward a legislative settlement began in 1978 precisely because of the potential impact of the lawsuit on non-Indian economic development and water uses. Early on in the negotiations, it became apparent that any water rights settlement would be tied to Central Arizona Project (CAP) water. This multibillion-dollar project is a canal approximately 335 miles in length that is intended to deliver Arizona's allocation of Colorado River water to central Arizona. In 1978, funding for the Tucson portion of the aqueduct was uncertain. A settlement based on providing water from CAP would ensure that the aqueduct would be built.

In 1982, the settlement passed Congress and was vetoed by President Ronald Reagan. Reagan objected to the bill on the grounds that the federal government had not been a party to the negotiations and also because of the costs of the settlement to the federal government. A cost-sharing agreement was established with local water users, and new legislation passed the House and Senate and was signed by President Reagan in October 1982.

The Southern Arizona Water Rights Settlement Act (SAWRSA) settles the water rights claims of the San Xavier Reservation and part of the Schuk Toak District.[36] The act provides for a total of 76,000 acre-feet of water, including 27,000 acre-feet of CAP water for San Xavier and 10,800 acre-feet of CAP water for Schuk Toak. Groundwater pumpage is limited to 10,000 acre-feet each year on San Xavier and to a minimal amount on Schuk Toak. Finally, the secretary of the interior is instructed to acquire 28,200 acre-feet of effluent from the city of Tucson to exchange for an alternative source of water such as CAP water.

Other federal responsibilities include construction of an on-reservation delivery system and payment of replacement costs for water in the event of no deliveries or late deliveries. Tribal responsibilities include subjugating the land if it is used for agriculture and also assuming responsibility for the operation and maintenance of the on-reservation system. The tribe has the right to lease the water, but only within the Tucson area. This provision both limits the potential market for the water if the tribe chooses to lease it and also prevents the tribe from transferring water to other parts of the reservation.

The act provides for a $15 million trust fund from which only the interest and dividends may be spent for the subjugation of land, the development of water resources, and the construction, operation, and maintenance of on-reservation facilities. The act also sets up a cooperative fund that is intended to assist the secretary of the interior in carrying out his obligation. The fund is composed of $5.25 million contributed by the state of Arizona, the city of Tucson, and various mining and agricultural corporations, plus another $5.25 million authorized by Congress.

Analysis of the Settlement

The implementation of Indian water rights settlements has yet to be subjected to rigorous scrutiny, particularly from the standpoint of Indian tribes. In fact, as one scholar notes, "Much of the analytical and partisan attention focuses on, and applauds, the act of settlement, not the implementation of an act." [37] This lack of analysis of the implementation of settlements reflects not only how recently most of these settlements have been enacted, but also how difficult they can be to evaluate. Many are complicated agreements involving water transfers and other management mechanisms that must be tested by time. However, SAWRSA has had a ten-year implementation period. In this section, we will look at the SAWRSA settlement and some issues that have arisen.

To date, the settlement has failed to deliver any water to the San Xavier Reservation. Although negotiations were continuing in late 1992 between the Tohono O'odham Nation, the San Xavier Reservation, and the city of Tucson over specific provisions in the act, water deliveries did not begin in October 1992 as was mandated by the act. Following is a discussion of three primary issues that have arisen during implementation: (1) groundwater pumping, (2) the development of large-scale farming on San Xavier, and (3) the water rights of the allottees.

Groundwater Pumping

Since 1945, approximately 8 million acre-feet of groundwater has been pumped from the upper Santa Cruz River basin, much of it from underneath and around the reservation. In the Tucson area, pumping increased from 29,000 acre-feet per year in 1935 to a peak of 439,000 acre-feet per year in 1976.[38] Pumpage in 1990 was estimated at 341,000 acre-feet. The overdraft for 1990 was estimated at 206,000 acre-feet of water.[39] The fastest rates of decline in the water table in the area are in the northern section of the basin in the Marana area and also in the vicinity of the San Xavier Reservation.[40]

Current estimates of pumpage around the reservation include figures from wells owned by Tucson in the Santa Cruz well-field, located just to the northeast of the reservation. In 1991, approximately 10,854 acre-feet of water was pumped from these wells.[41] Along the eastern edge of the reservation, the Farmers Investment Company (FICO) continues to pump groundwater to irrigate over 5,000 acres of pecan trees, a grove that stretches some seven miles long and about one mile wide.[42] Total pumpage in 1991 for FICO was estimated at 30,710 acre-feet per year.[43]

In addition, two mines are located directly south of the reservation—the American Smelting and Refining Company (ASARCO) Mission mine and the Cyprus Sierrita mine. In 1991, pumpage for the Cyprus Sierrita mine was estimated at 23,899 acre-feet.[44] In 1991, pumpage for ASARCO was estimated at approximately

8,326 acre-feet per year.[45] Under a lease negotiated in 1974, ASARCO also has rights to pump sufficient groundwater to support mining operations from three wells located on San Xavier.[46] In 1986, ASARCO pumped approximately 3,000 acre-feet of water from wells on the reservation but under full operation could pump up to 6,000 acre-feet per year.[47]

A conservative estimate of the total groundwater pumpage directly around the reservation is 73,789 acre-feet for 1991. Moreover, all of these groundwater uses have been "grandfathered" into use by the Arizona Groundwater Management Act in 1980. More significantly for the reservation, however, at the time the settlement was passed in 1982, both the mines and FICO were scheduled to contract to receive CAP water and were expected to cut back, if not eliminate, groundwater pumping. But these same interests who lobbied so heartily for CAP have rejected contracts for CAP water: FICO, ASARCO, and Cyprus Sierrita have refused to contract for their CAP allotments.[48] These water users will continue to pump groundwater because it is cheaper than CAP water and their rights are guaranteed under the Groundwater Management Act.

In contrast, on the entire San Xavier Reservation, "one lone well" is now in operation pumping from a depth of 680 feet irrigating two acres of land.[49] In 1986, the San Xavier Cooperative Farm shut down because of well failures. In July 1992, the local newspaper reported that "holes and fissures are clustered on the long-irrigated but now-closed farms on the northeastern end of the district."[50] In 1992, total water use on the reservation was minimal.

Both the Tohono O'odham Nation and the San Xavier Reservation are concerned not only about the current levels of non-Indian pumping, but also about the limits on groundwater pumping on San Xavier and Schuk Toak that are contained in the settlement act. Good-quality groundwater is needed on the reservation to support domestic and industrial uses. Water from CAP is not currently scheduled for treatment to drinking water quality and, if untreated, is only suitable for agricultural purposes. In addition, San Xavier may in the future want to conduct groundwater recharge projects, for which authority also is lacking under the act. Finally, the people of San Xavier want to see the water table stabilized underneath the reservation.[51]

The Farm

Although the settlement act does not mandate that the allocation of CAP water be used for on-reservation agricultural uses, it does provide for federal subsidy of an irrigation distribution system for CAP water "as long as such water is used for the irrigation of Indian lands."[52] The emphasis on farming in the settlement act has always been somewhat bewildering. Although the act states the water may be used for any purpose, the federal subsidy encourages agricultural use. In addition, although the costs of the water are subsidized under the act, the Tohono

O'odham Nation and San Xavier Reservation would incur substantial debt obligations for the development of a new large-scale farm on land with no history of irrigation.

Under a contract with the Tohono O'odham Nation, planning for the development of SAWRSA water was done by the Bureau of Reclamation, which in turn contracted with an engineering firm to perform the necessary economic, environmental, and other impact statements. It is this set of documents that recommends the farm. This engineering firm, which had recently constructed a 16,000-acre farm on Ak-Chin Reservation, advised San Xavier Reservation and the Tohono O'odham Nation that it would be unlikely to find an off-reservation market for the water and recommended a large-scale farming operation to put the water to use by 1992.[53]

The San Xavier Reservation itself at the time was embroiled in a proposal to lease much of the reservation to a non-Indian developer who wanted to build a non-Indian housing development on San Xavier. Much of the discussion over a proposed farm took place in this context, with supporters of the farm looking at it as a way to block non-Indian development of the reservation. The whole issue of a farm became caught up in the larger issue "of negotiating culture before the blade of backhoe and bulldozer."[54]

Public meetings were held in September 1987 and March 1988 to discuss the concerns of the residents of San Xavier about the proposed plans for the farm. Residents had four primary concerns about the farm development: (1) it would require an irreversible commitment of land to long-term agricultural uses, preempting other uses of both land and water; (2) it would destroy native plants and wildlife, which conflicts with strong cultural preferences for preserving lands in the natural state; (3) the Tohono O'odham Nation would commit to an indebtedness of nearly $26 million, with its ability to repay the development loans dependent upon the success of growing crops on lands with no history of irrigation; and (4) if the farm failed, it would subject the district to increased pressure to allow commercial and residential development to retire the debt to the federal government.[55]

The farm is not supported by San Xavier residents. Over $8 million has been spent in planning, and little has been resolved.[56] Some of the problems lie with the planning process used by the Bureau of Reclamation. As one author notes, the public hearings at Sells and San Xavier on the Environmental Impact Statement prepared for the farm "were orchestrated to receive comments on the draft EIS, not to provide responses. . . . The strategy backfired. Reclamation officials, taking no opportunity to respond, were chastised repeatedly at the San Xavier hearing and subsequently by incredulous editorial writers for a local newspaper, the *Arizona Daily Star*."[57]

There are also considerable doubts about the economics of the farm, with San

Xavier concerned that if it failed, the Tohono O'odham Nation would be "bankrupt."[58] In addition, the proposed tribal farm site may be the location of archaeological sites, including human remains, and would destroy many acres of wildlife habitat permanently. For these reasons, San Xavier residents remain staunchly opposed to the farm.

Allottee Water Rights

Of the more than 71,000 acres of reservation land, 40,000 acres is allottee land on the San Xavier Reservation. This land was allotted to individual Indians under the Dawes Act of 1884. Courts have recognized water rights for allottees, but the exact nature of the right has not been defined. Since the very start, the water rights of the allottees posed a thorny problem for negotiators for the simple fact that no one had a solution. One congressional staffer noted that, at this time, "there was some question at the federal level what the nature of the allottees' right is, whether by virtue of the fact that they have an allotted piece of property, whether the allotment carried with it a separate water right, or whether their water right is only derivative" of the water rights of the Tohono O'odham Nation.[59]

This question was ultimately decided by congressional staff members: "[W]e decided, the allottees, their rights are only derivative of the tribe, so that the tribe will have to take care of the allottees by giving them water out of their water and damages out of their damages."[60] In addition, these issues were never openly discussed. Congressional staff members hoped to avoid opposition from the allottees and also opposition from other Indian tribes that have allotted lands, including Montana tribes, on this issue.[61]

Opposition to this position did arise, but locally and late in the negotiation process. In 1982, Mark Ulmer, an attorney with Papago Legal Services, prepared a paper on SAWRSA for the Tribal Council.[62] Ulmer states that "from beginning to end the SAWRSA fails to express adequately the legally established water rights of allotted lands."[63] Among the concerns expressed by Ulmer are that the introduction did not cite the allottees, there was no requirement that the on-reservation distribution works serve the allottees, no rights of the allottees to the 10,000 acre-feet in groundwater were specified, and there was no mention of a right of allottees to receive damages.[64]

In hindsight, Ulmer's concerns were well founded, for considerable conflict has arisen between the Tohono O'odham Nation and the San Xavier Reservation over the issue of allottee water rights on San Xavier and the best way to meet these rights. One attorney commented recently that the SAWRSA settlement ultimately may fail because the settlement provided that "any entitlement of water of any individual member of the Papago Tribe shall be satisfied out of the water resources provided in this Title" and "the allottees have their own water rights and have not agreed with the settlement."[65] Negotiations are continuing on this issue in late 1992. Congressional amendments being sought by the allottees include authority over the Cooperative Farm on San Xavier, guaranteed access to groundwater, and a benefit fund for economic development and other purposes.

Conclusion

Judged according to the stated purposes in the act itself, the Southern Arizona Water Rights Settlement Act has failed by failing to provide a "fair and reasonable" settlement of the water rights claims of the San Xavier Reservation."[66] Moreover, it has failed "to provide the necessary flexibility in the management of resources" and also to "insure conservation and management of water resources in a manner consistent with goals and programs of the State of Arizona and the Papago Tribe."[67]

Substantial, and as of yet unresolved, issues have arisen during implementation. First, continued groundwater pumping by non-Indians in the surrounding area negates the original intent of the settlement, which was to reduce reliance on groundwater by both the Indians and non-Indians by structuring the settlement around CAP water. Under the act, only the Indians are legally bound to take CAP allotments, and only they have a limit on groundwater pumping. The Tohono O'odham will not be able to stabilize the water table beneath the reservation unless pumping by agricultural and mining interests in the area is curtailed.

Second, the planning for the farm and the subsequent controversy it has generated between the Tohono O'odham Nation and the San Xavier Reservation over water use on San Xavier are also unresolved. However, this tension was created largely by the act itself. When the terms of the settlement were crafted, there was little participation on the part of the Tohono O'odham, with "real negotiations" limited to "a handful of people, two handfuls."[68] As Ulmer noted: "Tohono participation was limited in the negotiations of the Settlement Act. . . . The whole thing was run on the mindset of lawyers and technical people, not in service to the community or to the underlying social and cultural values. The community level meetings were always held in English; more often than not there was no translation."[69] The current tension between the Tohono O'odham Nation and the San Xavier Reservation reflects that reality.

During negotiations, the act was crafted to ensure that CAP would be completed to Tucson, to lift the cloud the Tohono O'odham suit had placed on non-Indian economic development, and also to ensure continued groundwater pumping on the part of non-Indians in the Tucson basin. The act was not crafted to promote economic health on the reservation. The first set of goals have been met; the second has not. The Central Arizona Project is completed, and the cloud on growth has been lifted, leaving San Xavier as the only entity in the area with a strict limit on groundwater usage.

Third, the SAWRSA settlement is also flawed in the way the allottee claims are handled. The decision to transfer the responsibility for the claims of the allottees to the Tohono O'odham Nation, with no statutory language to ensure allottee participation (nor the time and resources to build that participation on the reservation), may ensure that the claims cannot be met under the terms of the act as it is now written. Amendments will be required on this issue also to ensure that the rights and claims of the residents of San Xavier are met through this settlement.

Judged from another perspective, the dimensions of Indian water rights discussed earlier, the settlement also fares none too well. When the dimensions are examined to determine how well they are represented in the settlement act, SAWRSA fares well on only two counts—the amount of water needed to fulfill the purposes of the reservation, under the quantity dimension, and funds provided for development, under the economic dimension. The award of 76,000 acre-feet is sufficient, and trust funds were established both to help the secretary of the interior meet his responsibilities under the act and also to fund on-reservation water development and use.

However, SAWRSA scores poorly on other counts. The supply of water—CAP—may not be a long-term reliable source of water, free from interruptions in supply, and of adequate quality. The Colorado River is overallocated, and no one is certain what will happen to water rights in the Colorado River basin once the Upper Basin states develop and use their full allotment of water. Droughts are also expected (not to mention climate change), and while San Xavier's water allotment does have a higher priority than agricultural users, there will be years of low, and possibly no, deliveries.

Moreover, San Xavier will not be able to turn to groundwater and pump as other interests may during shortage years. Also, no one in the state is certain of the long-term economic viability of the Central Arizona Project, with the recent refusal of agricultural and mining interests to take CAP allocations. Finally, because there are no provisions for the treatment of CAP water (thereby limiting use of this water to agriculture), the act scores low on the elements of adequate quality for all uses and also on flexibility in use. Consequently, because of these questions about CAP and the limits on groundwater pumping, SAWRSA scores low on reliability and concern for future generations.

Also, SAWRSA contains few provisions designed to enhance the management of water resources both on the reservation and in the surrounding community. In fact, the Tohono O'odham Nation and San Xavier's control over water use (an element of the management dimension) and also flexibility of use and the ability to use water without limits (both elements of the economic dimension) are all hampered by certain provisions of the act. These provisions include the limit on leasing to the Tucson area only, which certainly lowers the price if leasing is chosen as an option; the emphasis on agriculture found in the act, namely, the federal subsidy for the irrigation system only; and finally, the lack of treatment for CAP water. In addition, the Tohono O'odham still do not have a significant voice in water management decisions off-reservation.

As for ranking the spiritual dimension of the settlement act, the authors believe it is the province of the Indian people involved in each settlement to assess whether a water use is consistent with tribal culture, whether there is adequate concern for future generations, and whether the spiritual relationship with the Creator is respected.

Overall, SAWRSA does not rank highly on any of the elements with the exception of the amount of water and funds provided for water use. The management and economic dimensions in particular score the lowest. In fact, the only provision that mentions management states that the tribe must adopt a water management plan similar to the plan adopted by the state. A number of amendments will be required to address these issues before SAWRSA can be considered a successful settlement of Indian water rights claims.

In sum, Indian water rights settlements are a chance, an opportunity, to introduce flexibility into western water law and also to fulfill a long-standing trust obligation of the federal government to Indian people. The courts have repeatedly affirmed *Winters* rights, and tribal water rights will be an important factor in future water management efforts in the West. Negotiated settlements can improve the management of water resources—primarily by increasing coordination and cooperation among water users, irrespective of jurisdictional boundaries. To accomplish this coordination, however, partnerships between tribal governments and federal, state, and local agencies must be built.

The key to these settlements, and in improving water management in the West in general, is that all parties must participate fully in the negotiations. The residents of San Xavier and the Tohono O'odham Nation did not fully participate in the original negotiations, and it shows now as the settlement is implemented. Although the Central Arizona Project was completed to the Tucson area, other Indian interests were not served by the act. Western water politics, as usual, will not alone suffice. Unless all interests fully participate in the negotiation process, many of these issues may end up in court.

NOTES

1. Ada Deer, Menominee Tribe, Wisconsin, as quoted in Thomas Berger, *Village Journey* (Toronto: Collins Publishers, 1985), p. 184.

2. John Echohawk, Director, Native American Rights Fund, "Introduction," for the symposium, Settlement of Indian Reserved Water Rights Claims, sponsored by the

Native American Rights Fund and the Western States Water Council, September 1–3, 1992, Albuquerque, N.M.

3. Southern Arizona Water Rights Settlement Act of 1982, P.L. 97-293.

4. See Richard Collins, "The Future Course of the Winters Doctrine," *University of Colorado Law Review* 56 (1985): 481.

5. *Winters v. United States*, 207 U.S. 564 (1908).

6. *Arizona v. California*, 373 U.S. 546 (1963).

7. Western States Water Council, "Indian Water Rights in the West." Prepared for the Western Governors' Association, May 1984.

8. *Arizona v. San Carlos Apache Tribe*, 463 U.S. 545 (1983). See also Mary G. Wallace, "The Supreme Court and Indian Water Rights," in *American Indian Policy in the Twentieth Century*, ed. Vine Deloria, Jr. (Norman: University of Oklahoma Press, 1985), pp. 197–220.

9. Daniel Tarlock, "The Illusion of Finality in General Water Rights Adjudications," *Idaho Law Review* 25 (1988): 271.

10. Daniel McCool, *Command of the Waters: Iron Triangles, Federal Water Development, and Indian Water* (Berkeley: University of California Press, 1987).

11. Austin Nuñez, Testimony of San Xavier Reservation, Hearing of the U.S. Senate Select Committee on Indian Affairs, Washington, D.C., August 4, 1992.

12. Vine Deloria, Jr., *The Metaphysics of Modern Existence* (New York: Harper and Row, 1979), p. 135.

13. Ibid.

14. Interview with Priscilla Domingo, former Papago Water Commission Member, by Kate Vandemoer and Ramona Peters, in Sells, Arizona, October 21, 1983, p. 16. On file at Water Resources Research Center, University of Arizona, Tucson.

15. Interview with unidentified Tohono O'odham Indian, Cowlic Village, Sells District, Tohono O'odham Nation, by Kate Vandemoer and Ramona Peters, in Cowlic Village, Arizona, February 11, 1984. On file at Water Resources Research Center, University of Arizona, Tucson.

16. Deloria, *The Metaphysics of Modern Existence*, p. xiii.

17. Stephen Sanders, Chairman, Legal Committee of Western States Water Council, "Introduction," for the symposium, Settlement of Indian Reserved Water Rights Claims, sponsored by the Native American Rights Fund and the Western States Water Council, September 1–3, 1992, Albuquerque, N.M.

18. Arnold Appeney, former member of Shoshone Bannock Tribal Council, "Preparing to Negotiate," for the symposium, Settlement of Indian Reserved Water Rights Claims, sponsored by the Native American Rights Fund and the Western States Water Council, September 1–3, 1992, Albuquerque, N.M.

19. Howard Funke, Attorney, "The Negotiation Process," for the symposium, Settlement of Indian Reserved Water Rights Claims, sponsored by the Native American

Rights Fund and the Western States Water Council, September 1–3, 1992, Albuquerque, N.M.

20. Jana L. Walker and Susan N. Williams, "Indian Reserved Water Rights," *Natural Resources and Environment* 5, no. 4 (1992): 50.

21. Howard Funke, "Preparing to Negotiate," for the symposium, Settlement of Indian Reserved Water Rights Claims, sponsored by the Native American Rights Fund and the Western States Water Council, September 1–3, 1992, Albuquerque, N.M.

22. Dan Israel, Esq., "Identifying Parties and Issues," for the symposium, Settlement of Indian Reserved Water Rights Claims, sponsored by the Native American Rights Fund and the Western States Water Council, September 1–3, 1992, Albuquerque, N.M.

23. Vine Deloria, "The Lummi Indian Community: The Fisherman of the Pacific Northwest," in *American Indian Economic Development,* ed. Sam Stanley (The Hague: Mouton, 1978), pp. 87–158.

24. Hugh Holub and Don Bufkin, "The Santa Cruz River in Pima County: A Study of the Historical and Legal Factors Relating to Whether or Not the Santa Cruz River Was Navigable upon Arizona's Admission to Statehood." Submitted to Pima County Department of Transportation and Flood Control District, December 15, 1987. Manuscript on file at the Arizona Historical Society, Tucson, p. 32.

25. Testimony of the Papago Tribe of Arizona Before the Subcommittee on Water and Power Resources Committee on Interior and Insular Affairs on H.R. 4363, Tucson, Arizona, August 27, 1981.

26. Stetson Engineers, *The Interrelationships of Basin Ground Water and Surface and Subsurface Flow of the San Pedro River Basin, Arizona.* Report to the United States Department of Justice, 1987, p. B-3.

27. Testimony of Papago Tribe, August 27, 1981, p. 4.

28. G. P. Davis, *Man and Wildlife in Arizona* (Phoenix: Arizona Department of Game and Fish, 1986), p. 51.

29. Ibid., p. 52.

30. Holub and Bufkin, "Santa Cruz River," p. 3.

31. Ibid., p. 28.

32. Senate Subcommittee of the Committee on Indian Affairs, *Survey of the Conditions of the Indians in the United States, Hearings Before a Subcommittee of the Committee on Indian Affairs,* 71st Cong., 3d sess., 1931, pp. 8365–75.

33. Ibid.

34. See F. Lee Brown and Helen Ingram, *Water and Poverty in the Southwest* (Tucson: University of Arizona Press, 1987), p. 115.

35. Henry F. Manuel, Juliann Ramon, and Bernard Fontana, "Dressing for the Window: Papago Indians and Economic Development," in *American Indian Economic Development,* pp. 511–78.

36. Southern Arizona Water Rights Settlement Act, P.L. 97-293.

37. Thomas McGuire, "Indian Water Rights Settlements: Rhetoric of Implementation," *American Indian Culture and Research Journal* 15, no. 2 (1991): 139–69.

38. Tucson Active Management Area, *Management Plan for Second Management Period: 1990–2000* (Phoenix: Arizona Department of Water Resources, 1990), p. 12.

39. See also Susanna Eden and Mary G. Wallace, *Arizona Water: Issues and Information,* Issue Paper No. 11 (Tucson: University of Arizona, Water Resources Research Center, 1991).

40. TAMA, *Second Management Plan.*

41. Tucson Active Management Area, *1991 Pumpage Records from Non-Exempt Wells* (Phoenix: Arizona Department of Water Resources), pp. 32, 37, 38.

42. TAMA, *Second Management Plan.*

43. TAMA, *1991 Pumpage from Non-Exempt Wells,* pp. 8, 16–17.

44. Ibid., pp. 12–13.

45. Ibid., p. 3.

46. ASARCO, Inc., Lease with Tohono O'odham Tribe, negotiated by Ed Berger, Tribal Attorney, September 7, 1972, Sec. 1.

47. Brown and Ingram, *Water and Poverty in the Southwest,* p. 159.

48. See Anthony Davis, "The Central Arizona Project," *The Tucson Weekly,* May 27, 1992, p. 6.

49. Tom Shields, "Holes on O'odham Land May Be Utility-Caused," *The Tucson Citizen,* July 7, 1992, p. 1A.

50. Ibid.

51. See Testimony of Austin Nuñez, Chairman, San Xavier Reservation of the Tohono O'odham Nation, Hearing, Senate Select Committee on Indian Affairs, Washington, D.C., August 3, 1992.

52. SAWRSA, P.L. 97-293, Sec. 304 (e) (2).

53. McGuire, "Indian Water Rights Settlements," p. 154.

54. Ibid.

55. Dennis Rule, "Choices in Indian Water Management," draft thesis, Department of Hydrology and Water Resources, University of Arizona, 1988.

56. Shields, "Holes on O'odham Land May Be Utility-Caused," p. 1A.

57. McGuire, "Indian Water Rights Settlement," p. 159.

58. Tom Shields, "CAP Water? Hold It!" *Tucson Citizen,* November 27, 1989, p. 2A.

59. Interview with Deborah Sliz, Counsel, Committee on Interior and Insular Affairs, U.S. House of Representatives, by Jean Florman, Tom McGuire, and Mary G. Wallace, in Tucson, Arizona, September 11, 1983, p. 6. On file at Water Resources Research Center, University of Arizona, Tucson.

60. Ibid., p. 7.

61. Ibid.

62. M. Ulmer, *Discussion Paper: Southern Arizona Water Rights Settlement Act of 1981*. Prepared for the Papago Tribal Council and Papago Legal Services, January, 1982.

63. Ibid., p. 65.

64. Ibid.

65. Michael Curtis, "Indian Water Rights and Settlements," in *Understanding and Protecting Your Water Rights* (Virginia: The Cambridge Institute, 1992), pp. 2–20.

66. SAWRSA, P.L. 97-293.

67. SAWRSA, P.L. 97-293, Sec. 301, 5(A) and 5(B).

68. Sliz, interview, September 11, 1983, p. 17.

69. Interview with Mark Ulmer, formerly with Papago Legal Aid Services, by Kate Vandemoer and Ramona Peters, in Sells, Arizona, July 28, 1983, p. 4. On file at Water Resources Research Center, University of Arizona, Tucson.

PART II   INTERESTS

4

A FEDERAL PERSPECTIVE

Joseph R. Membrino

The secretary of the interior has the principal responsibility for the government's fiduciary obligations to Indians and Indian reservations. The secretary is also responsible for the use and management of the nation's public lands, mineral resources,
reclamation projects, and fish and wildlife resources. In addition, the Army Corps
of Engineers' water projects, the Forest Service's timber and land management responsibilities, and the Environmental Protection Agency's water quality regulatory
activities affect Indian trust interests. Where non-Indian programs affect Indian
trust resources, the conduct of agency officials must account for the federal fiduciary
duty to Indians as well. In the event of conflicts among agencies on legal issues, the
attorney general has the authority to establish an integrated federal position.

Acknowledging the importance of Indian reserved water rights has been less
difficult for the federal government than accommodating traditional federal goals
and objectives to them. Congress has assigned the secretary of the interior the task
of managing Indian, reclamation, public lands, and environmental responsibilities. The difficulty in the assignment arises from the competition among the Interior Department's programs for water. It is expressed by the political, economic,
and racial overtones in the adage "Water flows uphill toward money, away from
Indians." The Department of the Interior and the Army Corps of Engineers have
implemented massive federal programs for designing and constructing projects to
dam, divert, store, pump, and distribute water. Many federal water developments
in the West occurred with the knowledge that legitimate Indian uses and needs had
to be accounted for, although frequently those Indian interests were ignored or cir-
cumvented. The constituencies sponsoring those developments are in the non-

Indian community. From their ranks come the policy officials who conduct the Interior and Corps of Engineers programs and the congressional delegations that authorize them. In the Interior Department, four assistant secretaries claim an interest in reserved water rights settlements: Indian Affairs; Water and Science; Fish, Wildlife and Parks; and Policy, Budget and Administration. Water and Science represents the reclamation constituency. Fish, Wildlife and Parks is the Interior Department's environmental secretariat. Policy, Budget and Administration serves as the department's internal office of management and budget.

Non-Indian Challenges to Indian Reserved Rights

Indian reserved water rights frequently are seen as conflicting with the federal land and resource management programs that serve non-Indian constituencies. Critics assert that the reserved right itself creates such a conflict with the structure and management of state appropriative rights that the only acceptable way to resolve the conflict is to eliminate the reserved right. For example, in the Colorado Ute Indian Water Rights Settlement Act of 1988, there was enormous pressure to make the water supply allocated to the Indians in satisfaction of their reserved rights a state water right.[1] In the *Big Horn River* adjudication of 1988, the state of Wyoming argued that the court should limit the reserved right of the Indians on the Wind River Reservation only to that amount of water actually appropriated by the Indians.[2] The state advanced this argument even though state water users had notice prior to their development of water in the Wind River basin of state permit applications—secured by federal agents for the Indians. The amount of water identified in the state permits was more than was eventually awarded to the Indians by the Wyoming courts under the reserved rights doctrine. These examples suggest that the states' advocacy against Indian reserved water rights has less to do with a perceived legal incompatibility between state appropriative and reserved water rights, and more to do with the goal of divesting Indians of the economic benefits that reserved water rights provide.

The legal positions taken by adversaries to Indian reserved water rights claims described in these examples have been argued repeatedly in state and federal court and have been rejected. In fact, there is no legal conflict between an Indian reserved right and a state appropriative right. Both appropriative and reserved water rights can be quantified, assigned a priority date, recorded in a binding decree, and administered effectively.

Impacts of Water Rights Conflicts on Federal Programs

The growth in water rights adjudications since the United States Supreme Court's decisions in *Colorado River Water Conservation District v. United States* (1976) (also known as the Akin case) and *Arizona v. San Carlos Apache Tribe* (1983) has had a major impact on federal water interests.[3] The government now has no choice about whether to adjudicate its water rights. Program agencies that were used to having the political initiative in Congress on goals and objectives for water use and planning now have to react to general stream adjudications in the courts or risk loss or subordination of their water rights. As adjudications intensified, officials in the Department of the Interior recognized their legal obligation to account for the Indian trust resource. Departmental policies and practices that had favored non-Indian interests or ignored Indian interests had to be reviewed. Laws regarding fish, wildlife, and environmental protection required formulation of claims that were based on more conservative development and management of federal water projects.

The inherent risk in litigation and ignorance or preconceptions about the water needs of other federal programs often lead agency officials to advocate aggressively not only for their programs but also against those of their colleagues in other agencies. Not surprisingly, federal officials reflect the behavior of their constituents' private interests in their instinct to defend an agency practice and assign responsibility for conflict elsewhere. But as adjudications began to proliferate in the mid 1970s, Indians and non-Indians alike attempted to find alternatives to the adjudication process to ensure the resolution of disputes.

Conflict Resolution: The Ak-Chin Settlement

The following history is an example of the dynamic decision-making process federal officials engage in when addressing Indian water needs. In 1978 Congress enacted the Ak-Chin settlement (Public Law 95-328). At the time, the Ak-Chin Indian Community's 20,000-acre reservation in south-central Arizona was wholly dependent on groundwater for irrigation and domestic use. Unfortunately, the community's emerging agricultural economy could not survive because irrigation of farmland surrounding the Ak-Chin Reservation was depleting the aquifer on which the Indians depended for water. The Interior Department recommended to the Justice Department that a suit be brought against the neighboring non-Indian farmers to enjoin the further depletion of the groundwater and to establish the Indian reserved water right in the aquifer.

Before the suit could be filed, a settlement proposed by the Ak-Chin Indian Community was introduced in Congress. The settlement provided for both an interim water supply to meet the emergency needs of the Indians and a permanent water supply. The interim supply was to be produced from a well field to be developed on nearby federal lands. The source of the permanent supply was not identified. Failure to meet the delivery obligations under the proposal would result in federal liability measured by the replacement cost of water not delivered. The administration was supportive of the Ak-Chin claim to water but was opposed to the proposed remedy in the bill because of the problematic nature of the water supply and the attendant cost. After attempting to accommodate some of the Interior Department's concerns, Congress enacted the settlement.

The strong opposition of the Office of Management and Budget to the cost of the settlement was not enough to persuade the president to veto the settlement. As the initial delivery deadline under the act approached, the Interior Department's concerns about being unable to meet the delivery obligation proved to be well-founded. The interim source of supply turned out to be inadequate and in any event could only be developed at enormous expense to the federal government. Although failure to meet the deadline could be looked upon as the fault of the secretary of the interior, everyone shared the blame. The secretary had advised Congress about both the cost and the uncertain source of supply. But Congress had proceeded regardless with a plan that the Ak-Chin Community had advocated. The government could not turn its back on the settlement because the statutory damages remedy in Public Law 95-328 made federal liability practically inescapable. Fully aware that the Ak-Chin Indian Community had an unbreakable grip on the government's wallet, officials of the Department of the Interior professed the commitment of their minds and hearts to an equitable solution.[4]

Although the Ak-Chin Indian Community had a legal remedy—monetary damages—for the government's failure to perform under Public Law 95-328, the community recognized that even a successful lawsuit would not produce any water for them. For its part the Interior Department was persuaded that, aside from the liability risk, neither the federal trust responsibility nor politics with the influential bipartisan Arizona congressional delegation would be well-served if the United States were a defendant in a damages action. Instead, the Ak-Chin Indian Community and the Interior Department negotiated an agreement in principle to revise the government's obligations under Public Law 95-328. Essentially, the agreement provided for the government to pay damages for failure to make timely delivery of the interim water supply and revised the funding and delivery schedules for the permanent water supply. Whether the agreement in principle would succeed depended upon its adoption by both the administration and Congress.

The Interior Department took the initiative to make it clear that the revised settlement in the agreement did not in principle reflect an unwillingness by the executive branch to carry out instructions from Congress. The success of the Indians at Ak-Chin in their farming enterprise and the economic benefits it provided for the Ak-Chin Community had made a favorable impression on both the Carter and the Reagan administrations. The unfortunate irony for Ak-Chin was that its farm economy depended on a depleting groundwater supply and the remedy provided in the 1978 act simply could not be implemented feasibly.

In correspondence to the Arizona congressional delegation and the governor of Arizona, the secretary of the interior described the history of the settlement and the agreement in principle and urged cooperation in finding a common solution to a shared problem. This strategy was unusually constructive but not easily accomplished. The constructive element of the strategy was its premise that "we have a problem"—not just the Interior Department, but Congress, the state, and the Ak-Chin Indian Community as well. The strategy preempted finger pointing.

Yet the difficulty in the strategy was its insistence that interests not normally associated with Indian affairs contribute to a revised settlement. Many were surprised and displeased that the secretary's determination to provide a permanent water supply to Ak-Chin instead of paying damages would affect their interest in water. The secretary concluded that all resources under his authority, not just those in the Bureau of Indian Affairs program, should be examined as potential means for meeting the needs at Ak-Chin. One source of water was the lower Colorado River, which was under the exclusive management and allocation authority of the secretary of the interior.[5] Irrigation districts and cities in the lower Colorado River basin with water delivery contracts under section 5 of the Boulder Canyon Project Act objected to the suggestion that the secretary had the authority to cancel the right to unused portions of their contract allocations. Officials in the department's reclamation program also argued against supplying water from canceled contracts for Indian use. Interestingly, the director of the Arizona Department of Water Resources concurred with the conclusion that the secretary could cancel contracts for unused water but argued that the water should be used for the Central Arizona Project, not Indian water rights settlements. At the end of the day, and with some accommodation by the federal government to the non-Indian parties, a revised settlement was enacted in 1984.

Federal Strategy for Resolution of Water Conflicts

While the Ak-Chin settlement is noteworthy as the first settlement in the post-Akin era, it was a settlement exclusively between the federal government and the Ak-Chin Indian Community. There was no cost sharing by nonfederal interests and no pending litigation involving non-Indian water users, although the Interior Department's recommendation to the Justice Department that suit be filed against non-Indian pumpers in the vicinity of the Ak-Chin Reservation was a major factor in Congress' consideration of the settlement proposal.

Between the first and second Ak-Chin settlement acts, another dispute over Indian water rights was pending in southern Arizona. The dispute pitted the United States and the Tohono O'odham Nation (formerly the Papago Tribe) against the city of Tucson and myriad corporate and individual water users. The response of the federal executive to the Tohono O'odham settlement negotiations was a signal event for Indian reserved water rights.

61

A lawsuit had been pending since 1975 over the nature and extent of the Tohono O'odham Nation's reserved water rights in the aquifer underlying both the city of Tucson and the San Xavier District of the Tohono O'odham Nation's reservation. Except for an allocation of water that will be delivered from the Central Arizona Project, Tucson is wholly dependent on groundwater for its municipal needs. In 1982, the Tohono O'odham Nation and local interests negotiated a settlement bill that was passed by Congress. The president vetoed it because federal policy-level officials had not participated in the negotiations and there was no provision for sharing the settlement costs by the local beneficiaries of the settlement.

Following a review of options for managing Indian water rights negotiations after the Tohono O'odham settlement veto, the secretary of the interior established an Interior Policy Advisory Group on Indian water claims on July 14, 1982. The practical and political impossibility of making any one of the assistant secretaries first among equals in managing Indian claims resulted in a decision to make the solicitor into the chair of the advisory group. The advisory group was staffed with career and political appointees who formulated policy positions for consideration by the advisory group, coordinated the presentation of issues involving other federal agencies and the Office of Management and Budget, and served as plenipotentiaries for the Interior Department in negotiations with Indian tribes and non-federal interests. A federal team supervised by the advisory group participated in subsequent Tohono O'odham negotiations, cost sharing was provided for, and the Southern Arizona Water Rights Settlement Act was approved by the president.

The essential result in the Tohono O'odham settlement is not much different from that of Ak-Chin. Both settlements require the United States to acquire and deliver a permanent water supply to Indian reservations and make the government liable in damages measured by the replacement cost of water when delivery deadlines are not met. Final settlement leaves the federal government exclusively responsible for performance; the non-Indian community is held harmless. The nonfederal share of the cost ($5 million) represents only a small fraction of the ultimate cost of the settlement to the federal government.

The Tohono O'odham settlement is important, then, not so much for the differences between the vetoed bill and the final settlement, but because it was a vehicle for a major federal policy pronouncement on Indian water rights. Since the veto of the first Tohono O'odham settlement, participation of federal policy officials and nonfederal cost sharing are integral to future settlement negotiations if they are to receive federal approval.

The Interior Policy Advisory Group format was also used to address the second Ak-Chin, Fort Peck, Colorado Ute, and Pyramid Lake conflicts, among others. The advisory group was dismantled in the last year of the Reagan administration.

Federal Non-Indian Program Interests

Indian water rights settlements are sometimes viewed as opportunities to accomplish non-Indian goals and objectives. The primary inducement to non-Indian interests in the Colorado Ute Indian Water Rights Settlement (P.L. 100-585), for example, was the construction of the Animas–La Plata Project in southwestern Colorado. The project had been authorized in 1968 in the same act that authorized the Central Arizona Project (P.L. 90-537). The Animas–La Plata Project proved to be controversial and of questionable feasibility. Neither the Carter nor the Reagan administration was in favor of its construction. Nonetheless, proponents of the project viewed it as an opportunity to make use of a portion of the water allocated to the Upper Basin of the Colorado River in the Colorado River Compact. After prolonged negotiations to scale down the project and provide for nonfederal cost sharing, the Animas–La Plata Project was made an integral part of the Colorado Ute settlement. Some observers question whether the project will ever be built. Others criticize the settlement process as having been overwhelmed by the controversy over the Animas–La Plata Project at the expense of the government's advocacy of the Indian interest.

The Federal Fiduciary Role

Frequently, the Interior Department is invited to make its objective the facilitation of water rights settlements. The role of facilitator is one that falls naturally to the Interior Department because of its stature as a cabinet agency and the diverse interests its programs serve. But the role of facilitator is ancillary to the fiduciary role; it should not supplant it. Advocacy is as essential in negotiations as it is in litigation. The department has been most effective both for the federal interest generally and in its role as trustee for Indian water resources when it has been an advocate in the settlement process. For example, in the negotiation to revise the Ak-Chin settlement discussed above, the federal government saved millions of dollars and secured a practicable water supply for the Indians by advocating the position that the secretary of the interior had the authority to reallocate unused Colorado River water for Indian use.

Tribal Trust Funds

A major influence on the dynamic process of negotiation of reserved water rights is the introduction of tribal trust funds as part of a settlement. Trust funds raise considerations for Indian tribes that are independent of reserved water rights. Tribes generally are not well-off, and they generally cannot expect immediate economic benefit from a water rights settlement. Their concern in litigation or negotiation is in securing a long-term agreement for reservation water supplies. But when a trust fund is proffered, tribal leadership becomes subject to a different array of constituent pressures that are created by the prospect of immediate financial relief from the trust fund. Negotiators responsible for the Indian water resource at stake in negotiations should carefully manage the introduction of a trust fund concept into negotiations to avoid distorting the focus of the negotiations or distracting the tribal constituents with the opportunity for short-term monetary relief at the expense of a permanent interest in water. If Indian water rights are going to command attention of the administration and Congress only as a vehicle for advancing objectives such as the creation of trust funds to cash out Indian water rights in whole or in part, or featherbedding water projects that are unfeasible, Indian tribes may realize little benefit from their water resources.

Water Marketing

One subject that has caused considerable controversy in water rights settlements is water marketing. For many Indian tribes without the capital or organization to engage in large-scale water development, the opportunity to market water for off-reservation use enables them to participate in regional economies while raising capital to provide for on-reservation economic growth. The economic potential for water marketing lies at the heart of the conflicts over control of Indian water rights by state authorities. At the same time, that potential has influenced federal officials to promote marketing of not only Indian water, but also water developed by the Bureau of Reclamation and the Army Corps of Engineers.

The following are observations about some of the legal and policy aspects of the marketing issues. First, the Supreme Court in *Sporhase v. Nebraska* (1983) concluded that for the purpose of the Interstate Commerce Clause, "water is an article of commerce."[6] Most commerce clause cases, including *Sporhase,* turn on the issue of whether the sovereign can restrict commerce in view of the constitutional authority of Congress in that matter. In the case of Indian water marketing, tribes are attempting through their sovereign and proprietary interests to put water into commerce over the objections of state and private water interests. No substantial justification has been identified to restrict Indian water marketing except an interest in controlling the potential economic gains tribes could realize from water marketing. Under *Sporhase,* that is not a legitimate justification because, as the Court stated, "a state's power to regulate the use of water in times and places of shortage for the purpose of protecting the health of its citizens— and not simply the health of its economy—is at the core of its police power. For Commerce Clause purposes, we have long recognized a difference between economic protectionism, on the one hand, and health and safety regulation, on the other. The Court also would not justify one state's attempt to restrict interstate commerce because of another state's unreasonable burden on commerce." [7]

Second, *Sporhase* is instructive on claims of state primacy over off-reservation transfers of Indian water rights. The Court rejected Nebraska's argument that federal law, particularly section 8 of the Reclamation Act of 1902, authorized states "to impose otherwise impermissible burdens on interstate commerce" in water.[8] The Court held that Congress's deference to state water law does not indicate any intent to "remove federal constitutional constraints on such state laws. The negative implications of the Commerce Clause, like the mandates of the Fourteenth Amendment, are ingredients of the *valid* state law to which Congress has deferred."[9] The Court made that conclusion having fully considered the facts that Congress had not created a federal water law for reclamation projects and that states are permitted to make compacts over water rights under Article I, Section 10, of the United States Constitution.

In the case of Indian water rights, Congress has created a federal water law of Indian reserved rights. Indian reserved water rights are not subject to state appropriation doctrines; they are not dependent upon state law or procedure for their existence.[10] In addition, states that have made compacts on interstate waters consistently disclaim any adverse impact on Indian water rights.[11] Attempts to do otherwise have not been well received. Congress has refused for almost twenty years to approve a compact allocating water from interstate streams between California and Nevada because of provisions that would adversely affect Indian water rights. Such action by Congress can hardly be described as deference to state primacy over Indian water rights.

Third, in addition to the limits on state burdens on commerce in the Interstate Commerce Clause is the Indian Commerce Clause, which has the distinct and central function of ensuring Congress the plenary power to legislate regarding Indian affairs.[12]

Fourth, the Supreme Court has ruled that means used to quantify Indian reserved water rights "shall not constitute a restriction of the usage of them."[13] The Wyoming Supreme Court in the Big Horn River adjudication also expressed that conclusion in holding that the quantification of the Indian reserved water rights in terms of practicably irrigable acreage subsumed use of water for domestic, stock water, and municipal uses. It also held that the water could be used for other purposes such as mineral and industrial development. The solicitor has also concluded that "neither law nor sound policy forbid marketing Indian water rights outside the boundaries of Indian reservations."[14]

Clearly, states have a considerable stake in regulating water use by their non-Indian citizens who reside outside Indian reservations. That interest extends to the use of Indian reserved water rights by those citizens. The question really is about the nature and extent of that interest. In view of *Sporhase* and the Indian reserved rights doctrine, the claim of authority by the states probably is more limited than they are prepared to concede. As a practical matter, state transfers of Indian reserved water for off-reservation use will occur generally as a first use of undeveloped water. In that case, the impact of such use on state water administration will be no different than that of a senior appropriator making a priority call for water under state law. Although junior users may be displaced under that circumstance, it is because the state law of prior appropriation and the federal law of Indian reserved rights operate similarly in that regard.

While there is nothing inherent in the reserved water right itself that would restrict placing it in commerce, the effect of the Indian Non-Intercourse Act on Indian water marketing needs to be considered.[15] The Non-Intercourse Act is protective legislation for the benefit of Indians, enacted early in this country's history to regularize dealings with Indian tribes through a federal authority and to prevent the improvident alienation of Indian land. If any legal bar exists to Indian water marketing, it is the Non-Intercourse Act. The bar would exist not because the Non-Intercourse Act affects the substance of the reserved rights doctrine but because no conveyance under the act is valid without congressional approval. The Non-Intercourse Act addresses only transfers of interest in lands; it makes no express mention of water rights. Parties in negotiations that contemplate water marketing generally have agreed that relief from the prohibition in the Non-Intercourse Act in the context of water marketing should be provided for expressly in federal legislation to approve the settlement. Examples are the Southern Arizona Water Rights Settlement Act (P.L. 97-293 Title III), the Fort Peck–Montana Compact, the Colorado Ute Indian Water Rights Settlement Act (P.L. 100-585), and the Salt River Pima-Maricopa Indian Community Water Rights Settlement Act of 1988 (P.L. 100-512).

Another view is that the special provision for water marketing in specific settlement legislation should be read to reflect an agreement to restrict extant marketing authority in a way calculated to best serve the interests compromised in the settlement. The Tohono O'odham settlement limited Indian water marketing geographically. The Fort Peck–Montana Compact includes provisions for interstate water marketing in accordance with state law and for joint ventures in water marketing by the state and the Fort Peck tribes. The Colorado Ute settlement provides that off-reservation use of tribal water changes the water right to a Colorado state water right. Support for this view is found in the lack of inherent limitations on marketing in the reserved rights doctrine as it has been judicially determined to date.

In addition, 25 U.S.C. 477 codifies the provision of the Indian Reorganization

Act regarding the incorporation of Indian tribes. It provides that an Indian tribe's corporate power shall include the power to hold and dispose of property of every description, real and personal, and limits the power to lease land to ten years. Thus, to the extent that the Non-Intercourse Act is a bar, the requisite congressional authority to lease may exist in 25 U.S.C. 477. Congress has also provided general authority to lease Indian land in 25 U.S.C. 415. If the prohibition against the alienation of land in the Non-Intercourse Act has been construed to include water, perhaps the authority to lease land in 25 U.S.C. 415 should be construed to authorize the lease of water. This approach would require reconciling the provision in 25 U.S.C. 415, which authorizes leases for up to ninety-nine years, with 25 U.S.C. 477, which authorizes only ten-year leases of tribal corporate property. In any event, a property interest of such importance as tribal water rights probably would not be considered to have been implied as marketable under 25 U.S.C. 415 or 477.

In terms of federal policy considerations, the economic potential of Indian water marketing is substantial. The Department of the Interior published the *Report of the Task Force on Indian Economic Development* in July 1986, which followed up on and assessed the *Report and Recommendations of the Presidential Commission on Indian Reservation Economies* of November 1984.[16] The task force observed that water development on Indian reservations would require large amounts of federal capital that would probably not be available in view of the federal government's general reduction in investments in water projects. But the task force did conclude that off-reservation leasing of Indian water rights has the potential for becoming a significant new source of revenue for some Indian tribes.

The essential reason for objecting to Indian water marketing is that water not now used by Indians because of lack of financing or political support for its development on the reservations is used by other water users in priority. It is in the interest of those users to advocate against both Indian water marketing and efforts by Indians to develop water for on-reservation use. As long as the economic and political influence of the non-Indian community remains unchecked, water will continue to be used at the expense of Indian economic development.

The irony in the contention against Indian water marketing is that there is a vigorous water market in non-Indian communities throughout the West. Moreover, the Department of the Interior's Bureau of Reclamation has had an aggressive water marketing program since the 1960s, when it introduced a comprehensive plan to make contracts with energy producers for water from reclamation reservoirs in the Missouri River basin. The goals of the industrial water marketing program included generation of revenues for the reclamation fund and reduced dependence on foreign energy supplies. Between 1969 and 1971 the secretary of the interior entered into option contracts for the use of 658,000 acre-feet of water annually for industrial purposes.[17] The Interior Department's water marketing program included contracts that provided for interstate water marketing. In 1982, in view of the continued expectation that many of the authorized reclamation projects for irrigation in the Missouri River basin would not be constructed, the Department of the Interior contracted with the Energy Transportation Systems, Incorporated (ETSI) Pipeline Project to provide water for interstate transportation of coal to steam-generating power plants.[18] In the *ETSI* case, the Department of the Interior and the states of Montana, North Dakota, and Wyoming supported South Dakota's issuance of a permit for ETSI to take water from Oahe Reservoir, a federal facility in that state, for interstate use in the government's water marketing program. Missouri, Iowa, and Nebraska challenged the contract on a number of grounds, including the fact that the interstate transportation of water under the contract would remove it entirely from the Missouri River basin. The Interior Department lost in the Supreme Court, not on that specific issue or the merits of the water marketing program generally, but because the 1944 Flood Control Act, under which the Oahe Reservoir had been constructed, did not authorize the secretary of the interior to "enter into a contract to withdraw water from an Army [Corps of Engineers–supervised] reservoir for industrial use without the approval of the Department of the Army." [19]

At the end of the Reagan administration, the Department of the Interior announced a new water marketing policy. Under the policy, the department agreed to facilitate marketing proposals involving water stored or conveyed in federal facilities. The policy raised the attendant question of whether and how the massive federal subsidy in the reclamation program will be recouped by the federal treasury when water is transferred to higher-value economic uses through marketing. The policy was promulgated in part in response to a resolution of the Western Governors' Association that the Interior Department develop a policy to facilitate water transfers involving water or facilities of the Bureau of Reclamation.

The non-Indian arguments against Indian water marketing lack credence in view of this background. They also reveal an essential conflict with both Indian and national economic interests by asserting that Indians should not market because the private interest will suffer but that non-Indians should be free to market even if federal financial interests will be adversely affected.

For Indians to enjoy any measure of economic benefit from the reserved water rights doctrine, the federal government will have to represent the Indian interest vigorously in the water marketing debate. This requires at a minimum that federal policy officials reject the premise asserted by nonfederal negotiators that reserved water rights may be marketed off-reservation only as if they were state water rights. Access by Indian tribes to water markets is in both the federal fiduciary and national economic interests. Legal authority for that access exists. It remains for the federal trustee, in concert with Indian tribes, to assert it.

Conclusions

Indian reserved water rights are increasingly important to both Indian and non-Indian communities in the West. Resolution of Indian claims to water requires acceptance, legally and economically, of tribal interests in western water supplies. The federal government's roles as trustee of Indian water rights and manager of the nation's natural resources uniquely suit it to leadership in Indian water rights and water resources management.

NOTES

1. P.L. 100-585, 102 Stat. 2973 (1988).

2. 753 P.2d 76 (Wyo. 1988), affirmed sub nom. *Wyoming v. United States,* 492 U.S. 342 (1989).

3. 424 U.S. 800 (1976); 463 U.S. 545 (1983).

4. It is interesting to compare the subsequent history of the Ak-Chin settlement with that of the Fallon Paiute-Shoshone Indian Reservation. In 1978, the same Congress had enacted a law (P.L. 95-337) requiring the secretary of the interior to make his "first priority" the development of irrigation on the Fallon Indian Reservation that had been owed to the tribes since 1906. The Fallon Indian Reservation lies within the bounds of the controversial Newlands Reclamation Project in Nevada. Irrigation development under the terms of the act proved to be technically difficult, environmentally sensitive, and very expensive. Unlike the 1978 Ak-Chin act, there was no deadline in the Fallon statute and no provision for damages in the event the deadline was not met. Eleven years later, development had not occurred. Eventually, Congress enacted a revised settlement with the concurrence of the Fallon tribes (P.L. 101-618, 104 Stat. 3289).

5. Boulder Canyon Project Act (43 U.S.C. 617 et seq.); *Arizona v. California,* 373 U.S. 546 (1963).

6. 458 U.S. 941 (1983).

7. Ibid., p. 958, n. 18.

8. Ibid., p. 958.

9. Ibid., p. 960; emphasis in original.

10. *Cappaert v. United States,* 426 U.S. 128, 145 (1976).

11. Snake River Compact, Article XIV A.1 (Act of March 21, 1950, 64 Stat. 29); Upper Colorado River Basin Compact, Article XIX (a) (Act of April 6, 1949, 63 Stat. 31); Colorado River Compact, Article VII; Rio Grande Compact, Article XVI (Act of May 31, 1939, 53 Stat. 785).

12. *Cotton Petroleum v. New Mexico,* 490 U.S. 163 (1989).

13. *Arizona v. California,* 439 U.S. 419, 422 (1979).

14. Letter from Solicitor William H. Coldiron to Patricia Nagle, Chairperson, Colorado River Board of California, March 29, 1983. On file with author.

15. 25 U.S.C. 177.

16. U.S. Department of the Interior, *Report of the Task Force on Indian Economic Development* (Washington, D.C.: Government Printing Office, 1986); *Report and Recommendations of the Presidential Commission on Indian Reservation Economies* (Washington, D.C.: Government Printing Office, November 1984).

17. *Environmental Defense Fund v. Andrus*, 596 F.2d 848 (9th Cir. 1979).

18. ETSI *Pipeline Project v. Missouri*, 484 U.S. 495 (1988).

19. Ibid., p. 917.

5

FEDERALISM AND SELF-DETERMINATION: STATE GOALS IN INDIAN WATER RIGHTS DISPUTES

Peter W. Sly

The vast federal proprietary and trust landholdings in the West will present dynamic issues of federalism and water rights throughout the 1990s. In this decade, western states are becoming increasingly concerned with water management. The federal government will not fund major new water projects, yet its regulatory presence in western water matters is increasing.

In this climate, Indian water rights disputes provide both opportunities and dangers for states. States and tribes may work together to foster federal funding of some water projects. Some states may have common hydrologic interests with tribes. Some states fear increasing federal regulatory control as a result of uncertain Indian water rights claims. All states have four major interests in Indian water disputes: regulatory and adjudicatory simplicity, the protection of proprietary and fiscal interests, the maintenance of the integrity of state water law, and interstate interests.[1]

Regulatory and Adjudicatory Simplicity

In the exercise of its regulatory powers, the state acts in water matters as a "traffic cop." As with any exercise of state police powers, simple, certain, and clear rules are desirable. In resolving conflicts over the use of a finite resource, all water managers seek to remove uncertainty. Western water laws are built on efforts to increase certainty: for example, the requirement that a water right must be put to continuous beneficial use to remain protected. Uncertain, potentially senior rights, such as reserved water rights, affect all junior rights on the system. Uncertainty in the amount of water rights is especially disruptive to current efforts to make water more transferable. To avoid uncertainty, states have sought uniform administration, simplification of general stream adjudications, and negotiation where feasible.

Uniform Administration

States have an interest in ensuring that recognition of Indian water rights does not create a duplicative, overlapping, and potentially inconsistent system of water administration in the same drainage as state rights. It is this interest in uniform administration that the Supreme Court recognized in a series of cases concerning the powers of state courts to adjudicate Indian water rights under the McCarran Amendment.[2] Since 1983, it has been clear that the courts of all states have the power to adjudicate Indian reserved water rights.[3] Federal courts also have powers to adjudicate Indian water rights but generally defer to state courts under principles of comity.

The power of state courts to adjudicate reserved water rights includes the power to administer a judicial decree that recognizes federal water rights. State executive agencies may, at least under court supervision, administer Indian water rights that affect the rights of non-Indians.[4] States do not have the power to determine the internal allocation of Indian water rights within the tribe. The Supreme Court has struggled with continuing questions of local, tribal, and federal regulatory powers over checkerboard reservation areas.[5]

From the Desert Land Act through the 1902 Reclamation Act and the McCarran Amendment, Congress has generally declined to establish a duplicative system of federal water regulation overlapping intrastate systems of water rights. States are concerned that federal regulatory powers over federal water rights may upset this historic federal deference to intrastate water rights administration.

Simplifying Stream Adjudications

States have an interest in reducing the complexity and costs of general stream adjudications. These unique, mammoth proceedings have high fiscal, personnel, and political costs to states. State positions in these complex cases have been twofold: to keep the adjudication as simple as possible and to negotiate when feasible.

In a general adjudication, the water rights of each user against every other user are determined in a judicial forum.[6] To meet the requirement for jurisdiction over federal rights, the general stream adjudication must be "comprehensive." States resist federal Department of Justice attempts to broaden stream adjudications to include minor parties and rights, because of the large costs of participation in these complex and lengthy proceedings. Recent state court decisions in Idaho and Arizona have expanded the scope of those stream adjudications. In Idaho, the state supreme court required the inclusion of minor parties and adjudicated tributaries in the Snake River adjudication.[7] In the Arizona Gila River adjudication, the court included groundwater underlying federal reservations within the scope of the adjudication, although Arizona law does not currently permit the court to similarly treat nonfederal groundwater rights.[8] Involvement of thousands of parties and complex groundwater rights in these stream adjudications will lengthen the proceedings and undermine the possibilities for settlement. The Arizona courts have taken a practical approach to service of process.[9]

The question of whether the United States must share in the administrative costs of stream adjudication is pending before the Supreme Court.[10]

Dispute Resolution

In recognition of the costs of general stream adjudication, western states and tribes have actively sought negotiation of federal and Indian reserved water rights claims. The Conference of Western Attorneys General, after conferring with the Native American Rights Fund, published a comprehensive legal study of reserved water rights negotiation in 1988.[11] The Western Governors' Association has taken an active role urging federal approval of negotiated settlements. Montana and Colorado have been active in dispute resolution and in encouraging settlement and quantification of uncertain federal and Indian reserved water rights. Arizona, California, Idaho, Nevada, New Mexico, and Utah have also been party to recent Indian water settlements.

Negotiation for all three governments—state, tribal, and federal—can be as difficult as litigation. Effective negotiation requires that each government keep its internal house in order through the negotiation. The federal government faces internal conflicts in representing Indian tribes, both with respect to other federal interests and with competing tribes on the same drainage. As tribal governments wrestle with their relationship to allottees and other individuals on the reservation, they are increasingly recognizing a distinction between their sovereign and proprietary roles. The states face internal conflicts as they seek protection of their specific proprietary interests and in representation of non-Indian water users.

Protection of State Proprietary and Fiscal Interests

Proprietary Rights

As proprietor, the state's interest is as a water user. States can assert a proprietary interest based on beneficial use of water on state properties: for example, parks, hospitals, prisons, and schools. These state proprietary interests are site specific and may conflict with each other.

States also have proprietary rights for developed state water projects that rely on state bonding authority and tax-exempt status. The largest example is the

California State Water Project; Colorado, Montana, and Utah also have state projects. State water development agencies act somewhat like the U.S. Bureau of Reclamation, selling their developed water by contract to water districts and users. When it acts as a water purveyor, the state has both a representative and a proprietary interest on behalf of its contractors.

States also have proprietary claims for fish and wildlife. In most states, fish and wildlife agencies can assert claims for fish and wildlife preservation, which may overlap with similar federal claims. Most states now have programs for protection of in-stream flows. In-stream flow protection is complex when developed alongside existing systems of vested water rights. States are concerned that federal in-stream requirements resulting from the Endangered Species Act, Clean Water Act permits, regulations, salinity control, or non-Indian reserved water rights in wilderness areas will upset these state systems. Indian rights based on irrigation uses may not be consistent with state in-stream flow laws.

All western states assert a "public interest" in water by constitution or statute. State water allocation decisions are subject to a broad balancing of interests, including the "public trust" in some states.[12] It is not clear whether the state interest under public trust doctrine is proprietary or regulatory.

An evolving area is state water rights for school trust lands. At statehood, Congress granted sections of public land to the western states as a trust to fund public education. These state school lands must be administered to maximize revenues for state schools. States contend that their enabling acts and constitutions require sufficient waters to maximize revenue from those school trust lands. Ironically, this claim has some similarities to claims for federal reserved rights that frequently have been opposed by states.

Many states separate proprietary and regulatory roles. A state agency that acts in a proprietary capacity will be separately represented in a stream adjudication. In Montana, for example, the Department of Natural Resources and Conservation has a proprietary interest. The agency's role of assisting the water court in verification of inflated claims has been limited.[13] In California, the state Departments of Land, Fish and Game, and Water Resources are each separately represented in water rights hearings held before the Water Resources Control Board. Likewise, the Arizona Land Department is separately represented in the Arizona adjudications.

State Fiscal Interests

States have an interest in the economic well-being of Indian reservations, many of which are pockets of extreme poverty. It has been estimated that 80 percent of the government services provided to Indians come from state governments.[14] States encourage water development that can ensure tribal economic self-sufficiency consistent with the prosperity of neighboring communities.

State taxing agencies have a fiscal interest in the exercise of federal reserved water rights. Federal reservations are generally tax exempt. State and local tax revenues may be affected if new use of water on a tax-exempt reservation reduces tax revenues from existing junior priority water uses on taxable land.

Finally, states have a concern with water settlements that obligate the state to fund water supply as part of the settlement. All states recognize some cost-sharing obligations. However, Indian water conflicts are a consequence of conflicting federal policies for public lands, water, and Indians. States believe the federal government should fund Indian water rights settlements that result from inconsistent prior federal policies and practices.

Protection of State Water Rights

The state role as guardian of the state's water law system is complex. Particularly in litigation, states will act to protect the state system of water rights law against Indian rights. In the 1989 Big Horn case, eight out of fourteen western states filed *amicus* briefs in the Supreme Court urging that Indian water rights be limited to those necessary on the reservation. The practical forces pushing states toward representation of private interests are Indian/non-Indian population distribution, landholding patterns, and state water institutions.

1. The proportion of Indian and nonmember population within the reservation. Nonmembers who live on the reservation (whose ancestors were invited on the reservation by the federal government) cannot vote for the tribal government or sue it, and have no effective civil rights.[15] Because of the lack of nonmember enforcement powers against tribal governments, states take a representative role when the nonmember population is significant. Examples of reservations with a significant nonmember population include Yakima, Uintah and Ouray, Nez Perce, Flathead, and Wind River. For those reservations that are Indian enclaves, state interest in on-reservation water rights is limited to off-reservation effects. Examples of reservations primarily populated by Indians are Navajo, Hopi, San Carlos Apache, and Pyramid Lake.
2. Off-reservation effects and checkerboard landholdings. When exercise of a reserved water right has spillover effects off the reservation and on non-Indian lands, the state has strong interests.[16] For example, the Pueblos of New Mexico are interspersed with many other uses in the Rio Grande drainage. Because of the limited nature of the water resource, states oppose setting water aside for future uses on hypothetical projects that undercut the certainty of existing uses. In the regulatory context, the Ninth Circuit Court has recognized that respective state and tribal powers over non-Indian use of excess waters may turn on the extent to which the affected drainage is self-

contained within the reservation.[17] If the affected drainage is entirely within the reservation, the tribe has a greater interest; conversely, as the Indian rights are interspersed with and affect other rights in the drainage, the state's interest increases. In multistate basins, such as the Colorado, Missouri, Columbia, or Truckee, the federal government asserts an interest.

3. Existence of state water institutions to spread the cost. In some states, large water districts can spread among individual users the costs of participation in stream adjudications. In Arizona, the Salt River Project takes a major role in Indian water rights litigation and negotiation. The Metropolitan Water District of Southern California takes a similar role for southern California water interests. All users in the upper Snake River are represented by a single district in Idaho's adjudication. Those states without such large entities are more likely to represent private rights against Indian claims.

Representative Federalism in Negotiation

As a practical matter, "representative federalism" may be required for effective negotiation of Indian water rights. Negotiation is not feasible if all of the thousands of potentially interested parties are active participants in the discussion. To represent private vested rights, a state must strike a balance between (1) the need for a resolution of the conflict between state and federal water rights and (2) the right of the individual water user to be heard. Some states limit their role to regulatory fact-finding and separate representation of state proprietary interests. For example, in Arizona and New Mexico, private parties protect their own rights and control the course of the water rights adjudication. By contrast, Montana and Wyoming, as representative of private users, have directly negotiated settlements of conflicting federal-state water rights, subject to legislative and judicial approval of the settlement.

Montana has taken the strongest representative role in negotiation by creating the Reserved Water Rights Compact Commission to negotiate with the federal government and Indian tribes on behalf of the legislature and all water users claiming state rights. The legislature suspended adjudication of federal claims pending these negotiations. Any agreement must be approved by the legislature and the tribe and must be entered in the stream adjudication. Therefore, the agreement will be a state legislative act that recognizes the respective rights of the signatory governments and does not adjudicate the rights of individual users. The Fort Peck agreement has been adopted by the state legislature and the tribes but has not been approved by the State Water Court or Congress. The state agreed to a tribal water code that will allocate water within the tribe.

States have required that private parties not be injured by any settlement. To achieve this goal, states can choose to take a representative role; however, they cannot be compelled to do so because of due process constitutional limitations.

States can be compelled to exercise their regulatory authority over fishing in a manner that recognizes Indian rights.[18] However, there is no vested property right to fish, as there is in water rights.

Representative Federalism in Litigation

Wyoming has taken a strong adversary role to the tribes in the Big Horn litigation, serving as a de facto representative of private water users. The state's interest is regulatory, proprietary, and representative. Similarly, although perhaps more limited, the New Mexico legislature funded technical, hydrological, and legal costs for acequias and the city of Ruidoso in a general stream adjudication in 1988, thus lending funding support to the non-Indian water users.

By contrast, in Arizona, the Department of Water Resources has been held to an adjudicatory/regulatory role in the Gila general adjudication. In this role, the department assists the court by compiling hydrologic reports. The Arizona Supreme Court determined that the Department of Water Resources cannot undertake a representative role, nor is the department permitted to rank or quantify competing claims.[19]

Interstate Goals Vis-à-Vis Other States

Under interstate compacts and principles of equitable apportionment, each state has an interest in maximizing the economic use of interstate streams within its borders. State interests may be implicated by Indian claims that have an interstate aspect. The states may be friendly or adverse to Indian claims, depending on the location of these claims in an interstate basin.

Conclusion

In litigation and in legislation, state interests and roles concerning Indian water disputes are complex. States balance these competing goals in various ways, depending on hydrology, population and landholding patterns, and state water institutions. All states share a common interest in regulatory simplicity. The strong state interest in certainty of rights to the limited water resource has led states to explore negotiations with Indian tribes. Ultimate self-determination for both states and tribes may be best served by negotiations that can tailor an agreement to present and future existing needs without the costs, friction, and delay of litigation. To the extent that western states and tribes work cooperatively on sharing management of the resource, they can together define and limit the federal role.

NOTES

1. See Peter W. Sly, *Reserved Water Rights Settlement Manual* (Washington, D.C.: Island Press, 1988).

2. 43 U.S.C. 666.

3. *Arizona v. San Carlos Apache Tribe,* 463 U.S. 545 (1983).

4. *In Re General Adjudication of the Big Horn,* 835 P.2d 273 (Wyoming, June 5, 1992).

5. See *Brendale v. Yakima Indian Nation,* 106 L.Ed.2d 343 (1989); *South Dakota v. Bourland,* 949 F.2d 984 cert. granted No. 91-2051.

6. See *Nevada v. United States,* 463 U.S. 110 (1983).

7. *Idaho ex rel. Higginson v. United States,* 764 P.2d 78 (Sup. Ct. Id., 1988).

8. 15 Indian L.Rptr. 5099 (September 9, 1988, order in *Gila Adjudication,* Maricopa County Superior Court, appeal pending).

9. *In Re Gila River,* 830 P.2d 442 (Az. Supreme Court, March 19, 1992).

10. *U.S. v. Idaho,* No. 92-120, cert. granted October 19, 1992; see 832 P.2d 289 (Id. 1992).

11. Sly, *Reserved Water Rights Settlement Manual.*

12. See *Delta Water Cases,* 182 Cal.App.3d 82 (1986).

13. See *In re DNRC,* 740 P.2d 1096 (1987).

14. Theodore W. Taylor, *American Indian Policy* (Mt. Airy, Mass.: Lomond Publishers, 1983), p. 107.

15. See Charles F. Wilkinson, *American Indians, Time and the Law* (New Haven, Conn.: Yale University Press, 1987), pp. 111–19; cf. *Duro v. Reina,* S.Ct. 2053 (1990).

16. See *Rice v. Rehner,* 463 U.S. 713 (1983); and *In Re Yakima River,* Yakima Co. Sup. Ct., No. 77-2-01484.5, Memo Opinion, May 12, 1992.

17. *United States v. Anderson,* 736 F.2d 1358 (9th Cir. 1984).

18. *Washington v. Washington State Commercial Passenger Fishing Vessel Ass'n,* 443 U.S. 658 (1979).

19. *United States v. Superior Court in and for Maricopa County,* 697 P.2d 658 (Ariz. 1985).

6

NON-INDIAN WATER USERS' GOALS: MORE IS BETTER, ALL IS BEST

John B. Weldon, Jr.

The doctrine of prior appropriation has governed water use by non-Indians in most western states for over a century. Under the doctrine, a water user is entitled to that amount of water which the water user has diverted and put to a beneficial use. The water user's date of priority, as against all competing users, is the original date of the appropriation. With relatively few exceptions, the tenets of the doctrine of prior appropriation have remained constant and unswerving since the doctrine's inception in the mid to late 1800s.

In sharp contrast to the doctrine of prior appropriation, the body of law governing Indian water rights has gone through a number of revolutionary changes over the last hundred years. In the 1800s, it was generally believed that Indian tribes were subject to the prior appropriation doctrine to the same extent as all other water users. However, in the *Winters* case, the Supreme Court of the United States held that in creating the Fort Belknap Indian Reservation in Montana, Congress by implication had reserved enough water from the Milk River to "support the purpose" of the reservation. The priority date associated with the reserved water rights for the Fort Belknap tribe was the date of the creation of the reservation.

Since *Winters*, the Supreme Court has entertained a number of legal issues pertaining to reserved water rights for Indian tribes. Without a doubt, the decision that has had the most significant impact upon both Indian and non-Indian water rights is *Arizona v. California* (1963). In *Arizona*, the Court adopted practicably irrigable acreage (PIA) as the legal standard for quantification of the reserved water rights of five Indian tribes in western Arizona and eastern California.

Prior to the Court's decision in *Arizona,* Indian water awards had been based primarily upon notions of the amount of a tribe's reasonable or actual need, calculated at least in part according to the extent of a tribe's present water use.[1] With the Supreme Court's acceptance of the practicably irrigable acreage standard, however, it became clear that if PIA were utilized on a grand scale to quantify reserved water rights for Indian tribes, the amount of a tribe's present use might account for only a small portion of the tribe's overall water entitlement. As a result of these legal developments and the ensuing inflation of Indian water rights claims, hostility developed between the tribes and non-Indian appropriators, who viewed the tribes' claims as a potential threat to the exercise of their own water rights.

To remove the threat posed by the reserved rights claims of the tribes, several efforts were made to quantify Indian reserved rights through federal legislation.[2] Due largely to the opposition of the United States government and various Indian interest groups, however, these attempts were unsuccessful. As it became clear that a legislative standard of quantification for Indian reserved rights was an unreachable goal, uncertainty among non-Indian appropriators as to the tribes' respective shares of an ever-shrinking water supply redoubled.

In an attempt to alleviate this uncertainty, water rights adjudications were instituted throughout the West. In Arizona, non-Indian appropriators initiated the Gila and Little Colorado River adjudications in the 1970s. In addition, settlement negotiations were undertaken with a number of Indian tribes in Arizona for the purpose of obtaining a final quantification of the tribes' water rights. Non-Indian appropriators throughout Arizona have continued to play a significant role in these endeavors over the last fifteen years with a number of goals in mind: to establish their own water rights claims, to quantify federal reserved and Indian water rights, and to build cooperative relationships between Indian and non-Indian communities.

Establishing the Validity of Water Rights Claims

Because of the substantial quantities of water claimed by Indian tribes under the reserved rights doctrine, and because of the early priority dates often associated with Indian reserved rights, the exercise of such rights may significantly curtail water uses by junior non-Indian appropriators. To minimize this negative impact, appropriators must actively seek to establish the validity of their own water rights, thereby insulating those rights from attack by both Indians and non-Indians. This objective is best served through participation in a comprehensive adjudication of rights to use the water source in dispute.

The adjudication process provides an opportunity for Indian and non-Indian water users to assert and defend their water rights claims against all other users of the water source. Those water rights claimants with the most senior priority will utilize the adjudication process to define their water rights, confirm such rights, and protect them from attack by junior claimants. Those claimants with more junior priority will utilize the process to define their water rights, confirm them, and attack senior rights to increase the supply of water available to satisfy junior rights. At the conclusion of the process, a court will determine the extent and priority of each claimant's water right and enter those determinations in a final, binding decree. From that time forward, rights to the water source will be administered according to the determinations embodied in the decree.

Quantification of Federal Reserved and Indian Water Rights

Division of the Water Supply

Probably the primary reason for the growing number of water rights adjudications and Indian water rights settlements in the West is the pressing need of both Indian and non-Indian parties to achieve certainty as to their respective shares of a scarce natural resource. The quantification of Indian reserved water rights is crucial to the accomplishment of this goal.

Because of the enactment of the McCarran Amendment in 1952, the United States, on behalf of itself and its Indian wards, can be joined without its consent as a party in comprehensive water rights adjudications in both federal and state courts. In addition, Indian water rights settlements, which are often incorporated into a binding court decree and sanctioned by Congress as part of funding legislation, provide further opportunities for both Indian and non-Indian parties to permanently establish a particular tribe's portion of a water source.

Determining Specific Water Rights Entitlements

Over the last thirty years, changes in the law governing Indian water rights and in engineering technology have contributed heavily to the inflation of Indian water rights claims. As discussed previously, the first few attempts by the courts to quantify Indian reserved water rights after *Winters* were grounded upon notions of reasonable or actual need, calculated at least in part according to the extent of a tribe's historic water use.[3]

In 1963, however, the Supreme Court adopted PIA as a standard for quantification of the water rights of a number of tribes in Arizona and California. Following the Supreme Court's decision in *Arizona,* judicial water awards to Indian tribes began increasing steadily for two primary reasons. First, the PIA standard is based upon the number of acres on a reservation susceptible to sustained farming through irrigation, rather than upon any notions of reasonable or actual need or of present water use. In many cases, the application of the PIA standard has resulted in an award to a tribe of a higher quantity of water than would have been obtained through an assessment either of actual or reasonable need or of present use. Second, because an assessment of whether land is "irrigable" substantially depends upon the agricultural engineering technology available, improvements in this technology over the years have resulted in increased water awards for the tribes. Technological improvements have included utilization of micro sprinklers and drip irrigation on marginal lands. In addition, the fine points of the PIA standard have been refined over the years to reflect changing soil suitability standards, varying economic conditions and forecasts, and changing standards for determining the economic feasibility of water projects.

To prevent the continued expansion of Indian water rights due to changing legal doctrines or improvements in technology, non-Indian water users have sought to obtain an expeditious and legally binding quantification of Indian water rights through comprehensive water rights adjudications or Indian water rights settlements. Both of these undertakings, if handled capably, can result in a fixed determination of the legal characteristics of an Indian tribe's water right. Once such a determination has been made, it is considered final, and neither subsequent modifications in the law nor improvements in engineering technology will result in the expansion of a tribe's water right.

Potential Damages Claims by the Tribes

Once an Indian tribe's water rights have been established either by court decree or by a negotiated settlement, neighboring water users are put on notice as to the legal characteristics of the tribe's water rights and, as a result, are in a position to refrain from interfering with such rights. As long as the extent and priority of Indian water rights remain unknown, competing water users are subject to a wide range of interference claims by the tribe yet have little or no ability either to defend themselves or to effectively change their water-using practices to mitigate the tribe's damages.

When the extent and priority of Indian water rights are determined by a negotiated settlement, the settlement will often include a provision waiving all past, present, and future claims for water rights or for injuries to water rights by or on behalf of the tribe, other than those claims specifically provided for in the settlement agreement itself. Such provisions allow the tribe a cause of action for breaches of the settlement and at the same time give non-Indian parties to the settlement the assurance that the tribe will be precluded in the future from revisiting the legal status of its water rights through subsequent litigation.

Federal-State Water Policy Changes

One of the inevitable outcomes associated with the quantification of Indian reserved rights is a reduction in the amount of water available for non-Indian uses. To minimize this reduction, and the effects of this reduction upon agricultural and municipal economies, a number of changes in western water policy will need to be considered.

Water Transfers/Water Marketing

In an attempt to find a quick and easy remedy to the problem of water shortage that could be caused by the exercise of Indian reserved rights, a number of water users have advocated water transfer or water marketing arrangements between Indians and non-Indians. Several examples of water marketing can be found throughout the West. In Wyoming, for instance, the state has agreed to pay the Arapaho and Shoshone tribes $5 million to refrain from exercising certain aspects of their reserved rights during the 1989 irrigating season to maintain a water supply adequate to satisfy the needs of non-Indian users. In Arizona, the Colorado River Indian Tribes are currently seeking non-Indian markets for excess portions of their water right entitlement, as calculated under the PIA standard in *Arizona v. California.*

While some non-Indian appropriators favor water marketing as a solution to their water shortage woes, a number of non-Indians throughout the West view water marketing as an unnecessary evil. Many non-Indian appropriators are strongly opposed to the idea of having to pay for water that they have used freely for generations, particularly where, absent federal funding, the tribes will be unable to build the water storage and delivery systems that would allow them to fully utilize their water rights. Rather than participating in water marketing arrangements with the tribes, many non-Indian appropriators would prefer to use political clout in Congress to prevent the tribes from obtaining the funds necessary to exercise their reserved rights. At best, it can be said that the use of water marketing arrangements between Indians and non-Indians as a solution to water shortage problems in the West is controversial and will require extensive study over the next several years.

Cooperative Water Project Development

To resolve the problem of water shortage caused by the exercise of Indian reserved rights, non-Indian appropriators will need to consider the benefits to be derived from participating in cooperative water development projects with Indian tribes. These projects may include groundwater recharge and water conservation programs, as well as joint funding of water development projects aimed at making optimal use of the available water supply.

Recharge projects often involve an arrangement between Indian and non-Indian water users that in years of plentiful surface water supply, all water users will recharge the groundwater supply with unneeded or excess surface water. In subsequent shortage years, recharge water will be pumped to make up for the inadequate surface water supply. Conservation programs generally involve the pooling of Indian and non-Indian financial resources to line canals, increase the efficiency of distribution systems, and increase on-farm efficiency. Similarly, cooperative water development projects, such as the Animas–La Plata Project in Colorado, provide opportunities for Indians and non-Indians to share the costs of the construction of water storage and delivery systems for the purpose of making optimal use of their water supplies.

Cooperative Relationships between Indian and Non-Indian Communities

As an alternative to the judicial quantification of Indian reserved rights, the negotiated settlement of these rights offers many advantages to both Indians and non-Indians. From a non-Indian perspective, the negotiation of Indian reserved rights is less expensive than litigation, reduces the likelihood of an excessive water award to the tribe, and often eliminates or substantially reduces damages claims by the tribe for past interference with its reserved rights. From an Indian perspective, water rights settlements often permit an Indian tribe to take advantage of an immediately available water supply, rather than wait for the conclusion of extended water rights litigation. In addition, through the cooperative efforts of the tribe and non-Indian parties to the settlement, funding for the implementation of the settlement and the development of the tribe's water resources can often be obtained from Congress.

In recent years, Indian and non-Indian water users, as well as the federal government, have invested substantial time and expense in undertaking the settlement of tribal water rights claims. As a result of these efforts, a number of innovative Indian water rights settlements have been concluded throughout the West. These include the Ak-Chin, Tohono O'odham, and Salt River Pima-Maricopa settlements in Arizona; the San Luis Rey/Rincon Bands settlement in southern California; the Animas–La Plata/Colorado Ute settlement in Colorado; and the Fort Peck Compact in Montana.

Ten years ago, a group of non-Indian appropriators in the Phoenix, Arizona, metropolitan area initiated water rights settlement negotiations with the Salt River Pima-Maricopa Indian Community. These negotiations have culminated in a settlement agreement that (1) sets forth the water resources to be used in providing the Salt River Community with a more assured source of supply; and (2) waives all past, present, and future claims by or on behalf of the Salt River Community for water rights or injuries to water rights, other than those claims specifically reserved in the agreement.

In addition to the substantial water contributions of non-Indian parties to the settlement agreement, Congress has enacted enabling legislation that authorizes the appropriation of over $58 million to fund the settlement.

The Salt River Pima-Maricopa Indian Community Water Rights Settlement is illustrative of the benefits to be derived from a cooperative undertaking by Indians, non-Indians, and the federal government to permanently settle the water rights claims of an Indian tribe. Through settlements such as this, Indian tribes can turn the dream of developing their water resources into a reality, while relieving non-Indian appropriators of their uncertainty as to the extent of Indian water rights and the potential impact of those rights upon neighboring non-Indian users.

NOTES

1. See *Walker River Irrigation District*, 104 F.2d 334, 339–40 (9th Cir. 1939). The court accepted the special master's estimate of the Walker River tribe's water right, based almost completely upon historic use, "as a fair measure of the needs of the Government as demonstrated by seventy years of experience." In addition, see *United States v. Ahtanum Irrigation District*, 236 F.2d 321, 326–27 (9th Cir. 1956); and *Conrad Inv. Co. v. United States*, 161 F.2d 829, 832 (9th Cir. 1908). In *Ahtanum* and *Conrad*, the Ninth Circuit Court based its quantification of Indian reserved rights upon the tribes' reasonable present and future needs.

2. See, for instance, H.R. 5561, introduced March 24, 1977, "A Bill to provide water to the five Central Arizona Indian Tribes for farming purposes, to settle their surface water rights, and for other purposes"; and H.R. 9951, introduced November 3, 1977, "A Bill to require adjudication and quantification of all claims to rights to the use of water based upon federal reserved rights for Indian reservations." See also the "Proposal by the Western Regional Council," Committee on Energy and Natural Resources, U.S. Senate 389 (June 1984), which called for "an exhaustive study of Indian water rights aimed at providing a data base for the 'informed and intelligent' quantification of the rights." In addition, see the "Water Rights Coordination Act," Committee on Energy and Natural Resources, U.S. Senate 390, a proposal by the Western Conference of the Council of State Governors, which would have recognized Indian reserved rights exercised prior to the act but "thereafter would establish an eight-year period within which Indians would have to exercise or lose their *Winters* rights."

3. *Walker River*, 104 F.2d at 339–40. See *Ahtanum*, 236 F.2d at 326–27; and *Conrad*, 161 F.2d at 832.

PART III PROCESS

7

NEGOTIATING WATER SETTLEMENTS: TEN COMMON THEMES

Daniel McCool

Indian claims to water are among the most contentious issues in the American West. Acting Assistant Secretary of the Interior Wayne Marchant recently wrote that Indian water claims based on the *Winters* doctrine could "severely disrupt the existing regimen of water use."[1] Congressman John Rhodes of Arizona and three of his colleagues made a similar statement recently: "Indian water rights are among the most complex legal issues in the West, and the uncertainty of case law causes economic and social hardship on both the Indian and non-Indian communities affected by these water claims."[2] The most succinct response, however, came from Congressman Bill Richardson of New Mexico: "There is no more divisive issue in the West than the dispute between Indians and non-Indians over water."[3]

Litigation has been the traditional mode of conflict over water rights, resulting in court battles that sometimes last for decades. In recent years there has been an increased emphasis on negotiation as a form of conflict resolution in this area. It is important to note that negotiation has not replaced litigation as a means of resolving Indian water claims—currently there are over fifty general stream adjudications involving Indian water rights—but negotiation can be used as an alternative in some situations.

Beginning in the late 1970s, the federal government began a policy of actively encouraging negotiations to settle long-standing legal conflicts over Indian water rights. Settlements were negotiated for the Ak-Chin Reservation in 1978 and 1984, the Tohono O'odham (formerly Papago) reservation in 1982, and Fort Peck the following year. By the late 1980s, two dozen tribes were in various stages of negotiation over water. In 1988, the policy of negotiating Indian water settlements achieved an unprecedented level of success with the signing of three major settlement bills. In that year, settlements were signed by the Ute Mountain and Southern Ute tribes in southern Colorado, the mission bands along the San Luis Rey River in southern California, and the Salt River Pima-Maricopa Indian Community in central Arizona.

Although participants in such settlements are quick to deny that any precedent has been set, the three 1988 settlements embodied a number of themes and strategies that are commonly found in subsequent settlements. Moreover, even though every reservation is unique (hence every settlement is unique), the common themes found in the 1988 settlements typify the process, and the outcome, of many Indian water settlements. Ten themes characterize the three 1988 settlements: deference to the states and the Law of the River; efficiency, conservation, and the environment; limits to marketing and leasing; flexible and comprehensive negotiations; "wet water" for Indians; the search for "new" water; cost-sharing and pork barrel; presidential opposition; the "Indian blanket"; and sovereignty with comity. To varying degrees, these themes can also be found in the water settlements signed in 1990 (Fallon Paiute-Shoshone and Truckee-Carson–Pyramid Lake; Fort Hall; Fort McDowell) and 1992 (Northern Utes; San Carlos Apache).

Deference to the States and the Law of the River

Much attention has been devoted to the conflict between state water law (and its recognition by Congress) and the *Winters* doctrine. Many policy makers have voiced fears that Indian water rights would undermine the existing fabric of law and tradition that controls water in the arid West. The most alarmist among them have argued that any recognition of reserved rights would result in the wholesale transfer of state-granted water rights to Indian reservations. One of the incentives to negotiate is to prevent such a situation from developing. Indeed, the three settlement acts, and the accompanying discussion and debate, repeatedly stress the importance of deferring to existing tradition and law, including a deference to state control over water rights. In drafting the San Luis Rey bill, the House Committee on Interior and Insular Affairs noted that it had "been careful in the drafting of this legislation to ensure that the existing format for making water available from the Colorado River is not violated."[4]

Deference to the Law of the River was a critical part of the conflict over whether the Colorado Utes would be able to sell or lease their water off-reservation (the off-reservation leasing issue is discussed below). Senator James McClure of Idaho claimed that the early version of the bill, which permitted off-reservation sale or lease, would have "established the basis for litigation to break the Law of the River. That was unconscionable."[5] Several congressmen from California wrote a dissenting committee view that also argued against changing existing law regarding the sale and lease of water: "We do not believe that it is in the national interest to disrupt the long established structure of Colorado River Basin rights and priorities."[6] The offending language had to be modified before the bill could pass. Section 5 of the final version of the bill provides that "nothing in this section is intended to affect, in any way, the various State, Federal, or international laws affecting the Colorado River or its tributaries."[7]

Throughout the debate on the bills the deference to tradition and existing law was a constant theme. However, successful negotiation required that at least some new ground be broken and some traditions be altered, which did not please all parties. In the Salt River case the Interior Department objected to language in the bill that affirmed and validated several existing private water contracts that had traditionally been under the exclusive domain of state water law: "The Congress' affirmation of these contracts, which essentially are private agreements on water rights within the State of Arizona, would raise questions as to whether the Congress would reverse 85 years of Reclamation law with regard to non-interference with State control over its water."[8] The contract validation language became law despite the protest from the Interior Department. For the most part, however, the negotiators worked within the existing framework of law rather than attempt any major modifications. To date, no settlement has required a major departure from established state and federal concepts of water law.

The Management Era: Efficiency, Conservation, and the Environment

Any law that affects water rights will have an impact on the environment. The legislators who were sensitive to environmental issues left their mark on the settlement debate and in some cases on the final settlement acts. Moreover, the tenor of the debate often reflected the current emphasis on efficient management. These issues were particularly salient to the Colorado Ute and San Luis Rey settlements. In regard to the former, the environmental impact of the Animas–La Plata Project was a major concern. A reauthorized version of this project was the "keystone of the settlement," in the words of Congressman (now Senator) Ben Nighthorse Campbell of Colorado.[9] Phase II of the updated version of the project provided some additional fish and wildlife features, but this did little to mollify the project's environmental critics. Organized opponents that testified before Congress against the project included the American Rivers Conservation Council, the National Wildlife Federation, the Colorado Wildlife Federation, the Environmental Policy Institute, and the Sierra Club. Congressman George Miller of California was one of the most vocal opponents to the reauthorizing language in the bill:

The environmental problems this project will cause are classics: It is a huge user of electric energy. Water for the main storage reservoir must be pumped over 500 feet uphill, and then more pumping is required to get the water, under pressure, to irrigable lands. Yearly project pumping power requirements total 135 million kilowatt hours. The main project dam and reservoir will destroy important elk and mule deer habitat. Irrigation water will be used primarily as a supplemental water supply to enable mostly non-Indians to grow relatively low-value crops, such as alfalfa, at high elevations.[10]

Project supporters argued that the Animas–La Plata Project had already been modified to minimize environmental impact. Congressman Campbell of Colorado argued that the settlement "recognizes these [environmental] concerns because the project, which is an off-channel storage reservoir, was designed to be the least environmentally damaging."[11]

Perhaps the best example of an environmental consciousness comes from the San Luis Rey settlement. The centerpiece of this bill is a plan to line the unlined portions of the All American Canal to increase its efficiency. This will save 80,000 to 100,000 acre-feet of water every year, of which 16,000 acre-feet will go to the mission Indian bands. The local interests that will receive the remaining conserved water agreed to pay for the lining of the canal. The House Committee on Interior and Insular Affairs emphasized that the "lining of the existing canal in place will have substantially less overall adverse environmental impact than construction of a new lined canal."[12] Senator (now Governor) Pete Wilson of California succinctly described the significance of this new approach to water problems:

I rise in support of what I consider to be the most important California water legislation for this Congress. . . . [I]t signals the arrival of a new era in our seemingly never ending battle to provide for California's water needs. Instead of authorizing the construction of a new dam—something that has long been California's answer to water shortages—we are instead authorizing new conservation measures. . . . [T]he benefits from this project in terms of water conserved will flow to southern California consumers, and they are the ones who will be footing the bill for this project.[13]

The final version of the bill also authorized the secretary of the interior to use groundwater from public domain lands. Part of the incentive to search for innovative ways to increase the water supply was to avoid taking water from the Central Valley Project. Originally the bill proposed the use of water from the Central Valley Project, but congressmen from the project area objected, so negotiators had to find another source of water. The San Luis Rey settlement also contained a provision to protect the Salton Sea wildlife area.

Environmental considerations have continued to play an important role in negotiations. The Colorado Ute settlement has been modified several times in an effort to mitigate environmental damage, especially in regard to endangered species of fish. Fish habitat was also a major issue in the 1990 settlement for the Pyramid Lake Paiutes. And conflict over environmental issues held up the settlement for the Northern Ute Tribe of Utah for over three years. It is becoming increasingly difficult to pass settlement bills that depend upon large water projects with significant environmental impacts.

Limits to Marketing and Leasing

By far the most contentious issue during the debate over the Colorado Ute settlement act was the question of whether the tribes could sell or lease their settlement water off-reservation. This is a very complex issue and can only be summarized here. The Indian tribes and the Department of the Interior envisioned water sales and leasing as a way to generate revenue for the tribes. This was not the first time that such off-reservation water use had been endorsed by legislation, but it was unprecedented in the extent to which off-reservation activity could take place. This was deeply troubling to the Lower Basin states. An early version of the bill attempted to establish a neutral stance on the subject. Several amendments to the bill were proposed, but none of them pleased Lower Basin congressmen, who noted, "While Colorado may have satisfactorily resolved some difficult local litigation there, it has done so by opening up a Pandora's Box on inevitable litigation in and among other Colorado River Basin States. . . . The legal controversy that such a transaction would precipitate boggles the mind." [14] The Lower Basin states argued that off-reservation sale or lease of Indian water would violate the Colorado River Compact: "Any interbasin or interstate transfer of the water rights of the two Ute Indian Reservations would be impermissible under the Law of the River." [15]

The bill was finally amended to require that Indian settlement water be treated as a Colorado state water right, subject to all the limitations of existing law. Congressman Campbell of Colorado explained: "The amendments clarify the tribes' rights by providing that if the tribes' water is used off-reservation, then their rights are to be treated as if they were non-Indian water rights arising under Colorado State law. . . . In short, the tribes' ability to use their water off their Reservations will be the same as their non-Indian neighbors." [16] This approach was opposed by other legislators, who argued that it set a dangerous precedent and meant that if the leased water fell into disuse the tribes would forfeit the water—a requirement that does not apply to *Winters* doctrine rights. Senators Daniel Inouye and Bill Bradley, of Hawaii and New Jersey, respectively, led the fight to insert language into the Senate Resolution on the bill to "assure absolutely the reversion of that State right back to a reserved right whenever the water ceases to be used beneficially off-reservation. With this language, Congress assures that these tribes will not lose their water right through inadvertent or hostile action." [17]

93

DANIEL MCCOOL

The final version of the Ute settlement act did little to resolve basic legal questions surrounding off-reservation leasing and ensnared Congress in a bitter debate over the nature of the *Winters* doctrine. The Senate Select Committee on Indian Affairs and the Senate Committee on Energy and Natural Resources, both of which had jurisdiction over the bill, clashed repeatedly over these points of law.

Off-reservation use of settlement water was also an issue in the San Luis Rey bill, but not to the same extent as the Ute bill. Section 107 of the bill prohibited off-reservation sale or lease but permitted the exchange of water under certain conditions. Off-reservation water marketing was permitted in the Salt River Pima-Maricopa bill, but only for specified in-state uses and specific amounts.

Viewed as a whole, the congressional response to off-reservation water marketing was a conservative one. Prior to 1988, some water settlements permitted limited forms of water marketing, but in these three bills Congress for the most part chose to restrict Indian uses of water and respect existing state limits to such activity. The case law on off-reservation marketing remains unclear, and the politics of marketing will continue to be contentious. Nevertheless, the Interior Department has expressed limited support for marketing as a way of promoting tribal self-sufficiency.[18]

The 1990 and 1992 settlements placed similar restrictions on tribal water marketing. Out-of-state leasing of tribal water has yet to be authorized by any settlement. Whether a less restrictive approach to off-reservation marketing is adopted in future settlements remains to be seen. According to a leading Indian spokesman, off-reservation marketing will be "the key to Indian water settlements in the future."[19]

Flexible and Comprehensive Negotiations

One of the reasons for the complexity of these settlement bills is that all affected parties were invited to negotiate. In addition, once they were brought to the table, all parties were expected to participate in a lengthy process of give and take. The passage of the three settlement acts followed years of negotiation, which in turn had followed years of litigation. One of the congressional staffers involved in the formulation of the bills noted that every element in the settlement was a product of extensive dialogue among all of the parties that had an interest in the bill. Once these parties were brought together at the bargaining table, it was made clear that everyone had to give up something in order to gain something. The resistance to any loss, especially among non-Indian parties that did not recognize the legitimacy of *Winters* claims, had been a stumbling block in the past. A 1982 Interior Department memorandum complained that "frequently the non-Indian competing water users are not interested in reasonable negotiations."[20] This attitude had

94

changed demonstrably by 1988; non-Indian interests agreed to make sacrifices, especially in terms of the financial burdens of implementing the settlement acts.

The debate over the settlement bills also required that all parties be flexible in their position. The bills progressed through a number of versions that modified significant aspects of the bill. This was especially true of the San Luis Rey bill and the Colorado Ute bill. An example from the former concerns the source of water that was to be used to meet the needs of the Indian tribes. Congressman Ron Packard of California noted that "the water supply for this bill has taken a circuitous route from the Central Valley to the All American Canal, and finally to reliance upon ground water from the public domain."[21] The Ute settlement act also required parties to renegotiate several important elements in the bill. In the case of the Salt River bill, the parties renegotiated the funding sources for Colorado River water. In short, the final settlement acts were substantially different from the original bills; all parties had to be willing to accept changes in their position as the price for a legislative solution to their water problems.

Wet Water for Indians

The literature on Indian water rights often makes a distinction between "paper" water and "wet" water. The former consists of a legal right to water that is not available for use. In contrast, the latter refers to water that can actually be utilized by a·tribe to produce a benefit. This usually requires funding to build water diversion facilities. In the three settlement bills the tribes were clearly not interested in more paper water; they wanted not just a legal right to water, but also the means to effectively utilize that water for beneficial purposes. In all three bills this was accomplished through two mechanisms.

The first was a commitment on the part of the federal government and non-Indian parties to build appropriate water facilities on Indian reservations. For example, the Senate Select Committee on Indian Affairs noted that "a premise of the [Salt River Pima-Maricopa] Settlement Agreement is that reservation land which will be irrigated by Settlement water needs to be developed and improved to achieve an efficient level of irrigation. . . . Community farmlands, generally maintained by the United States, have fallen into neglect in past decades and the United States should appropriately bear the burden of the costs of land and irrigation improvements required by the settlement."[22] The bill provides $10 million in federal funds to rehabilitate and construct reservation water facilities and contributes an additional $9 million to facilitate water exchanges and transfers. The Colorado Ute bill sets aside $60.5 million for tribal water resource development, and in addition the state of Colorado agreed to build a $5 million pipeline to the reservation town of Towaoc (for the last forty years the town has had to truck in water). In the case of San Luis Rey the settlement requires that the U.S. Bureau of Reclamation be responsible for delivering water to the Indian bands and authorizes the agency to use the aqueducts of the Metropolitan Water District of Southern California.

The second part of the wet water strategy was to set up tribal development funds to help finance future water development. All three settlements acts contain a provision of this nature. For the mission bands the federal government set up a $30 million development fund, to be used by the Indian Water Authority (a tribal government entity also established by the act) for water development and operation. Some of the trust fund money will also be used to support the lining of the All American Canal, depending upon how much of the conserved water the Indians use. The Colorado Ute bill authorized the expenditure of $49.5 million of federal money, and $10.5 million in state and local contributions, for tribal development funds (one for each Ute tribe). For the Pima-Maricopa Indians the government set up a Salt River Community Trust Fund with $26 million in federal funds and $3 million in funds from the state of Arizona. All three settlement acts forbid the tribes from distributing the proceeds from the trust funds to tribal members on a per capita basis; the clear intent of Congress is that all trust fund monies are to be spent on water-related activities.

The basic thrust of these efforts is to convert paper water into wet water on American Indian reservations. This has been touted as one of the advantages of negotiations as opposed to litigation, which often produces only paper water. As a result, the tribes will finally see some real benefits from the *Winters* doctrine (assuming the acts are fully funded and implemented). Of course, the tribes had to sacrifice also; as part of the settlement they gave up their *Winters* doctrine claims. For many years the doctrine was the only viable means the tribes had to obtain water; relinquishing their prize weapon has an emotional as well as a legal impact on tribal members. Subsequent settlements have also required tribes to waive all *Winters* rights.

The Search for "New" Water

The settlement acts did not merely reallocate existing supplies of water. For the most part such an approach is still not politically feasible in the American West. Rather, the negotiators in each case found alternative sources of water other than those traditionally in use in the affected area.

In the case of San Luis Rey, the bill originally attempted to use water from the Central Valley Project, but when this proved politically unacceptable the proponents of the bill suggested lining the All American Canal and using groundwater from public lands. The answer to the Colorado Ute situation was to build the Animas–La Plata Project. Senator William Armstrong of Colorado argued that the project "has become the answer to resolving their Indian water rights claims without economic disruption of the region."[23] The water claims of the Pima-Maricopa Indians were resolved by the purchase of 22,000 acre-feet of Colorado River water. In the original bill the federal government was to pay for the purchase of this water, but local entities agreed to bear this burden after the Reagan administration objected to the expense.

Cost Sharing and Pork Barrel

Perhaps the most significant reform in water development policy in this century is the advent of cost sharing. The debate over cost sharing has dominated the water policy-making process for the last decade; no area of water policy has been left untouched, including the attempt to negotiate settlements to Indian water rights disputes. All three of the settlement acts authorize a cost-sharing formula that provides funds from state and local as well as federal sources. However, it would be an error to assume that pork barrel politics has no role in the formulation of settlement bills. The federal commitment is substantial, and there is at times an obvious effort to please as many people as possible through a variety of subsidies and appropriations.

The question of cost sharing was especially significant to the Colorado Ute settlement because it depends on the construction of the Animas–La Plata Project and the completion of the Dolores Project. The 1985 Supplemental Appropriations bill required cost sharing before construction could begin on the Animas–La Plata Project. The following year an agreement was worked out that split the project into two phases. Phase I will cost the federal government $379 million, while nonfederal entities (several water conservation districts and the state of Colorado) will pay $69 million. Phase II, costing $132 million, will be funded entirely by nonfederal sources. In terms of the entire settlement bill, state and local interests will pay about 39 percent, much of it in up-front financing of construction costs.

The cost-sharing agreement for the Salt River bill requires state and local contributors to pay for about 54 percent of the settlement's financing, including the purchase of Colorado River water and payment into the Salt River Community Trust Fund. This will total about $78 million (only $3 million of that is paid by the state of Arizona). Local entities also give up some water rights worth several million dollars. The San Luis Rey settlement requires local interests to pay for the entire cost of lining the All American Canal.

Despite these state and local contributions, the federal government will still incur a sizable financial liability. The settlement acts contain a confusing array of federal subsidies, including loan deferrals, loan forgiveness, and interest-free loans, as well as new authorizations for direct spending. The least expensive of the settlement acts, at least in terms of federal expenditures, is the San Luis Rey. The federal government agreed to deposit $30 million into the tribal development fund; local interests will cover the cost of lining the All American Canal. The Salt River settlement is a good example of a rather complex combination of new and old water and federal and nonfederal spending. As Senator Dennis DeConcini of Arizona explained, "[I]t is important to note that in order to accomplish the provisions of this legislation and the terms of the settlement agreement, significant sums of money are required."[24] The Justice Department complained that the federal expenditures for the settlement were excessive: "[T]he level of contemplated federal funding . . . far exceeds the exposure of the United States in pending litigation. Measured in this manner, it becomes apparent that the thrust of the package is something other than the settlement of litigation. . . . Essentially, the package presents a project initiative and must rise or fall on that basis."[25] Due to such complaints the federal commitment was reduced from $88 million to $58 million.

The most traditional of the settlements, in terms of a dependence on new project construction and federal money, is the Colorado Ute bill. As Senator Pete Domenici of New Mexico pointed out, the Animas–La Plata Project was designed to distribute benefits to a wide variety of constituents: "The beneficiaries of the Animas–La Plata are diverse. They include residents of two States, three Indian tribes, municipalities, farmers and ranchers, business owners, and sportsmen."[26] The federal share of the project, including the settlement agreement, is about $340 million. Critics argued that the project will irrigate land at a cost of $5,800 per acre to produce low-value crops that are already in surplus. They also expressed concern that, although Phase II of the project is supposed to be funded by local interests, it remains authorized as a federal project. This creates the possibility of a federal "bailout" in the future. Critics such as Congressman Miller of California also charged that the project "perpetuates the worst of the repayment myths associated with reclamation projects. It allows power users to subsidize irrigation costs and delay repayment to the Treasury for many years to come."[27]

The Bush administration consistently voiced its opposition to significant funding increases for federally financed water development, but Congress—forever looking for a chance to bring home the bacon—consistently pushed for more spending on water projects. President George Bush repeatedly threatened to veto appropriations for more new water projects but always yielded when legislators threatened to cut funding for the supercollider—one of Bush's home-state pet projects.[28] President Bill Clinton has promised to dramatically increase funding for infrastructure, which could result in a new lease on life for the federal water development program.

Presidential Opposition

The principal reason why state and local interests have such a large role in funding the three settlement acts is because of the influence of the Reagan administration, which fought at every turn to minimize the federal funding for these bills. The Reagan administration opposed the original version for the Salt River bill and insisted that nonfederal sponsors pay for the purchase of Colorado River water; the bill was amended accordingly. The Reagan administration also insisted on the cost-sharing provisions in the Colorado Ute bill and complained about the generous payback schedule. And, during the negotiations over the San Luis Rey agreement, the president made it clear that nonfederal entities would have to pay for the lining of the All American Canal.

The Bush administration continued to oppose federal funding for water settlements. As one official put it, "these should be water settlements, not monetary settlements." Despite his complaints that the settlements passed by Congress in 1990 and 1992 were much too costly, Bush nonetheless signed them. There are two reasons why both Ronald Reagan and George Bush signed settlement bills they did not like. First, many western Republican legislators urged them to sign; second, administration officials believed that continued litigation could cost even more. President Clinton may agree to increased spending for water settlements as part of his policy of increased funding for the country's infrastructure.

The Indian Blanket

Since the advent of the reclamation program in 1902 there have been attempts to generate support for primarily non-Indian water projects by including an Indian component, a strategy often called the "Indian blanket." All three of these projects create benefits for non-Indians—that is the nature of successful negotiations. In the case of the San Luis Rey and Colorado Ute settlements, much more water is provided to Anglos than to Indians. The latter is the best example of the Indian blanket strategy, however. Congressman Miller of California made this argument during the debate in the House:

> Let's be honest about what we're buying if this bill is enacted. Are we really buying an Indian water rights settlement? . . . We are buying a Bureau of Reclamation water project. . . . [W]e are buying a water project that will benefit non-Indian alfalfa farmers much more than it will ever benefit the Ute Mountain Utes and the Southern Utes. I believe this bill is flawed because it forces the American taxpayer to settle legitimate Indian water rights claims by bootstrapping construction of a $600 million water project that will primarily benefit non-Indians.[29]

In future negotiations over Indian water rights, it will be interesting to see how many conflicts are resolved by creating new sources of water that primarily deliver to non-Indians. This is one way to generate local support for "sacrificing" something to the Indian tribes. If a trend back to the pork barrel approach to water develops, there may be many opportunities to attach Indian water projects to

Anglo projects, especially if the Indian funds can be linked to the new "green pork" environmental expenditures that are popular with many contemporary legislators.

Sovereignty with Comity

In all discussions between tribes, states and localities, and the federal government, sovereignty is an important issue. Throughout the negotiations over these settlement acts, the various governmental entities attempted to protect their control over their water. However, there was an obvious realization that sovereign interests had to be considered in light of the needs of the other parties. The term *neighbor* was used repeatedly in the negotiations to describe the relationship between the various parties to the agreements. A statement by Leonard Burch, chairman of the Southern Ute Indian Tribe, typifies this sentiment: "We are pleased that, together with our neighbors, we can . . . solve what otherwise will be a long and bitter lawsuit affecting all of southwest Colorado."[30] There were also repeated comments concerning the recent nature of this newfound spirit of neighborliness.

Conclusion: A "New Vision"?

Legislators often wax hyperbolic when extolling the benefits of their handiwork, and the settlement bills are no exception. The Arizona delegation was particularly effusive, calling the Salt River bill "a historic agreement" (Senator DeConcini), a "milestone in our Nation's effort to resolve crucial questions over the allocation and use of scarce water supplies" (Congressman Morris Udall), and a "spirit of visionary cooperation among Indian and non-Indians" (Congressman Rhodes).[31] A more somber assessment is provided by Senator Inouye of Hawaii, chairman of the Senate Select Committee on Indian Affairs, who noted that their effort "represents an ongoing debate regarding what the law of Federal reserved water rights and Indian reserved water rights is or should be. These matters remain unresolved."[32]

Negotiation is not a panacea. Certain conditions must be present before fair, consensual negotiations can take place, and such conditions cannot be created in some situations. Furthermore, once an agreement is signed, there is no assurance that it will be implemented. Indeed, so many settlements are experiencing problems that the Department of the Interior has organized "implementation teams" to monitor settlements. Several settlements have been modified because of unworkable compromises that resulted from prolonged negotiation. The signatories under the 1988 Colorado Ute settlement have experienced nearly continuous problems because of conflicts over endangered fish species, conflict with the Navajo, and opposition from environmentalists. And water users under the San

Luis Rey settlement have experienced difficulties finding a suitable source of water. In some cases, the negotiation strategy has not resulted in the benefits expected.[33]

Rather than a panacea, negotiation may simply be the lesser of two evils. Numerous Reagan appointees at all levels of the federal court system have made litigation a more risky proposition for Indian tribes. The case of *Wyoming v. U.S., et al.* (1989) illustrates this problem. The Supreme Court voted 4 to 4, without comment, to uphold a ruling by the Wyoming Supreme Court that had pleased neither the Wind River tribes nor the state of Wyoming. The attorney for the tribes noted that high-stakes Indian water cases are becoming "very dicey."[34]

Many tribes are now participating in formal negotiations. Given the significance of the issue, it will take a sincere commitment from all parties to preserve the comity and mutual respect that are prerequisites to successful water rights settlements.

NOTES

1. *Congressional Report,* "Facilitating and Implementing the Settlement of Colorado Ute Indian Reserved Water Rights Claims in Southwest Colorado, and For Other Purposes," 100th Cong., 2d sess., House of Representatives, Report 100-932, 1988, p. 17.

2. Ibid., p. 29.

3. *Congressional Record,* October 3, 1988, p. H9348.

4. *Congressional Report,* "San Luis Rey Indian Water Rights Settlement Act, Reclamation States Drought Assistance Act of 1988, and for Other Reasons," 100th Cong., 2d sess., House of Representatives, Report 100-780, 1988, p. 44.

5. *Congressional Record,* October 14, 1988, p. S16251.

6. *Cong. Report,* "Settlement of Colorado Ute Indian Reserved Water Rights Claims," p. 28.

7. Ibid., p. 10.

8. *Congressional Report,* "Salt River Pima-Maricopa Indian Community Water Rights Settlement Act of 1988," 100th Cong., 2d sess., Senate, Report 100-495, 1988, p. 17.

9. *Congressional Record,* October 3, 1988, p. H9345.

10. Ibid., p. H9347.

11. Ibid., p. H9346.

12. *Cong. Report,* "San Luis Rey Indian Water Rights Settlement Act," p. 41.

13. *Congressional Record,* October 19, 1988, p. S16837.

14. *Cong. Report,* "Settlement of Colorado Ute Indian Reserved Water Rights Claims," pp. 26–27.

15. Senate Select Committee on Indian Affairs and Senate Committee on Energy and Natural Resources, *Colorado Ute Settlement Bill: Report on S. 1415,* 100th Cong., 1st sess., December 3, 1987, p. 384.

16. *Congressional Record,* October 3, 1988, p. H9352.

17. *Congressional Record,* October 14, 1988, p. S16250.

18. Daniel McCool, "Water Marketing and American Indians," *The Forum for Applied Research and Public Policy* 5 (Spring 1990); Office of the Solicitor, U.S. Department of the Interior, Memorandum for Water Policy Advisory Group, October 22, 1984.

19. John Echohawk, comments made at the conference, Setting a Tribal Agenda for the 80s, sponsored by the American Indian Resources Institute, Washington, D.C., April 5–6, 1989.

20. "Water Resources, . . ." U.S. Department of the Interior, undated memorandum, circa 1982.

21. *Congressional Record,* October 3, 1988, p. 3237.

22. *Cong. Report,* "Salt River Pima-Maricopa Indian Community Water Rights Settlement Act of 1988," p. 11.

23. *Congressional Record,* October 14, 1988, p. S16245.

24. *Congressional Record,* March 4, 1988, p. S2050.

25. *Cong. Report,* "Salt River Pima-Maricopa Indian Community Water Rights Settlement Act of 1988," pp. 21–22.

26. *Congressional Record,* October 14, 1988, p. S16253.

27. *Congressional Record,* October 3, 1988, p. H9346.

28. *Congressional Quarterly Weekly Report,* June 23, 1990, p. 1949.

29. *Congressional Record,* October 3, 1988, p. H9346.

30. Select Committee on Indian Affairs and Committee on Energy and Natural Resources, *Colorado Ute Settlement Bill,* p. 246.

31. *Congressional Record,* March 4, 1988, p. S2050; September 13, 1988, p. H7499; March 8, 1988, p. H726.

32. *Congressional Record,* October 14, 1988, p. S16248.

33. Daniel McCool, "Intergovernmental Conflict and Indian Water Rights: An Assessment of Negotiated Settlements," *Publius,* in press; McCool, "Indian Water Settlements: The Prerequisites of Successful Negotiation," *Policy Studies Review,* in press.

34. *U.S. Water News,* "Irrigable Acreage Standard for Reserved Rights Upheld," October 19, 1989, p. 19.

8

THE 1985 FORT PECK–MONTANA COMPACT: A CASE STUDY

Mary McNally

The Fort Peck–Montana Compact, an agreement to settle *Winters* rights claims, was the result of five years of negotiations between the Montana Reserved Water Rights Compact Commission, the Fort Peck tribes, and various federal entities. It has been widely noted because of the magnitude of the recognized right (a diversion right of 1,050,472 acre-feet), the purposes for which the water may be used (including provisions for water marketing), and its unique administrative and regulatory elements. The compact was also significant in that it was an early example of a negotiated settlement between a state and Indian tribes. Although negotiations are increasingly recognized as an alternative to litigation, there has been little documentation of the complexities and compromises such a process entails. The Fort Peck–Montana Compact offers an opportunity to examine how negotiations worked in one case. In the interests of simplification and illumination, emphasis will be on the way two key provisions of the compact (quantification and water marketing) evolved through three drafts into their final form.

Montana's statewide water adjudication, initiated in the early 1970s, was an effort to rationalize and modernize the state's prior appropriation system. The task was a daunting one, on a number of levels. Although the prior appropriation doctrine was well established in practice and in fact, Montana lacked an adequate water management system, had few centralized records, and had little reliable information on the uses or claims to state water.[1] The sheer magnitude of the undertaking was also impressive, as Montana encompasses some 140,000 square miles, a variety of landscapes and climates, eighty-five water basins and sub-basins, and a multitude of "interested" parties. A significant portion of the land within the state's boundaries is controlled and managed by federal agencies or Indian tribes.[2]

The movement toward systematic adjudication in state courts was actively opposed by Indian tribes during the 1970s, and tribal leaders tried unsuccessfully to exclude Indian reserved rights from the drafted legislation. When these efforts appeared to be headed for failure, the Justice Department filed suit in federal court in April 1979. The suits sought to ensure a federal forum and were filed only after attempts to exempt Indian tribes from the pending state initiative failed. However, the immediate impact was dramatic: some 3,400 Montana water users were served notice, and it was suggested the number of defendants might reach 10,000 or more. Thus, while reserved water rights were not necessarily well understood by the general public, they were suddenly very visible.

It was amid this contentious climate that Senate Bill 76, the amended state water plan, was approved in May 1979. It divided the state into water districts and created independent water courts to adjudicate all claims and to issue decrees. The bill included all claimants of Indian reserved water rights as "necessary and indispensable parties" under the authority granted the state by the McCarran Amendment. The legislation also created the Reserved Water Rights Compact Commission and authorized it to negotiate with tribes to conclude compacts. A subsequent amendment (House Bill 667, passed in 1981) suspended all proceedings to adjudicate reserved rights in state courts while negotiations or ratification efforts were in progress.

The Fort Peck tribes had opposed state adjudication but had also indicated their willingness to consider negotiations. Several characteristics of the reservation and its tribal leadership are pertinent to understanding the context within which negotiations were initiated. First, the reservation is located on the main stem of the Missouri River, just below the massive Fort Peck reservoir. Thus, while surface and groundwater supplies may be variable in some locations on the reservation, the Missouri offers a seemingly ample supply of water. Second, the leadership of the Assiniboine and Sioux tribes of Fort Peck (Chairman Norman Hollow and key council members) was experienced, had considerable tenure in office, and endorsed negotiating efforts. The tribes' land base and natural resources, combined with their location relative to the Missouri, suggested that, if quantified, their right to water could be a substantial one.[3]

Fort Peck Compact Negotiations

The Reserved Water Rights Compact Commission, created by Senate Bill 76, had nine members appointed by the legislature, the governor, and the attorney general. The first chair of the commission was Henry Loble, a lawyer with extensive background in water law who had previously served in the state legislature. In addition to commission members and tribal representatives, a number of state and federal agencies were regular participants or observers at these meetings. The governor, attorney general, and state Department of Natural Resources and Conservation (DNRC) sent representatives to meetings, as did the Departments of the Interior (specifically the Bureau of Indian Affairs, Field Solicitor, and Bureau of Reclamation), Defense (Army Corps of Engineers), and Justice.

The first formal meeting between the commission and the Fort Peck tribes took place in December 1980. The chronology of events between the initiation of talks and the ratification of a final compact in 1985 included the drafting of an initial version in 1982, which both the tribes and the commission agreed would be submitted to the state legislature for ratification. The commission's failure to submit the compact led to a breakdown in negotiations for a year. When talks resumed in late 1984, the state presented the tribes with a revised compact that differed significantly from the original. It took less than six months to move from that second proposed agreement to the final one. The three versions of the compact, and the evolution of provisions relating to the two key issues of quantification and water marketing, provide insight into key substantive issues and points of disagreement.

Round I: The 1983 Draft

The first draft, to which both the commission and the tribes agreed, stipulated that the tribes could divert up to 1,806,318 acre-feet annually, or the quantity necessary to supply a consumptive use of 903,159 acre-feet, whichever was less. The quantified right was based on estimates of irrigable lands and available surface water supplies, as opposed to being a full-blown practicably irrigable acreage (PIA) analysis.[4] For example, a preliminary tribal evaluation of irrigable lands (in 1981) indicated that approximately 500,000 acres were irrigable. The study was based on existing soil surveys, only included land below the 2,300-foot contour level, and was premised on the belief that the Missouri River would be the source of water supply. The tribes' figures compared favorably with the state's estimate of 487,000 irrigable acres, and the parties were eventually able to agree on consumptive use requirements and diversion measurements.

Actual diversions were based on the percentage of Indian-owned land within the base area, which consisted of parcels of land below the 2,300-foot contour, classified on the basis of their productivity.[5] At the time the compact was drawn up, Indian-owned lands comprised about 58 percent of the total base area, resulting in a diversion right of 1,050,472 acre-feet annually. The determination of Indian-owned lands was subject to requalification by either the state or the tribes. In effect, while there was a ceiling on diversions and consumptive use, the right was flexible and could expand or contract to reflect changing patterns of land ownership within the reservation.

The ceiling of 1.8 million acre-feet was clearly a tremendous amount of water.

However, this quantity was the result of a number of reciprocal concessions. For example, the tribes focused on the Missouri River as the primary source for satisfying their claims. They agreed to refrain from drawing from the Milk River, recognizing that this basin was the area of maximum difficulty for the state, and subordinated their rights to existing uses on a number of reservation streams and tributaries. Protection of existing non-Indian water users had been a priority for the commission, and it is evident that the tribes viewed these concessions as a suitable exchange for a more generous award of Missouri River water and the authority to market water.

Interest in water marketing reflected the broader forces reshaping water allocation and management practices in the West. But tribal interest in water marketing was further enhanced by the particular realities that characterized resource development in Indian Country. During the decades when water and regional development were the cornerstones of federal water policy, such developments generally ignored, or even usurped, Indian claims to water. This gap between water rights in theory and fact persists, often even after these rights are recognized and quantified.[6] For example, agriculture has been the predominant use of water on many reservations, but future investments in irrigated agriculture often do not make economic sense.[7] Other options for tribal development of water resources are frequently limited, not least because of insufficient capital and limited local demand. It is evident that reserved rights may remain largely useless to many tribes, in a practical and economic sense, unless they can be marketed.

The extent to which the tribes can market water goes to the heart of many controversies over Indian reserved rights: the purposes for which water may be used; the extent of tribal authority to control and manage resources; and the ability of the tribes to capture the full value of their quantified rights. While there is some agreement that tribes may utilize their right on-reservation for a variety of purposes, the very concept of water marketing is extremely controversial, particularly when it involves off-reservation leasing and when it may impact existing water users.

The Fort Peck tribes' insistence on the right to market water was a matter of principle and practicality. The history of irrigated agriculture on the reservation, specifically the Fort Peck Irrigation Project, combined with current economic realities, suggested limited economic potential for agricultural development. The tribes were utilizing only a fraction of their quantified right (approximately 20,000 acre-feet per year) and had no illusions about developing it immediately. Instead, water marketing offered the tribes the potential to realize more of the economic value of their right, in both the short and the long term.[8] And while there was no immediate demand for water in the upper Missouri River basin, South Dakota's ETSI Pipeline Project had demonstrated the potential value that might be realized from specific marketing arrangements.

The legal and political precedents recognizing tribal water marketing authority in the mid 1980s were limited and mixed at best. The Wyoming District Court decision on the rights of the Wind River tribes, handed down in 1983, held that the tribes could sell or lease their water, but such sale or lease could not be for export off the reservation.[9] Meanwhile, under the Southern Arizona Water Rights Settlement Act of 1982, Congress authorized the Tohono O'odham Nation to market its water, subject to the approval of the secretary of the interior. And several other western tribes were including related provisions as part of other settlement proposals.[10]

This first Fort Peck–Montana Compact recognized the right of the tribes to transfer water, subject to some restrictions. For example, out-of-state marketing arrangements were subject to valid state law; off-reservation diversions were geographically restricted and the right was to be used for beneficial purposes. But within some broad parameters there appeared to be considerable latitude for the tribes to develop transfer or marketing arrangements.

The draft of the initial compact was completed in the spring of 1983 but was never submitted to the state legislature. A number of factors appear to have worked against smooth approval. Both the attorney general's office and DNRC had representatives present at the negotiating sessions, but their objections seemingly did not adequately surface until the last minute. For example, reservations expressed by the director of DNRC at a meeting in May of 1983 concerned the magnitude of the quantified right, the tribes' use and diversion of water off the reservation, the split jurisdiction and administration of water rights, and the precedent this first compact might be setting. In addition, the attorney general's office was in the midst of arguing the *Adsit* case, and there was concern that specific aspects of the compact might weaken the state's position.[11]

Skirmishes over political turf and legal complications were compounded by the changing personality of the commission itself. Henry Loble resigned in early 1983 to become state district court judge, and Gordon McOmber, newly appointed to the commission, took over as chair. Although Mr. McOmber had considerable legislative experience, he lacked Mr. Loble's legal expertise and experience with water law. This transition took place at a rather critical juncture: the commission had worked on the compact for over three years and seemingly felt it was ready to go. Suddenly it appeared that substantial objections remained and, indeed, were reinvigorated. In the end it was evident that legislative approval would be unlikely, so the commission elected not to submit the compact for ratification.

Round II: The State's Proposal to Fort Peck (1984 Draft)

The failure to ratify the initial Fort Peck Compact led to a breakdown in negotiations that lasted for over a year. Prior to meeting again with the tribes, the commission drafted a compact that was characterized as more "politically prag-

107

matic." The state's revised version differed from the 1983 draft in significant ways, primarily in the quantity of water involved and in the use of tribal water rights.

For example, it was proposed that the tribes divert the lesser of 840,000 acre-feet or the quantity necessary to supply a consumptive use of 420,000 acre-feet. Diversions from groundwater were expected to make up a significant portion of this total diversion right. Provisions tying actual diversions to the percentage of Indian-owned lands were eliminated.

Concerning the use of tribal water rights, provisions that had allowed off-reservation diversions upstream from the Fort Peck Dam and from any tributary of the Missouri (with prior legislative consent) were eliminated, and a new sub-section required that off-reservation diversions comply with all state laws. Through a number of revised provisions the state effectively asserted broad juris-dictional and regulatory control. For example, under a new section it was held that the "state shall have exclusive jurisdiction to administer and enforce the allocation of all rights to the use of water allocated under state law, tribal law or federal law on or off the Reservation." [12]

The revised compact was not warmly received. The tribes argued that the state had taken back every one of its important concessions (in the areas of quantity, marketing, and administration) but had retained every concession the tribes had made (e.g., protection of existing uses). The tribal position on the smaller quantity proposed by the state was that it was completely fictitious and had no connection to the 500,000 acres both parties had earlier determined might be irrigable. In addition, the stipulated groundwater withdrawals were admittedly hypothetical, since the groundwater source was purely "fictional." Conflicts over off-reservation water marketing were both substantive and procedural. Both parties differed as to whether or not the tribes could claim marketing authority for using their re-served rights and how much control the state would have under such circum-stances.

Round III: Fort Peck–Montana Compact Concluded (1984–1985)

It was evident, given the state's redrafted proposal, that the diversion of 1.8 million acre-feet allowed under the first compact was simply too much for the state to accept. After some discussion the tribes agreed to settle on a firm quantity, as opposed to the earlier system that allowed for adjustments based on changing patterns of land ownership. But that quantity and source (surface versus ground-water) were still at issue.

In early January the commission proposed recognizing a fixed tribal right of 1,050,000 acre-feet but required that 210,000 acre-feet of that come from ground-water.[13] The proposal was unacceptable to the tribes because, as the state admitted, absolutely nothing was known about the source, storage capacity, or annual safe yield of the groundwater under the reservation. The tribes sought to modify the state's position, suggesting that they have the option, if groundwater could not be found, to take the remainder out of the Missouri River. But the stalemate persisted.

There were also serious obstacles in regard to water marketing. The prospect of off-reservation diversion and use of the tribal water remained highly controversial. The commission's revised position on control over water marketing represented a substantial departure from earlier understandings, but the state was adamant in arguing that such a right was not clearly understood to be within the scope of Indian reserved water rights.

Meanwhile, Montana had its own concerns with water marketing. By 1984 the Montana legislature was drawing up proposed initiatives outlining a water leasing program, and the commission was concerned with ensuring compatibility between tribal water marketing provisions and emerging state guidelines.[14] The new statute designated DNRC as the sole entity with authority to market water and seemed to assert regulatory control over reserved rights. It appeared that the tribes would have parity with any other applicant seeking to market "state" water—and nothing more.

This caused protracted disagreement. The tribes argued that such restrictions negated the potential value of water marketing authority and effectively subjected the tribes to broad discretionary state approval for use of their own water resources. Such an outcome was unpalatable. For its part, the commission was concerned about the precedent that the Fort Peck Compact, and any marketing provisions, would set for other tribes.

The impasse over quantification and water marketing was resolved at a meeting in February. In an effort to reach some agreement in principle, the tribes offered the following suggestions:

1. The parties should return to the 1983 provisions dealing with marketing, and the tribes would abide by state regulations regarding out-of-state water transfers;
2. The tribes would agree to be subject to the same ceiling as DNRC on the quantity of water they could market;
3. Joint marketing arrangements between the tribes and the state were agreeable;
4. The tribes would accept a 950,000 acre-feet ceiling on surface water diversions and the 100,000 acre-feet diversion requirement from groundwater sources.

This initiative was the catalyst for getting things moving. The inclusion of groundwater brought the ceiling on diversions from surface water below the "magical" 1 million acre-feet total, which appeared to be a major objective for the state.

And the tribes ended up with the largest amount of water ever confirmed for a reservation.

A series of counterproposals yielded basic agreements on water marketing as well. The state offered some compromises (e.g., allowing the tribe to divert and market from the Fort Peck reservoir or below with minimal state interference) and conditionally agreed to the proposed quantification.[15] One of the state's conditions included a marketing cap for the tribes of 50,000 acre-feet per year or 25 percent of the state ceiling. After further debate, the parties compromised on an alternative that set the tribes' cap at 50,000 acre-feet per year and linked further increases to changes in the state ceiling.[16]

The water marketing provisions worked out in the final compact are complex and innovative and distinguish between on- and off-reservation use. The tribes are prohibited from permanently alienating their water rights (in all cases) but may transfer or lease their rights for up to fifty years. Otherwise there are few restrictions constraining on-reservation marketing activities. The off-reservation provisions are more involved, however. For example, outside of the reservation, tribal water use must be for a beneficial use as defined by applicable state laws; diversions must comply with state laws regulating facilities siting; and use of the right outside the state is subject to all applicable state laws. Different restrictions also apply to specific geographic areas and water sources. For example, the tribes may lease water from the main stem of the Missouri but must provide the state with advance written notice of any proposed transfer and offer the state the opportunity to participate. In addition, different provisions will apply to potential water transfers depending on whether the diversions are from upstream or downstream of the Fort Peck reservoir, from the reservoir itself, or from the tributaries of the Missouri. For example, while all existing uses on tributaries of the Missouri that flow through or adjacent to the reservation were protected, the tribes can enter into deferral agreements with future off-reservation water users of these tributaries, excepting the Milk River.[17] What all this means in terms of tribal water marketing prospects remains to be seen. In essence, they have considerable latitude on-reservation, but the economic value of their off-reservation marketing authority is difficult to estimate.

The meetings of February 27–28, 1985, proved decisive. The parties were under considerable time pressure because the revised compact had to be submitted to the state legislature by mid March if it was going to be considered during the forty-ninth biennial session. Both sides seemed anxious to have a settlement. The commission had been negotiating with various tribal groups and federal agencies for five years but had yet to successfully conclude an agreement. The tribes had understood that they had reached an agreement two years earlier, only to have it dissipate on the state level.

This time the outcome was different. The Fort Peck–Montana Compact (S.B. 467) was introduced to the state legislature, and hearings were held in April 1985. In addition to the testimony of representatives of the compact commission and the tribes, representatives from various state agencies and offices (including DNRC, the attorney general's office, and the governor's office) also spoke in support of passage of the bill. There were no opponents, and Senate Bill 467 was approved by the Senate and House by the end of April. The compact was subsequently ratified by the Tribal Executive Board and signed by the governor.

Conclusion

The compact is only in the initial stages of being implemented, and many provisions have yet to be tested. In addition to issues of interpretation and feasibility, broader questions about implementation remain. The water marketing provisions in the compact require congressional approval (or exemption from the Indian Non-Intercourse Act), but such approval appears problematic in the short term. Congress has yet to develop a consistent position with regard to the marketing of Indian reserved rights. There are precedents for congressional approval: examples include the 1984 Ak-Chin settlement and the 1988 Salt River Pima-Maricopa Indian Water Rights Settlement Act. But there are also significant obstacles. This was evident in the treatment of both the San Luis Rey and Colorado Ute settlements, when the language pertaining to water marketing provisions was substantively changed as the bills moved through Congress.[18] The Montana state legislature passed a resolution in 1985 urging congressional approval of the water marketing arrangement in the compact; but there was no congressional action until November of 1991, when the Fort Peck Indian Tribes–Montana Compact Act of 1991 (S.B. 1602) was introduced by Senator Max Baucus of Montana. Hearings were held, and the bill was reported out of committee in August 1992, but it subsequently died. As a result, the dimensions of this critical element of the compact have yet to be fully clarified or developed.

NOTES

1. The inadequacies of Montana's "nonsystem" prior to 1973 are well documented by Albert Stone in "Montana Water Rights—A New Opportunity," *Montana Law Review* 34 (1973): 57–74.

2. Four federal agencies control 29 million acres, and seven Indian reservations encompass an additional 8.2 million acres.

111

3. The reservation encompasses some 2 million acres. Although it was subject to allotment during the early 1900s, approximately 900,000 acres remain in trust.

4. Practicably irrigable acreage is the standard developed to quantify Indian reserved rights in *Arizona v. California,* 373 U.S. 546 (1963). Determining PIA involves classifying lands based on their suitability for irrigation, identifying a water supply, and documenting the technical and economic feasibility of irrigation.

5. The base area consisted of 501,755 acres. The tribes and the state had compromised on a water duty of 3.6 acre-feet per acre. Thus, the actual diversion right in 1983 consisted of 291,798 acres (approximately 58 percent of the 501,755 that were Indian-owned) multiplied by 3.6 acre-feet per acre, for a total of 1,050,472 acre-feet.

6. See, for example, Steven Shupe, "Water in Indian Country: From Paper Rights to a Managed Resource," *University of Colorado Law Review* 57 (1986): 562–92.

7. See, for example, Robert A. Young and Roger Mann, "Cheap Water in Indian Country: A Cost-Effective Rural Development Tool?" chapter 12, this volume.

8. Water marketing can encompass a wide variety of options, from outright leasing of rights to deferral or conservation agreements. From the transcripts it appears that the tribes had thought about leasing arrangements (including exporting water off-reservation) and deferral agreements whereby they might benefit from future development on tributaries.

9. This finding was upheld by the Wyoming Supreme Court in 1988. The supreme court decision noted that the tribes had not sought permission to export water and that the United States had conceded that no federal law explicitly permits the sale of reserved water to non-Indians off the reservation; see *Big Horn, In re rights to use water in,* 753 P.2d 76 (Wyo. 1988).

10. For example, the San Luis Rey settlement (representing the claims of five California mission Indian bands), introduced in 1985, sought explicit authority to market water.

11. *Northern Cheyenne Tribe v. Adsit,* 668 F.2d 1080 (9th Cir. 1982). On appeal this decision was consolidated with two others and was ruled on by the U.S. Supreme Court in *San Carlos* (1983).

12. Proposed 1984 Fort Peck–Montana Compact, Article 5, Allocation, Enforcement and Administration; specifically, Sec. C, State Administration.

13. The 210,000 acre-feet amounted to the difference between the tribes' diversion right in the original compact based on Indian-owned irrigable acreage and the state's proposed ceiling of 840,000 in the second draft.

14. Recommendations included permanently repealing bans on the out-of-state export of water and the use of water for coal slurry purposes, and initiating a limited water leasing program.

15. Conditions included counting in-stream flows against the surface cap of 950,000 acre-feet; subordinating tribal rights to existing uses; and making an agreement that the tribes would have no veto right over new permits on the north/south tributaries.

16. If Montana exceeds 200,000 acre-feet per year, the tribes' percentage would increase to a maximum of 50 percent of anything over 300,000 acre-feet.

17. These include the Poplar River and Big Muddy and Porcupine creeks. These users must first obtain a state water permit and would be subject to state jurisdiction.

18. Compare, for example, S.B. 795, introduced March 19, 1987, Section 7 (b) with P. L. 100-675 (1988), the San Luis Rey Indian Rights Settlement Act, Section 106 (c).

9

THE SALT RIVER PIMA-MARICOPA SETTLEMENT: AN OVERVIEW

William H. Swan

The Salt River settlement was reached the old fashioned way—by tough negotiations —by representatives of seven municipalities, a major reclamation project, irrigation and water conservation districts, the State of Arizona, the United States and the Indian community. The settlement is a testament to the art of political compromise, and all those who participated can be rightly proud of their role in its development.
Congressman Morris Udall of Arizona[1]

Although SRP [the Salt River Project] is fully prepared to proceed with litigation to protect the Valley's water rights, we question whether litigation is the optimum alternative for resolution of Indian water claims. The socioeconomic impacts of water allocations between Indians and non-Indians are so significant that it may be imprudent for these conflicts to be resolved by the judiciary on an ad hoc basis. Our judicial system is not designed or equipped to address the fundamental question of water reallocation.
Jack Pfister, former general manager, Salt River Project[2]

Although Arizona has produced a number of Indian water rights settlements, the Salt River Pima-Maricopa Indian Community Water Rights Settlement of 1988 is unique for several reasons. First, it presented an extremely complex snarl of disputes and plumbing arrangements that challenged the creativity of the parties involved. Second, one goal of the settlement process was to provide to the Salt River Pima-Maricopa Indian Community the sources of water to which it believed it was entitled. The Salt River Indian Community wanted to have for its use the indigenous water supplies to which its alleged rights attached, not imported water. And third, the settlement unavoidably highlighted areas of dispute among the non-Indian participants that had to be resolved to arrive at a comprehensive settlement package.

In addition to the need to resolve local water-related issues, the settlement participants faced the necessary task of negotiating with the federal executive branch over the nature and scope of the federal monetary contribution. Although the initial settlement arrangement was flatly opposed by the Reagan administration, a series of compromises led to the package that was eventually approved by Congress and accepted by the president.

Background

To understand the Salt River settlement, it is critical to have an understanding of the interrelationship between the creation of the reservation and the development of one of the first and most successful reclamation projects in U.S. history, the Salt River Project.

In the 1870s, Pima and Maricopa Indians from the Gila River Reservation in south-central Arizona migrated in search of better agricultural water supplies to the Salt River valley. In 1879 the president created a reservation for Pima and Maricopa Indians along the Salt River. With a strong agricultural heritage, the Indians of the Salt River Reservation continued over the years to grow crops with water diverted from the Salt River, along with a growing population of non-Indian neighbors in the Salt River valley.

After the 1902 Reclamation Act, local water users convinced the secretary of the interior to develop a reclamation project in the Salt River valley. The cornerstone of the project was to be a high dam on the Salt River northeast of Phoenix, at the confluence of the Salt River and Tonto Creek. After authorizing the Salt River Project, the secretary pursued three goals: (1) he initiated plans for the construction of Roosevelt Dam and Granite Reef diversion dam; (2) he purchased privately owned canal and ditch companies in the valley area; and (3) he compelled local water users to initiate a water rights adjudication to clarify who held valid rights to water in the Salt River valley.

In 1905 the local water users initiated a water rights proceeding entitled *Hurley v. Abbott,* which eventually resulted in a 1910 stipulated decree known as the Kent Decree. In 1907 the federal government filed a complaint in intervention, advancing its own rights and also claims on behalf of Indians residing on the Fort McDowell and Salt River reservations. In present-day litigation the government has asserted that it only claimed prior appropriation rights on behalf of Indian farmers on the two reservations, as opposed to federal reserved water rights. However, the Salt River Project and other non-Indian users assert that the government intended to litigate once and for all the water rights of the two reservations. Although the Supreme Court's *Winters* decision was issued in 1908, the government did not amend its complaint on behalf of the Indians, and in 1910 the government and the other parties stipulated to the Kent Decree in which relatively small amounts of water were allocated to existing farming uses on both reservations.

When Roosevelt Dam was completed in 1911, the flow of the Salt River through the Salt River Reservation was essentially stopped. Normal flow and developed water supplies were diverted at Granite Reef diversion dam into project canals, and the Salt River Indians thereafter could not resort to self-help in diverting additional amounts from the river.

Since the Indians continued to complain about insufficient supplies of water, U.S. Indian Service officials attempted to include some of the reservation's allotted lands in the Salt River Valley Water Users' Association so that such lands would be eligible to receive project water. However, a debate within the Department of the Interior arose as to the legality of such action—focusing primarily on the legality of imposing Reclamation Act liens on Indian lands—and the effort was eventually dropped.

Sensing some inequity, Congress enacted legislation in 1916 that directed the secretary of the interior to provide water, from works constructed under the Reclamation Act, to 631 ten-acre allotments on the reservation.[3] Thereafter the Indian Service attempted to utilize appropriated funds and the authority of the 1916 Act to obtain entitlements to water from the Salt River Project. However, even though the project was not officially opened until 1917, the U.S. Reclamation Service responded that all of the anticipated project supply had already been allocated to non-Indians.

The position of the Reclamation Service reflected a decision made by the secretary of the interior in 1914 in regard to the boundaries of the project. Recognizing that there would be insufficient developed water to supply all irrigable lands in the valley, the secretary appointed a board to study which lands should be included in the project and to make appropriate recommendations. Although the board's preliminary findings mentioned irrigable lands on the Salt River Reservation, the final recommendations provided for a project boundary that excluded the entire reservation. Those recommendations were accepted by the secretary in his 1914 decision, which established the initial project boundaries.

After the project was officially opened in 1917, the secretary transferred, in that year, the care, operation, and maintenance of the project to the Salt River Valley Water Users' Association (which later became the Salt River Project [SRP]). Thereafter the Water Users' Association constructed in the 1920s and 1930s three additional dams on the Salt River below Roosevelt Dam. Also, in the early years of the project, relatively small tracts were added to the project service area, but no effort was ever made to include Indian lands.

In the 1920s, two important agreements were consummated with nonproject irrigation districts. First, SRP entered into an agreement with the Roosevelt Irrigation District (RID) whereby RID was allowed to place wells within the project service area to withdraw for its use project seepage water that was contributing to waterlogging. The secretary of the interior approved the SRP-RID agreement. Second, SRP entered into an agreement with the Roosevelt Water Conservation District (RWCD) whereby RWCD agreed to line a portion of one of the SRP canals to have for its use the saved seepage water. Again, the secretary approved the SRP-RWCD agreement.

In the 1930s, the Water Users' Association contemplated the construction of the first dam on the Verde River tributary of the Salt River. In an effort to satisfy the directive contained in the 1916 legislation, the secretary agreed to construct Bartlett Dam on the Verde River and agreed that the federal government would pay 20 percent of the construction costs to obtain water for the 631 Salt River Reservation allotments. The Bartlett Dam agreement provided that the government would have 60,000 acre-feet of storage in the reservoir and a right to take a maximum of 20,000 acre-feet per year for use on the reservation (providing a little more than 3 acre-feet per acre for the 6,310 acres of allotted land). In present-day litigation the Salt River Indian Community has asserted that the secretary should have provided enough water for 6 acre-feet per acre.

In the 1940s, SRP arranged for the construction of a second dam on the Verde River, Horseshoe Dam, located upstream from Bartlett Dam. With the addition of that dam, the project consisted of six dams on the two rivers, only two of which had been constructed by the federal government.

From the 1930s to the 1970s, the Indian Community survived off of three sources of water: (1) Kent Decree water, (2) Bartlett Dam water, and (3) developed groundwater. With these three sources, the Indian Community irrigated between 10,000 and 15,000 acres of land per year, although the reservation contains an undisputed 29,000 acres of irrigable land, much of which lies under or in close proximity to the SRP gravity system.

In the 1970s, the Indian Community embarked upon an effort to obtain additional water entitlements. It started down the path of litigation at the same time that it helped to initiate settlement discussions with SRP in the late 1970s. For a variety of reasons, those negotiations came to an end in the early 1980s, and for a time the parties focused only on litigation.

In 1983, the secretary of the interior finalized his Indian water allocations from the Central Arizona Project (CAP), authorized by Congress in 1968, which was under construction. Along with other Indian reservation allocations, the secretary allocated 13,300 acre-feet of high-priority CAP water to the Salt River Indian Community (CAP water is imported from the Colorado River; Arizona has an entitlement of 2.8 million acre-feet per year).

In 1985, negotiations were again initiated between the Indian Community and SRP. In 1986, the Department of the Interior agreed to formally participate in the negotiations that eventually led to the 1988 settlement.

The Pressure of Litigation

Unlike the situation in other states, in Arizona the state does not have the authority to represent its citizens in Indian water rights negotiations. Consequently, if the water users do not get together in an effort to resolve their differences, settlements cannot be negotiated.

Experience had demonstrated that the heat of litigation often presents the best catalyst for settlement. Following that approach, the Salt River Indian Community in the late 1970s and early 1980s initiated a number of lawsuits against many different entities to obtain either a greater water entitlement or monetary damages. The Indian Community's suits asserted the following kinds of claims:

1. The Indian Community and its allottees sought damages against the United States in the claims court based on allegations concerning deprivation of water rights.
2. The Indian Community sued SRP and the secretary of the interior in an effort to challenge the 1914 project boundary decision and the 1935 Bartlett Dam agreement. The Indian Community asserted that reservation lands were excluded from the Salt River Project on the basis of racial discrimination.
3. The Indian Community challenged the legality of the RWCD and RID agreements, arguing that it was unfair to allow project-related water to go to these users without including reservation lands in the project.
4. The Indian Community sued SRP, valley cities, and other entities alleging unlawful impact on the Indian Community's groundwater supply.

Other claims and challenges were advanced in other actions by the Salt River Indian Community. In addition, at the same time other forces had caused the development of a complete adjudication of water rights in the entire Gila River watershed. Although the Indian Community was not a participant in that proceeding, the United States was compelled to be a party to that state court action. In the Gila River adjudication, the government advanced a claim of approximately 190,000 acre-feet per year on behalf of the Indian Community, and many of the difficult water rights issues raised by the Indian Community would probably be ultimately decided in the Gila River adjudication if not decided elsewhere first.

The obvious importance of the above-outlined litigation inevitably created risk on both sides. For example, a pivotal issue was the effect of the 1910 Kent Decree. If the courts eventually decided that the federal government and the Indian Community were bound by the terms of the decree, in regard to the Indian Community's claimed federal reserved water right, then the Indian Community would probably not be entitled to any additional water. However, if the courts eventually determined that the decree was of limited scope and therefore was not binding in regard to the Indian Community's claimed reserved water right, then the Indian

119

Community would probably receive significant additional supplies due to the undisputed irrigability of the community's lands.

In the face of this risk, all parties eventually became convinced that their time and money was better spent in the direction of settlement, and the long negotiation process was initiated.

Terms of the Settlement

Given the complex and detailed nature of the settlement package, it is not feasible to explain all facets of the settlement in detail.[4] Basically, the settlement provides that the Salt River Indian Community will have the use of 122,400 acre-feet per year, developed from the following components:

1. Kent Decree water, with storage provided in CAP storage space in an enlarged SRP reservoir—18,776 acre-feet.
2. Contribution of stored water from SRP—9,074 acre-feet; or the choice of an alternative uncertain supply dependent upon SRP storage.
3. Bartlett Dam agreement water—20,000 acre-feet (with certain problems regarding the Bartlett Dam agreement resolved through amendments).
4. Entitlement of CAP water—13,300 acre-feet (to be leased to valley cities for a period of ninety-nine years).
5. Contribution from RWCD—8,000 acre-feet.
6. Contribution from RID—10,000 acre-feet.
7. Contribution from valley cities in the amount of 20,000 acre-feet from city lands within the SRP area, in exchange for the cities receiving 22,000 acre-feet of purchased Colorado River water to be imported via the CAP system. The imported water may be used by the cities on lands outside the SRP area.
8. Developed groundwater on the reservation—23,250 acre-feet (long-term average).

Due to the complex legal and plumbing arrangements surrounding each of the above-listed supplies (except groundwater), the settlement documents necessarily had to address and resolve a host of complicated issues and supporting arrangements. For example, the purchase of water from the Colorado River is made very complicated as a result of a number of factors. First, various contractual matters have to be resolved with the selling entity (the settlement legislation provides Reclamation Reform Act relief, for example). Second, the imported water goes to seven different valley cities, thus necessitating seven contracts for additional CAP-related water and seven additional CAP-related water accounts. Finally, to account for the difference between the amount of imported water and the amount to be delivered to the cities, a complex arrangement had to be put into place regarding the contribution of a portion of RWCD's CAP water allocation.

However, even though it presents unwanted complexities, the imported supply is to some extent the linchpin of the settlement. On the one hand, the cities with urbanized lands inside the SRP boundaries (essentially the same interest advanced and protected by SRP) are contributing additional SRP stored water to the settlement from an area of relative water abundance. On the other hand, the cities are obtaining a much-needed supply for use *outside* of the SRP area, where there is a greater need for a secure supply.

Similarly, the other components of the settlement involve complicated plumbing arrangements, transfers, or exchanges, all of which cause the settlement document to exceed seventy pages in length. In addition, there are about forty exhibits attached to the settlement agreement, and made a part thereof, which operate to either stipulate to the dismissal of the various lawsuits being settled or effectuate the numerous arrangements upon which the settlement is built.

In regard to monetary contributions, the local parties attempted to show somewhat equally balanced local-federal contributions in their initial settlement package, utilizing a value of $3,000 per acre-foot for contributed water supplies. The initial package included a federal contribution of approximately $80 million.

Since the initial legislative package was opposed by the Reagan administration on the basis of cost and other reasons, various proposed amendments were discussed in an effort to reduce the federal burden. Along with other minor adjustments, the parties eventually agreed that local cities would cover the cost of the acquisition of the imported Colorado River water. These adjustments resulted in a federal contribution of approximately $58 million, which was eventually accepted by Congress and the president.

The $58 million federal contribution is made up of several major components. First, the United States will deposit into a legislatively established trust fund approximately $30 million for the "design and construction of facilities to put to beneficial use the Community's water entitlement, to defray the cost to the Community of CAP operation, maintenance and replacement charges, and for other economic and community development on the Salt River Indian Reservation." [5] Second, the United States will deposit $17 million into the Indian Community's trust fund for the rehabilitation and improvement of existing facilities serving the Salt River Indian Community. Finally, up to $10 million will be spent by the United States under existing CAP authority to construct facilities for the use of CAP water on the reservation.

The components of the nonfederal contributions are (1) local water contributions (estimated value)—$96 million; (2) funds from the valley cities for the purchase of Colorado River water—$9 million; (3) lease of CAP water—$16 million; (4) contribution from the state of Arizona—$3 million; and (5) contribution from the Indian Community—$2 million. On the basis of these contributions, the parties see a contribution split of 68.4 percent from local sources and 31.6 percent from the federal government.

Conclusions

The Salt River settlement provides an important precedent in regard to other potential Indian water rights settlements in Arizona and in other states. Many of the remaining Indian water rights disputes in Arizona present situations of similar complexity, and therefore it is important that the non-Indian participants now recognize that settlements such as these can be accomplished with sufficient dedication of time, attention, and creativity.

Furthermore, the Salt River settlement is important from the perspective of risk assessment and federal contributions. Developments in the law and a judicially refined understanding of the practicably irrigable acreage analysis compel settlement participants to study and assess their litigation risks, and the risks of their opponents, to arrive at appropriate compromises. Without such assessments, participants may deceive themselves into believing that their relative positions are stronger than what a realistic assessment would support.

In regard to federal contributions, the Salt River settlement demonstrates that both Congress and the executive branch are becoming much more knowledgeable about Indian water rights settlements. Settlement participants now face a greater burden in justifying their demands for significant federal contributions, particularly in light of the concern over the budget deficit. In addition, this settlement raises the issue of the effect of historical reasons that may justify present-day federal contributions, in addition to the effect of the monetary risks that the government may face as a result of litigation.

In summary, as stated by Congressman Udall, the Salt River settlement "is a testament to the art of political compromise." Through a process of exhausting negotiations the participants have crafted a settlement package that presents a win-win situation for all parties involved and resolves many disputes that would have been the subject of litigation for years to come. Unfortunately, the complexity of the settlement provides a new source of burden and frustration, which has caused a number of people to question whether litigation might in fact be easier. Nevertheless, the settlement achieved what litigation cannot: a fair resolution of the Indian Community's claims to water and a package of financial assistance that will allow the Salt River Indian Community to move toward a position of self-reliance.

NOTES

1. *Congressional Record,* September 13, 1988, p. H7499.

2. *Arizona Waterline,* Winter 1984, p. 5.

3. Act of May 18, 1916, Chap. 125, 39 Stat. 130.

4. The Salt River Pima-Maricopa Indian Community Water Rights Settlement Act of 1988, P.L. 100-512.

5. P.L. 100-512, Sec. 9 (a) (3).

10

EQUITY, LIABILITY, AND THE SALT RIVER SETTLEMENT

Norman H. Starler and Kenneth G. Maxey

In late 1988, Public Law 100-512 authorized the implementation of a water rights settlement agreement among the Salt River Pima-Maricopa Indian Community, local non-Indian public agencies in Arizona, and the federal government.[1] The most difficult issues addressed during the negotiation of the settlement agreement and the implementing legislation were the appropriate level of settlement cost, its division between federal and nonfederal participants, and how best to measure these contributions.[2] During the latter stages of the negotiations, these issues became critical and shaped much of the character of the settlement.

The relative contributions of the settlement participants have been determined by three different analyses, illustrated in Table 10.1 and discussed in detail later in this essay. One analysis represents the initial position adopted by the nonfederal participants. A second analysis represents the federal assessment of those proposed contributions, the identification and measurement of other financial effects, and a summation of the final settlement cost sharing. The third represents a federal analysis of the settlement, based on the relative legal exposure of the non-Indian settlement participants compared to that of the federal government.

As a result of the two federal analyses, the contribution from the United States specified by legislation ratifying the settlement was significantly reduced. The Department of the Interior used the second analysis as a basis to advocate changes in legislation that would reduce the federal contribution and fashion a distribution of the costs consistent with its view of programmatic responsibilities and equity.

The analysis of legal exposure was used to analytically determine a limit on the federal contribution. Based on this computed limit, the Office of Management and Budget (OMB) advocated a further reduction in the federal contribution, both during the time Interior was formulating its position and while Congress was considering legislation necessary to ratify the settlement. Ultimately, Congress enacted the law along the lines advocated by Interior. Nevertheless, there are many potential water rights settlements, and the debate as to the appropriate federal role continues.

Our objective is to explain these different approaches in a manner that will facilitate the analysis of future Indian water rights settlement proposals. We feel that the two federal analyses provide a basis to measure the cost of potential future settlements.

The analysis of the relative contributions of the settlement participants was important in addressing equity issues and programmatic responsibilities involving the resolution of these Indian water rights claims. Once all of the proposed costs were counted in the first federal analysis, the second federal analysis was used to determine the relative benefits from settlement and provided a basis for determining the appropriate federal contribution. The difference between this amount and the amounts suggested in various proposals during the debate on the enabling legislation represents a quantification of equity. Congress made the ultimate determination of what the United States should contribute in the name of "equity."

Background

The Salt River Pima-Maricopa Indian Community was formed as a reservation in 1879. The reservation is located just east of Phoenix, Arizona, and is rapidly being surrounded by the urban development occurring in the metropolitan area. The economy of the reservation is basically agricultural with some light industry.

In the early 1900s, the U.S. Bureau of Reclamation undertook the construction of the Salt River Project. The project allowed storage of water for irrigation of land in the Salt River valley. The local organizations contracting for the benefits and repayment of the Salt River Project are the Salt River Project Agricultural Improvement and Power District and the Salt River Valley Water Users' Association (collectively known as SRP). Today, SRP basically is a power generating and marketing agency with a lesser interest in water. However, SRP is also a major water supplier to the growing cities in the Phoenix area.

For reasons that are unclear, the Salt River Indian Community and its members were never included in the Salt River Project. Thus, early in this century, the Indians of the Phoenix area did not benefit from federal water development as did their non-Indian neighbors. An attempt at partial redress was made through legislation enacted in 1916 to secure water for 613 ten-acre allotments within the reservation.[3] However, the federal government did not act on that authorization until 1935 through participation in the financing of Bartlett Dam on the Verde River to secure 20,000 acre-feet for those allotments.[4] The Kent Decree in 1910 secured a direct flow right for 700 miner's inches of water for the Indian Community, but no storage rights.[5] At no time was the *Winters* doctrine invoked as a legal strategy for securing additional water for the Indian Community.[6]

During the last two decades, the Indian Community began to abandon its dependency on the federal government and embarked on a course of self-development and litigation of its water and land claims.[7] Initially, the United States negotiated with the Salt River Indian Community in tandem with its neighbor in the Phoenix vicinity, the Fort McDowell Indian Community. When the United States offered $45 million to settle both claims, the Fort McDowell negotiations ended and the Salt River Indian Community negotiations continued among the nonfederal parties without U.S. representation. The dynamics driving negotiations were that the Indian Community would be willing to reduce their claim for over 202,000 acre-feet if they could end up with about 122,000 acre-feet, facilities to use their Central Arizona Project (CAP) water, and capital to rehabilitate their existing irrigation system and to develop their community economy.

A signed settlement proposal was presented to the federal government by the nonfederal parties in February 1988, and legislation was introduced in Congress to authorize the settlement (H.R. 4102 and S. 2153). Many of the water rights and damage claims were to be obviated by the implementation of the Salt River Pima-Maricopa Indian Community Water Rights Settlement and the associated legislation, Public Law 100-512.

Initial Nonfederal Cost-Sharing Analysis

Three general types of resources were to be contributed by the parties to the settlement—cash, rights to water, and use of facilities. The initial nonfederal settlement proposal would have required primarily cash contributions from the federal government, while the main contribution by nonfederal entities would have been in the form of water rights.

The nonfederal participants to the settlement, including the Salt River Indian Community, initially represented the relative cost sharing as 57 percent local and 43 percent federal (Table 10.1, section C, column 1).[8] Without considering the time value of money, the federal government would have contributed about $88 million in facilities, trust fund money, and water and would also have accommodated future allottee claims. Under the initial proposal, the nonfederal contribution of $117 million would have consisted of water rights, willingness to lease Central Arizona Project water from the Indian Community, and trust fund money.

TABLE 10.1. Distribution of Costs in the Salt River Pima-Maricopa
Water Rights Settlement (in dollars)

		Source of Data		
Contribution		Nonfederal Proposal (1)	Federal Analysis of Proposal (2)	Federal Analysis of Final Settlement (3)
A.	Nonfederal			
1	Value of water (32,000 AF)	96,000,000	57,600,000	57,600,000
2	Lease of SRPMIC CAP water to Phoenix	16,000,000		
3	State of Arizona contribution to SRPMIC trust fund	3,000,000	3,000,000	3,000,000
4	SRPMIC contribution	2,000,000		
5	Purchase of WMIDD water			8,560,000
6	M&I charge to be paid by cities for shipping WMIDD water		972,000	972,000
7	CAP O&M paid by cities for WMIDD water (25,000 AF)		13,120,000	13,120,000
8	Subtotal, nonfederal	117,000,000	74,692,000	83,252,000
B.	Federal			
1	Purchase of WMIDD water	14,000,000	8,560,000	(see A-5, 3)
2	Lost repayment from WMIDD		1,400,000	1,400,000
3	Lost full-cost revenues from WMIDD		1,800,000	1,800,000
4	Rehabilitate existing irrigation system	17,000,000	14,000,000	(see B-8, 3)
5	CAP facilities	20,000,000	15,170,000	10,000,000

TABLE IO.I. *(continued)*

Contribution	Source of Data		
	Nonfederal Proposal (1)	Federal Analysis of Proposal (2)	Federal Analysis of Final Settlement (3)
B. Federal (continued)			
6 Reduction of right-of-way costs		– 1,650,000	
7 Additional SRPMIC claims	10,000,000	10,000,000	
8 Agricultural development trust fund	16,000,000	16,000,000	48,000,000
9 Kent Decree storage	1,000,000	1,300,000	1,300,000
10 Allottee claims	10,000,000	10,000,000	
11 Reduction in CAP revenues due to WMIDD import		9,000,000	9,000,000
12 Ten-year discount in CAP O&M costs to SRPMIC		4,470,000	(in B-8, 3)
13 O&M savings from reduced operation of desalination plant		– 11,400,000	– 11,400,000
14 Subtotal, federal	88,000,000	78,650,000	60,100,000
C. Summary			
1 Total amount	205,000,000	153,342,000	143,352,000
2 Nonfederal (percent)	57	49	58
3 Federal (percent)	43	51	42

ABBREVIATIONS: AF=acre-feet; CAP=Central Arizona Project; M&I=municipal and industrial; O&M=operation and maintenance; SRPMIC=Salt River Pima-Maricopa Indian Community; WMIDD=Wellton-Mohawk Irrigation and Drainage District

Federal Analysis of the Proposed Settlement

As is shown in Table 10.1, column 1, the primary local contribution to the proposed settlement (section A) was to be water, while the primary federal contribution (section B) was expected to be cash. Of critical interest to the federal government was the $3,000 per acre-foot of "in kind" water contribution. Was that an accurate valuation of the water being contributed? Also, were all the costs of the settlement set out in the above analysis, or were there other unidentified costs? Were some costs that had been included in the settlement actually external to it? Were all of the costs accurate and measured as of a common point in time? Only after accurately measuring the present value cost of the settlement and how it would be shared could it be determined whether the settlement proposal was "fair" to the local entities, the members of the Indian Community, and the federal taxpayer.

The federal analysis of these questions provided a rich exercise in cost-sharing evaluation and equity considerations.[9] The results are shown in Table 10.1. Column 1 displays the initial nonfederal proposal. Column 2 shows a reanalysis in present value terms, to recognize the time value of money. Column 3 shows the costs of the final settlement as specified by Public Law 100-512; this is also in present value terms. A discount rate of 8.625 percent was used to evaluate all future costs identified in this paper. This was the planning rate applicable to the evaluation of federal investments in water resources in Fiscal Year 1988.

The present value cost of the original nonfederal proposal was estimated to be about $153 million. The share of the federal government under this proposal would have been 51 percent rather than 43 percent (Table 10.1, last row, columns 1 and 2; for the remainder of this chapter, we will use the convention of listing the table number, the row number, and then the column number or numbers [e.g., Table 10.1, C-3, 1&2] to identify the value of a particular contribution).

Valuation of Water

The city of Phoenix, SRP, the Roosevelt Water Conservation District, and the Roosevelt Irrigation District would have contributed about 32,000 acre-feet of water for use by the Salt River Indian Community. These settlement participants placed a value of $3,000 per acre-foot on the contributed water ($96 million), which they represented as a conservative approximation of the expected market price for water in Arizona.[10] This estimate was based on actual and estimated capital costs plus operations and maintenance costs associated with large water transactions in the recent past.

An initial evaluation of local water transactions by federal analysts resulted in an estimate of capital costs averaging $1,700 per acre-foot and capitalized operations and maintenance costs averaging $800 per acre-foot. Thus, a value of $2,500 per acre-foot was initially viewed as valid from the federal perspective.[11] However, the valuation of water supplies in Arizona water markets is far from an exact science. There is not yet in operation in Arizona a well-functioning, active water market for large blocks of water. Historically, the water market has been characterized by large, infrequent purchases of water rights by municipalities. Thus, $3,000 per acre-foot, $2,500 per acre-foot, or other estimates may or may not be reasonable.

The data available underscore the wide range of water prices faced by Arizona buyers and sellers.[12] Life-cycle development costs for new water supplies in Arizona ranged from about $1,700 to $3,500 per acre-foot, with an average of $2,500 per acre-foot.[13] Other estimates set development costs ranging from $2,900 to $6,000 per acre-foot.[14] In contrast, one transaction was reported where a limited partnership acquired a ranch in bankruptcy for $1.5 million with 10,000 acre-feet of associated groundwater rights ($150 per acre-foot).[15] This latter purchase is a fraction of the cost incurred by municipalities in purchasing land for "water ranches." However, it appears to have been a "distress" sale that simply underscores the volatility of water transactions in Arizona.

The dilemma for the federal government was what value to accept for the contributed water. In the end, a simple standard was adopted. The value of the contributed water was assumed to be the same as the acquisition cost for the proposed lease transaction between the Salt River Indian Community and the city of Phoenix ($1,200 per acre-foot) plus operations and maintenance costs ($600 per acre-foot, in present value terms). For 32,000 acre-feet, this totalled $57.6 million (see Table 10.1, A-1, 2).

Other Nonfederal Contributions to the Proposed Settlement

Phoenix–Indian Community Lease / The Indian Community would lease its annual Central Arizona Project (CAP) water supply of 13,300 acre-feet to Phoenix for $16 million ($1,200/acre-foot) and would pay the CAP operations and maintenance costs ($600/acre-foot in present value terms).[16] As of the effective date of the agreement, the city could elect to make a down payment of $8 million and pay the balance over four years with interest.

This lease was negotiated in the context of the water settlement for the purpose of providing capital for the Indian Community to use its water. Nevertheless, the Indian Community had the right to this CAP water without the settlement. It could have pursued authorization to lease its CAP water independent of the settlement. The city and the community were merely exchanging money and water; there was no settlement contribution involved. Therefore, this element was not considered as a contribution by the federal analysts (see Table 10.1, A-2, 2).

State of Arizona Contribution / The agreement would require the state to con-tribute $3 million to the Indian Community trust fund. There are two views as to what this represented. One view is that it represented avoided litigation costs in the Gila River adjudication (of which the Indian Community claims are an integral part). Another view is that the state contribution was a "balancing item" to provide the Indian Community enough funds to carry out its agricultural development program. Regardless, this was counted as part of the settlement cost in the federal analysis. Like all contributions to trust funds, its amount was not discounted because it was to be paid up front (see Table 10.1, A-3, 2).

Indian Community Contribution / The Salt River Indian Community proposed to "contribute" $2 million to the settlement, essentially by moving funds from unrestricted accounts to a restricted settlement account. In a sense, the Indian Community thus would be contributing money to itself. In the federal analysis, this contribution was not counted, since it was viewed as reducing the total cost of the entire settlement rather than contributing to the financing of the settlement (see Table 10.1, A-4, 2).

Additional Nonfederal Costs

Salt River Project users would incur additional costs due to their agreement to pro-vide 20,000 acre-feet of SRP water to the Indian Community and to accept in ex-change about 25,000 acre-feet of Colorado River water transported via the CAP. For this CAP-transported water, they would pay a conveyance fee of 25 percent of the CAP municipal and industrial water capital charge, about $6.58 per acre-foot per year, plus the full CAP operations and maintenance (O&M) charge of $55 per acre-foot per year. Since SRP water users were at the time paying only $8.50 per acre-foot for O&M charges to SRP, the increase in their O&M charges would be $46.50 per acre-foot. The present value of the capital charges is $0.97 million, and the present value of the incremental O&M charges is $13.12 million, which totals about $14.1 million in additional nonfederal costs (see Table 10.1, A-6&7, 2).

Proposed Federal Contributions

Several components of the proposed settlement were reestimated from the federal perspective. Elements that imposed costs and savings for the federal government but were excluded from the nonfederal analysis had to be considered. Again, all of these were converted to a present value basis at 8.625 percent, the water resources planning rate.

Purchase of Colorado River Water / The settlement proposal initially called for an estimated expenditure of $14 million (see Table 10.1, B-1, 1) by the federal government to acquire water rights for the settlement from the Wellton-Mohawk

Irrigation and Drainage District.[17] Originally, the $14 million estimate related to the expected cost of acquiring land, and an associated 36,000 acre-feet of water, within the Wellton-Mohawk Irrigation and Drainage District (WMIDD). The quantity of 36,000 acre-feet was a holdover from the time when both the Salt River Indian Community settlement and the settlement with the Fort McDowell Indian Community were proceeding in tandem.

Later estimates predicted that there would be an acquisition and retirement of 2,000 acres, which would produce a consumptive use savings of about 10,000 acre-feet. However, as part of the settlement, the Colorado River diversion entitlement for WMIDD would be reduced by 22,000 acre-feet, and 3,000 acre-feet would come from other system savings. This 25,000 acre-feet would be provided to the cities. If prorated to the Salt River Indian Community settlement, the estimated acquisition cost would be approximately $8.6 million (see Table 10.1, B-1, 2).

The position that WMIDD took on the acquisition of the land and water was detailed in its Resolution 601-87.[18] That resolution contained two additional requirements that initially went unrecognized by the nonfederal participants. First, the resolution asked that WMIDD's remaining repayment obligation to the United States be extinguished. Second, the resolution requested congressional exemption from acreage limitation laws and the associated "full-cost" payments to the federal government for water facilities.[19] Evaluated on a present value basis, these two requests resulted in an additional federal cost of $1.4 million (see Table 10.1, B-2, 2) and $1.8 million (see Table 10.1, B-3, 2), respectively.

A question arose similar to the one posed previously—the appropriate valuation of the federal contribution associated with the acquisition of the WMIDD supply. If the actual acquisition costs were used, then the federal contribution would be on the order of $11.8 million.[20] However, it was conceivable that the federally acquired water should be accorded the same value as the nonfederal water—$3,000 per acre-foot (if the nonfederal valuation was used) or $1,800 per acre-foot (if the federal valuation was used). For the 25,000 acre-feet that the cities wanted in exchange for 20,000 acre-feet of Colorado River water, that would equate to valuing the federal contribution between $45 and $75 million.

Again, in the final analysis, it was decided to use the actual acquisition cost (including foregone revenues) to evaluate the WMIDD supply and the associated federal contribution. However, the final negotiated settlement shifted the direct cost of acquiring this supply from the federal government to the local non-Indian settlement participants (see Table 10.1, A-5, 3).

Development and Rehabilitation of Irrigation Facilities / The federal government was requested to contribute $20 million ($15.2 million present value; see Table 10.1, B-5, 2) to the development of CAP water delivery facilities to serve 8,700 acres of presently undeveloped Indian Community lands. This figure was

133

revised downward in the final settlement to the amount projected in CAP construction budgets, or approximately $10 million (see Table 10.1, B-5, 3). In addition, the federal government was asked to contribute $17 million ($14 million present value; see Table 10.1, B-4, 2) for rehabilitation of the existing water distribution system for the Indian Community.

Reduction of Right-of-Way Costs / In the federal reanalysis of the cost-sharing proposal presented by the local participants, it was noted that the cost of acquiring right-of-way for the new facilities and the rehabilitation of the existing facilities was estimated at $35,000 to $75,000 per acre. The estimate was based on local market value for power line right-of-way. Ordinarily, this might not have presented any problem. However, a principal tenet of the settlement for the Indian Community was that their lands would be dedicated to an agrarian use. In this context, it made little sense to accept a right-of-way cost based on the "highest and best use of the land" when such use was obviated by Indian Community policy. It was observed that right-of-way costs for the acquisition of agricultural land associated with the construction of CAP distribution systems ranged from $330 per acre to $3,700 per acre. Therefore, this right-of-way cost could be reduced by $1.7 million (see Table 10.1, B-6, 2).

Additional Indian Community Claims / The proposed settlement called for a $10 million settlement of additional claims against the federal government (see Table 10.1, B-7, 2). Apparently, this claim was based on the failure of the United States to deliver surface water to allotted lands within the reservation (the $10 million claim) and for groundwater depletion (an additional $10 million claim that was being waived).

Contribution to the Trust Fund / The $16 million federal contribution to the agricultural development trust fund was a balancing item that would yield sufficient capital and interest income to achieve the agricultural development objectives of the Indian Community (see Table 10.1, B-8, 2).

Allottee Claims / These are claims of individual Salt River Pima-Maricopa Community members for past unavailability of water (see Table 10.1, B-10, 2). This ownership category is distinct from tribal ownership; some of these owners may not be members of the Indian Community.

Additional Federal Monetary Costs and Contingent Liabilities

Kent Decree Storage / To guarantee 4,000 acre-feet of water allocated to the Indian Community as part of its Kent Decree rights, the municipalities participating in the settlement agreed to give up 7,000 acre-feet of storage space in the

Modified Roosevelt Reservoir for which they are contributing construction funds under another agreement.[21] The nonfederal proposal recognized, but underestimated, this federal cost. The CAP cost-sharing commitment of these municipalities will be reduced by about $0.7 million in capital costs and about $0.58 million in operations and maintenance costs, meaning that the United States will incur $1.3 million in costs (see Table 10.1, B-9, 2) rather than the $1 million estimate in the nonfederal proposal.

In the event that the Kent Decree storage space was not completed, the proposed agreement would have required that the federal government provide, at its cost, replacement water. However, this unquantifiable future liability was eliminated from the final negotiated settlement at the insistence of the federal negotiators.

Reduction in Central Arizona Project Revenues / The Bureau of Reclamation has been constructing the Central Arizona Project, a principal feature of which is the CAP aqueduct system. The costs of the aqueduct system are allocated to both reimbursable and deferred repayment/nonreimbursable accounts. Under the settlement proposal, the delivery of additional Colorado River (WMIDD) water through the CAP aqueduct system for Indian purposes would increase the cost allocated to the deferred/nonreimbursable category.[22] This reallocation would reduce the CAP repayment stream annually and cause a net present value reduction of $9 million (see Table 10.1, B-11, 2).

Ten-Year Discount in Central Arizona Project Operations and Maintenance Costs to the Indian Community / Another unacceptable future cost to the federal government concerned O&M costs imposed by SRP on the Indian Community. Under the proposed settlement, the Salt River Project would operate and maintain the Indian Community's new and rehabilitated delivery system at charges related to its cost of delivery to other agricultural customers. This "normal cost" is subsidized by SRP power revenues. The initial form of the settlement agreement required that the United States reimburse the Indian Community to the extent that actual charges by SRP exceeded the current inflation-adjusted SRP costs (i.e., a net reduction in power subsidization). The effect would have been to replace the SRP power revenue subsidy with a federal direct cash subsidy of about $4.5 million (see Table 10.1, B-12, 2).

Savings on Yuma Desalter / The purchase of Colorado River water from WMIDD and its delivery to the Phoenix area would result in the removal of 10,000 acre-feet of salt-laden return flows into the Colorado River. The United States constructed the Yuma desalter to meet water quality requirements under a treaty with Mexico. This reduction in return flow would mean that the frequency with which the desalter is run could be diminished. Estimates of annual cost savings ranged from $2.5 to $28.5 million; a present value of $11.4 million was used (see Table 10.1, B-13, 2).

Summary of Federal Analysis

The initial federal analysis concluded that the present value cost of the proposed settlement was about $153 million (see Table 10.1, C-1, 2). Based on this analysis, the proposed cost shares shifted slightly. The nonfederal amount of about $75 million (see Table 10.1, A-8, 2) represented 49 percent (see Table 10.1, C-2, 2), and the federal contribution of about $79 million (see Table 10.1, B-14, 2) accounted for 51 percent (see Table 10.1, C-3, 2). This split would have been "equitable" if the relative benefits from settlement to the nonfederal and federal parties had been the same. It was determined that this was not the case. From a perspective of legal liability, the local water users were in a more risky situation than the federal government and would therefore benefit more from the proposed settlement.

Ultimately, there were compromises in the proposed settlement, and legislation was fashioned. The costs for this final settlement were distributed as indicated in Table 10.1, column 3. The costs of purchasing WMIDD water were transferred from the federal to the nonfederal side (see Table 10.1, A-5, 3). From the federal perspective, its commitment for the construction of CAP-related facilities was quantified as a maximum of $10 million (see Table 10.1, B-5, 3). The rehabilitation of existing systems, additional claims, the agricultural development trust fund, and the ten-year discount on O&M costs to the Indian Community were all to be accommodated within a $48 million trust fund (see Table 10.1, B-8, 3). Language was included in the legislation that was designed to remove the threat of allottee claims against the federal government (see Table 10.1, B-7&10, 3). The federal share ended up at about $60 million (see Table 10.1, B-14, 3), or 42 percent of the total costs (see Table 10.1, C-3, 3). This was a move in the direction of sharing costs according to benefits.

Federal Analysis Based on Legal Liability

During the debate on H.R. 4102, which later was passed as Public Law 100-512, OMB made it known that the legislation would impose an unfair share on the federal government. This agency stated that the role of the federal government as trustee is to protect tribal water resources and to provide counsel to tribes for quantifying and adjudicating their water rights. In those instances where there was a valid legal claim against the federal government for not discharging its responsibilities, the United States should expect to discharge its liability by either complying with court findings or by contributing to a settlement. When there is a negotiated settlement, OMB indicated that all parties should benefit from the negotiations. This means that the federal government should not contribute any more to the settlement of a water claim than the amount for which it is legally liable. Furthermore, OMB viewed contributions related to the use of water or to economic development as discretionary, programmatic matters that should compete for funds with other programs in the Department of the Interior budget independently of settlements extinguishing legal liability.

Based on the OMB analysis, $25 million represented the limit of reasonable federal participation in the settlement.[23] This conclusion is derived from the parameters in Table 10.2. Column 1 represents the costs to all parties if there were no settlement, including litigation costs, construction costs, and water gains and losses; column 2 represents the costs of the settlement reflected in the legislation; and column 3, the costs of the OMB proposal. Under the OMB proposal, the federal government would incur costs of $25 million rather than the $60 million as specified in the proposed legislation that ultimately became law (see Table 10.1, B-14, 3). The nonfederal costs would be more than $83 million (water rights, associated expenditures to exchange water, and a $3 million trust fund). The Indian Community would receive a total of about $120 million in the form of water rights, expenditures and exchanges related to guaranteeing water availability, trust funds, and construction.

Without a settlement, the federal government could expect to incur as much as $10 million in CAP construction costs (see Table 10.2, A-1, 1), other related construction costs of $5 million (see Table 10.2, A-2, 1), and litigation expenses of $2 million (see Table 10.2, A-3, 1), but would not have to pay a claim to the Indian Community or to the allottees. The likelihood of not having to pay a claim was determined in consultation with the Department of Justice. Of course, it was recognized that there were various scenarios under which the government could be liable for some amount of money. Nevertheless, it was assumed in this analysis that its position would be upheld in court, which meant it would incur legal expenses but not be liable for damages.

Under the settlement legislation, the cost to the federal government would be $60.1 million (see Table 10.2, A-5, 2). Thus, it would make an "excess" contribution of over $43 million (see Table 10.2, A-6, 2) in the settlement. Even if it were to contribute $25 million under the OMB proposal, the federal government would be contributing $8 million more than it would if there were no settlement (see Table 10.2, A-6, 3). For this reason, OMB felt that a $25 million federal offer was more than reasonable.

The local water users, if there were no settlement, would be at risk of losing the use of their water in ten years and would incur litigation costs. These costs were estimated at $101 million (see Table 10.2, B-3, 1). The cost of the settlement would be about $83 million, so they would gain about $18 million under both the legislation and the OMB proposal (see Table 10.2, B-4, 2&3).

TABLE 10.2. Multiple-Party Comparison of Gains and Losses in the Salt River
Pima-Maricopa Water Rights Settlement (in dollars)

Gains and Losses	Without Settlement (1)	P.L. 100-512 Settlement (2)	OMB Proposal (3)
A. Federal			
1 CAP construction costs	– 10,000,000		
2 Other construction costs	– 5,000,000		
3 Litigation expenses	– 2,000,000		
4 Settlement costs		– 60,100,000	– 25,000,000
5 Subtotal, federal	– 17,000,000	– 60,100,000	– 25,000,000
6 Change (with v. without)		– 43,100,000	– 8,000,000
B. Nonfederal, non-Indian water users			
1 Loss of 130,000 AF in ten years	– 99,000,000		
2 Litigation costs	– 2,000,000		
3 Subtotal, nonfederal, non-Indian water users	– 101,000,000	– 83,252,000	– 83,252,000
4 Change (with v. without)		17,748,000	17,748,000
C. Salt River Pima-Maricopas			
1 Gain of 130,000 AF in ten years	99,000,000		
2 Litigation costs	(federal)		
3 CAP construction settlement (value of water)	15,000,000		
4 Gain of 32,000 AF from cities		57,600,000	57,600,000
5 Cost of other water		34,752,000	34,752,000
6 Nonfederal contribution to trust fund		3,000,000	3,000,000

TABLE 10.2. *(continued)*

Gains and Losses	Without Settlement (1)	P.L. 100-512 Settlement (2)	OMB Proposal (3)
C. Salt River, Pima-Maricopas (continued)			
7 Federal contribution to trust fund		48,000,000	25,000,000
8 Subtotal, Pima-Maricopas	114,000,000	142,752,000	119,752,000
9 Change (with v. without)		28,752,000	5,752,000
D. Lawyers' fees	4,000,000		
1 Total, nonfederal (Parts B, C, D)	118,000,000	142,752,000	119,752,000
2 Change (with v. without)		24,752,000	1,752,000

ABBREVIATIONS: AF=acre-feet; CAP=Central Arizona Project

Without the settlement, the Indian Community would gain the use of the water lost by the non-Indian water users in ten years as well as the CAP-related federal construction projects, together totaling $114 million (see Table 10.2, C-8, 1). With the congressionally passed settlement, they would receive about $143 million (see Table 10.2, C-8, 2) for a gain of about $29 million (see Table 10.2, C-9, 2). With the OMB proposal they would gain about $6 million (see Table 10.2, C-9, 3).

In this analysis, the estimates for legal expenses to be incurred by all parties totaled $4 million (see Table 10.2, D, 1). It was assumed that the United States would pay all of the legal expenses for the Indian Community, but this may have been an oversimplification.

It should be noted that under the OMB proposal, there is a difference of $11 million between the sum of the federal and nonfederal contributions (which total over $108 million—$25 million federal plus $83 million nonfederal [see Table 10.2, A-5, 3, and Table 10.2, B-3, 3]) and the $120 million (see Table 10.2, C-8, 3) in benefits received by the Indian Community. This is because the cost to the federal government is offset by savings from the reduced operations of the Yuma desalination plant.

Nevertheless, Congress decided on the grounds of equity that the Indian Community deserved to gain $29 million from the settlement (see Table 10.2, C-9, 2) rather than the $6 million proposed by OMB (see Table 10.2, C-9, 3). This brought the net federal costs to $60.1 million (see Table 10.2, A-4, 2) versus the OMB position of $25 million (see Table 10.2, A-4, 3).

Conclusions and Implications

Ultimately, the negotiated cost sharing between the federal and nonfederal, non-Indian parties came down to both a subjective and an objective calculation of the risk, liability, and equity parameters involved. It remains an open question whether all the objectives of the federal government were met.

It should be recognized that the federal government is far from a homogenous entity in this situation. Various degrees of negotiation, compromise, and power politics occurred within and among the Interior Department, OMB, Congress, and the White House. For example, there were strong feelings within Interior that $55 million in net costs rather than the $25 million advocated by OMB was the "right" federal contribution.[24] In fact, the estimated federal cost of Public Law 100-512 is about $60 million, or about 42 percent (see Table 10.1, B-14, 3, and Table 10.1, C-3, 3). This was a measurable decrease from the 51 percent share envisioned by the original nonfederal proposal (see Table 10.1, C-2, 2).

The reason for the contentious debate was that there did not exist a common, agreed-upon policy on settling Indian water claims within the federal government. As we understand it, such a policy is being developed. The three analyses presented above were tools employed to justify positions in this debate. Undoubtedly, there is a wide range of potential policy objectives, cost-sharing criteria, and liability parameters that can be fashioned to define the appropriate federal participation in Indian water rights settlements. Based on our experience analyzing the Salt River Pima-Maricopa Indian Community Settlement Act and other settlements, we suggest that four basic building blocks should be considered in addressing this issue: (1) federal liabilities and exposure, (2) objectives of Indian and non-Indian parties, (3) equity, and (4) tribal self-sustainability.

Analysis of Liabilities and Exposure

A fundamental basis for assessing the proper distribution of settlement costs is to evaluate the relative legal liabilities and exposures (potential gains and losses) of all parties: the Indians, the federal government, and the nonfederal, non-Indian entities. This will provide a set of opportunity costs from which further evaluation can proceed. Settlement amounts could be authorized on a present value basis.

This would maintain the value of the settlement regardless of the outcome of the annual appropriations process. We recognize that annual appropriations to discharge authorized settlements would have to compete against other programs within Interior. As such, it would put a budget constraint on Interior's capacity to negotiate settlements.

Analysis of the Objectives of Indian and Non-Indian Parties

In the Salt River Indian Community settlement, the Indians wished to develop an infrastructure that would maintain the community in an agrarian status that would be economically self-supporting. The nonfederal, non-Indian participants wished to bring closure to Indian claims to achieve certainty for future urban development, which is dependent on adequate water supplies. Such legitimate objectives need to be explicitly defined and subsequent negotiations undertaken to meet these objectives in a satisfactory manner.

The federal role here can be considered analogous to its role in solving a standard water resources problem. Standard cost-sharing arrangements would be applicable here.

Equity Analysis

Unfortunately, the heritage of the nation's Indian policy is steeped in racism, economic deprivation, and unfulfilled (or broken) promises. In essence, as one scholar notes, "The government has given away the water twice: once through the states [by upholding the prior appropriations doctrine] and once though the federal courts [by the *Winters* doctrine]. More water has been legally allocated than is available." [25]

Without the capital to exercise a water right, settling a claim may not be considered advantageous by the Indians. For this reason, water rights settlements are viewed by Indians frequently as a vehicle to recover natural and economic resources not available to them over many years as well as to obtain unrestricted grants or program commitments (e.g., irrigation facilities) in order to use the water they receive from a settlement.

Due to the conflict between state allocation systems and *Winters* court rulings, the nonfederal, non-Indian water users often feel that the federal judicial system is impinging on their state sovereignty as well as reneging on past encouragement to reclaim the land. Thus, in their opinion, the federal government should contribute a major share to Indian water rights settlements.[26] Yet it can also be argued that the nonfederal, non-Indian water users received the benefits over many years from water that belonged to the Indians and that they should be prepared to contribute the major share to the cost of Indian settlements.

"Equity" is often an extralegal concept; redress for past sins becomes a subjective judgment. The concept of equity and redress cannot be discarded because of the difficulty to measure it. However, compensation should address future objectives and needs, not merely past transgressions. The extent to which restoration should be shared by local entities and the federal government must be decided on a case-by-case basis.

From the federal perspective, the amounts spent in previous settlements on water development and rehabilitation on a per-acre basis or provided in trust on a per-capita basis can provide some guidance as to how reasonable a proposed contribution related to equity may be. Again, competition with other programs in the budget process is a fact of life.

Building Self-Sustainability

If the federal government is ever to make progress in helping Indians obtain their objectives, building a sustainable economic structure in which to realize these goals is, in our opinion, of primary importance. Here we are borrowing from a concept advocated for the revitalization of urban communities by Robin Malloy.[27]

Malloy's philosophy is that the federal government's proper role is to correct for market failure and to promote individual liberty. Toward those ends, Malloy proposes that federal assistance to communities should be for those activities that (1) provide for basic human wants such as adequate housing and education, and (2) provide for import-replacing activities and export (trade) opportunities.[28] Therefore, federal resources should be deployed to ensure that the settlement of a water right confers on the tribe a resource from which it can benefit. This means that in many instances they need to be able to market their water. In fact, several tribes have expressed an interest in water marketing. The effort needed to include this opportunity in Indian settlements will vary from state to state but should not be underestimated. This does not mean, however, that water settlements should be used to provide the whole gamut of basic human needs necessary for economic development.

Nevertheless, Indian communities should not be forced to become what they do not want to be. In the case of the Salt River settlement, the Indian Community was attempting to preserve an agrarian and natural heritage in a situation where the lease of land for urban development would have provided them with the greatest economic return. Their concept was to develop an infrastructure whereby they could export specialized crops to the surrounding urban area and still maintain their cultural objectives. They plan to lease some of their CAP water to partially finance this activity.

Thus, we believe that the federal participation in water rights settlements should contribute to self-sustaining economic development but be consistent with Indian cultural preferences.

142

Epilogue

On March 12, 1990, the Department of the Interior published the "Criteria and Procedures for Participation of the Federal Government in Negotiations for Settlement of Indian Water" in the *Federal Register.* Its purpose is to establish a basis for communication among the Departments of Interior and Justice, OMB and the executive branch, and Congress. Many of our suggestions are incorporated in the analytical framework that will be used in implementation.

NOTES

The authors are affiliated with the Office of Management and Budget and the Western Area Power Administration, respectively. The views expressed are our own and do not necessarily reflect the policies of these agencies or any of the agencies mentioned herein. We are indebted to our colleagues for useful criticism but are, of course, responsible for any remaining errors and omissions.

1. P.L. 100-512, 102 Stat. 2549, October 20, 1988.

2. Salt River Pima-Maricopa Indian Community Water Rights Settlement, February 1988.

3. P.L. 64-80, 39 Stat. 123, May 18, 1916.

4. Contract Between the United States and the Salt River Valley Water Users' Association dated June 3, 1935. These contracts are on file at the Contracts and Repayments Branch, Bureau of Reclamation, Washington, D.C.

5. *Hurley v. Abbott,* Civil No. C4564, Water Commissioner's Report filed June 3, 1977.

6. *Winters v. United States,* 207 U.S. 564 (1908).

7. "Report to the Secretary of the Interior of the United States in Regard to the Responsibility of the United States to Support the Salt River Pima-Maricopa Indian Community Water Rights Settlement Agreement and the Legislation Relating Thereto," Shea and Wilks, Indian Community attorneys, Phoenix, Arizona, February 26, 1988.

8. Salt River Pima-Maricopa Indian Community Water Rights Settlement, Sec. 20.2, pp. 46–47.

9. The federal analysis drew on the work of many individuals. Most of the parameters presented in Table 10.1, columns 2 and column 3, can be found in "Analysis of Amendments to H.R. 4102," prepared by Kenneth Maxey, Office of the Assistant Secretary of the Interior for Water and Science, May 1988. This drew on "Draft Financial Analysis," February 1988, prepared by Norman Starler, Bureau of Reclamation, which is partially based on comprehensive material prepared by Robert Johnson in "Memorandum from Regional Director, Boulder City, Nevada, to Commissioner," Bureau of Reclamation, [Analysis of] Salt River Pima-Maricopa Indian Community and Fort

McDowell Indian Community Water Rights Settlement, October 8, 1986. On file with the authors.

10. "Report: SRPMIC Water Rights Settlement Agreement—Local Cost Share Contribution Considerations," enclosure to February 26, 1988, letter from Michael J. Brophy to Kenneth Maxey. On file with the authors.

11. Johnson, "Memorandum from Regional Director," October 8, 1986.

12. For an excellent discussion of using price data to evaluate water values, see Bonnie Saliba, David B. Bush, William E. Martin, and Thomas C. Brown, "Do Water Market Prices Appropriately Measure Water Values?" *Natural Resources Journal* 27 (1987): 617–51.

13. Johnson, "Memorandum from Regional Director," October 8, 1986.

14. Brophy, "Report," February 26, 1988.

15. Stephen Shupe, ed., *Water Market Update* (Santa Fe, N.M.: Western Water Network, March 1988).

16. The Indian Community has a water service contract with the Bureau of Reclamation for delivery of water from the Central Arizona Project. "Central Arizona Project Indian Water Delivery Contract Between the United States and the Salt River Pima-Maricopa Indian Community," December 11, 1980.

17. The Wellton-Mohawk Irrigation and Drainage District is the contracting entity for the Gila Reclamation Project in southwestern Arizona near the Mexican border. By contract, WMIDD has an entitlement to about 300,000 acre-feet of diversions from the Colorado River annually. This diversion right would be reduced (with a proportionate savings in consumptive use and reduced return flow) through the purchase arrangements negotiated for the Salt River settlement.

18. Resolution 601-87 dated December 22, 1987. On file with WMIDD.

19. "Full Cost" is defined in the Reclamation Reform Act of 1982, P.L. 97-293, 96 Stat. 1263.

20. Acquisition costs of $8.6 million plus foregone repayment of $1.4 million and foregone full-cost revenues of $1.8 million (see Table 10.1, B-1&B-2&B-3, 2).

21. See "Agreement Among the United States, the Central Arizona Water Conservation District, the Flood Control District of Maricopa County, The Salt River Agricultural Improvement and Power District and Salt River Valley Water Users' Association, the Arizona Cities of Chandler, Glendale, Mesa, Phoenix, Scottsdale, and Tempe, the State of Arizona, and the City of Tucson for Funding of Plan Six Facilities of the Central Arizona Project, Arizona, and for Other Purposes," dated April 15, 1986. Also, see Kenneth G. Maxey and Norman H. Starler, "Cost Sharing in Transition: The Case of Plan 6, Central Arizona Project," *Water Resources Bulletin* 23, no. 5 (1987): 749–59.

22. Section 402, P.L. 90-537, 82 Stat. 894, September 30, 1968.

23. This analysis is based on work by Norman Starler, under the auspices of OMB in March 1988. This work was the basis for internal communications and informal discussions through October 1988. Robert Tuccillo and Ronald Cogswell provided valuable

input. The framework was used at OMB by Mark Taylor and Richard Mertens in September 1987.

24. In a letter written to Congressman Udall, James Ziglar, assistant secretary of the interior, indicated that the proposed federal cost of $78 million ($75 in present value terms; see Table 10.1, A-9, 2) "far exceeded the government's legal exposure" and for this and other reasons was unacceptable (May 10, 1988). This letter is reprinted in *Report of the Senate Select Committee on Indian Affairs,* S.Rept. 2153, 100th Cong., 2d sess., August 10, 1988, p. 16. Furthermore, he stated that in his personal opinion, $78 million was too high and the $45 million offered previously for both the Salt River and Fort McDowell settlements was a "tad low." Response to questions, House Committee on Interior and Insular Affairs, *Joint Hearing on S. 2153 and H.R. 4102 Before the Committee on Interior and Insular Affairs,* 100th Cong., 2d sess., March 24, 1988, p. 68.

25. Daniel McCool, *Command of the Waters: Iron Triangles, Federal Water Development and Indian Water* (Berkeley: University of California Press, 1987), p. 254.

26. Ibid., p. 247.

27. Robin Paul Malloy, "The Political Economy of Co-Financing America's Urban Renaissance," *Vanderbilt Law Review* 40 (1987): 67–134.

28. By "import-replacing," Malloy is referring to those economic activities undertaken by a community to produce goods and services formerly imported from other communities or regions, particularly when the community's traditional economic base has been eroded. An example might be a traditional steel town where the steel mill has shut down and the community attempts to attract alternative industries, such as fiberglass production, as a substitute for former imports of a product and as a new export item.

11

PARTIES AND PERMANENCE: ALTERNATIVE DISPUTE RESOLUTION PRINCIPLES

John A. Folk-Williams

Over the past twenty years the study and practice of alternative dispute resolution has taken on new life. Drawing on experience from labor mediation, international relations, economic theory, social psychology, and the formal study of decision making, new models of negotiation and mediation have emerged at influential study centers.[1] They have been applied through a variety of alternative dispute resolution techniques in a wide range of contexts from domestic relations to business to public policy and international conflict.[2] At the same time, dispute resolution remains a very ancient art, and those gifted in its practice probably have the same intuitive skills as practitioners of biblical times. It is at once an art and a science with increasing application to the natural resources and environmental fields.

Alternative dispute resolution aims at meeting the needs of all parties. Ending conflict, building relationships that will be productive in the future, even negotiating an agreement, are only steps in the direction of meeting those needs. With this focus, the negotiation process, whether assisted by a dispute resolution professional or not, is a means to an end. The role of a facilitator or mediator in such a process is to use his or her knowledge of conflict and the technology of reaching agreements to assist the parties in fashioning a decision that meets a multiplicity of interests.

Understanding how the field of alternative dispute resolution can be relevant to the settlement of cases involving Indian water rights depends on familiarity with several elements: (1) an orientation to conflict; (2) a paradigm of negotiation;

(3) clarity about the meaning of consensus; and (4) principles of the process of reaching agreement or satisfying interests.

These four elements provide some useful ways of thinking not just about conflict but about the practical process of guiding parties to a satisfactory resolution. This role of guidance is often played by an impartial facilitator, a professional mediator. The use of such a professional is one of the defining characteristics of alternative or assisted dispute resolution.[3] Most of the negotiation process issues raised in this chapter are precisely those that a professional neutral is trained to understand and deal with. Even when not making explicit mention of this role, this essay assumes the role is played in some way, if not by a professional mediator, then by someone who is trusted by the involved parties to facilitate conflict resolution. The reality is that the professional role is new to this field and relatively untested. I will not spend time arguing for its greater usefulness but will simply elaborate on those issues that occur to a professional mediator by way of illustrating its potential value to the constituencies most concerned about the timely and equitable resolution of disputes relating to Indian water rights.

To understand better what the process consists of, one has to focus on the end result of negotiations. While it is true that parties want to escape the high cost and risks of certain kinds of conflict, their purpose in entering negotiations is not merely to end conflict but also to satisfy interests—to achieve some substantive goal. Our general cultural system in the United States depends on conflict to enable people to reach such goals. We invest authority in institutions and individual decision makers and compete for influence in shaping the specific decisions that affect us. Such a system depends on each side promoting its needs in an adversarial way. In practice, though, the parties engaged in this competition will often work toward a decision that satisfies their needs but leaves out of account any groups that have not been represented in the process. Eventually, those other groups may feel their interests being threatened by the implementation of that decision and will become active on the issue. Then they will do whatever is necessary to frustrate the original parties until a new decision is made that responds to the issues they have raised.[4]

This continuum of conflict and decision making is a normal state of affairs. But there are many conflicts in the natural resources field that are either so complex or unusual that the situation calls for not a new decision but a new forum for decision making. That is where alternative or assisted dispute resolution techniques come into play. Each conflict presents not only a problem of resource use but also an opportunity to bring antagonistic parties into a new relationship so that multiple needs are satisfied simultaneously.

It is crucial to understand what each party is after before encouraging the use of negotiation. A helpful framework for this has recently been publicized in the dispute resolution field.[5] This framework defines the objectives of parties in conflict as falling into three categories: those relating to power, rights, and interests. A power contest, like an election, is designed to determine who is stronger, who will win the office or the game. There is no point in trying to negotiate the outcome because the whole point of the process is to establish one's power, either through the ballot or on the battlefield. If one is principally interested in establishing a right to something, then litigation or a formal grievance procedure is the ideal tool. If one is chiefly desirous of satisfying an interest, then negotiation can come into play.

Conflict about interests almost always occurs in the context of struggles over power and rights, which are intertwined in practice, never neatly separated. But each party, in considering options about how to resolve a dispute, must make a strategic decision about what is more important. That party should enter negotiations only if satisfying interests is more important than establishing rights or determining who is more powerful. Indeed, parties often begin negotiations only after they have attempted to establish their power and rights. By this means they have demonstrated, while not fully prevailing on the issue, that they have enough power with respect to the question at hand that they cannot be ignored.

With this orientation to conflict and a framework for choosing negotiation processes, one can then turn to the issue of consensus, or unanimity. Is this feasible or practical? Consensus is always the goal in a well-designed negotiation process because of the fundamental dynamics of bargaining.

Effective negotiation assumes a degree of interdependence among the parties.[6] That is, no single party has the ability to effect its solution without the assistance of *all* the others. In this situation, one party may have the goal solely to preserve the status quo (i.e., to ensure that a new resource use does not take place) but cannot achieve this goal without the cooperation of the relevant decision-making agencies. Another party with the goal of changing the status quo (i.e., to win approval for a new resource use) cannot achieve what it wants without the cooperation of the same agencies. All of the parties probably do not know the exact limits of what each party can do at the outset, but it is necessary that each party knows it cannot reach its goals without some degree of acceptance from the others. In many, but not all cases, the parties have arrived at this point only after trying hard to win without negotiation. They have tried litigation or political influence or other methods open to them and thus have established the fact that they have power in this situation. They have also been forced to recognize that others have power as well and that, in fact, they must either cooperate with those other parties or face significantly higher costs or risks in another forum.

When the negotiation situation meets this paradigm, consensus (or unanimity) is the only possible rule of decision making. Anything less than consensus would mean that a party with the power to frustrate the outcome does not agree, and the agreement of the other parties will very likely come under attack.

149

With this model in mind, one has a criterion for determining who should take part in negotiations. Only those parties with enough power to have a decisive impact on the resolution should be included. These are precisely the parties whose consent is *necessary*. If other parties who do not meet this criterion are selected to participate, serious complications can result. The key parties will feel their time is being wasted by having to respond to the needs of nonessential groups. So the first step in negotiation is identifying just who it is who *needs* to be at the table with you.[7]

One can think of the parties as existing in a series of concentric circles. At the center is the circle of parties who must take direct part in negotiations. The absence of any one would result in a relatively meaningless agreement that would immediately be subject to attack. In the next circle out from the center are those parties who will be involved in the ratification process. In an Indian water settlement, there is a broad range of constituencies who will articulate positions about the agreement either in Congress or through lobbying in other forums to influence the ratification process. An example of this occurred during consideration by Congress of the Colorado Ute water settlement bill. Western state water interests and national Indian organizations, none of whom took part in the original negotiations, entered the legislative debate with different views on provisions having to do with interstate leasing of Indian reserved water rights. In effect, they forced a renegotiation of those provisions and changed the settlement agreement in significant ways.[8]

A third circle out would include groups that have no direct role in ratification but are essential to implementation. When, for example, the Ak-Chin settlement of 1978 was being implemented, the federal government had difficulty locating a water source that could be used to meet its obligations for water delivery. Parties crucial to this aspect of the agreement had not been included in the original talks, and a new negotiation had to be undertaken with irrigation districts that were able to provide a reliable water source.[9]

In a fourth circle, we would find those parties who have no direct role in any phase of the agreement but who have an interest in the issues and who might organize in opposition if either they are not kept informed or if questions arise during the process that they feel would affect their interests. In Indian water negotiations, for example, environmental organizations, nearby communities or water-using entities, down- or upstream water users, and others will want to know that their interests will not be affected, and the best way to do this is to develop a means of staying in touch with them, answering questions and listening to their ideas.

It is no small feat to take these interests into account, respond to their concerns, and arrive at a fully ratified and implemented agreement. The skills of alternative dispute resolution specialists are often helpful in sustaining communication in complex cases of this type. They provide the disinterested facilitation that gives everyone involved a sounding board and a way of communicating that reduces the risk of misunderstanding.

Once the negotiating situation is clear and the parties are organized to participate, all sides must be able to deal with the dynamics of the bargaining process that goes on during negotiations. Contemporary theorists describe the basic tension during the process as one between the creation of value and the claiming of value.[10] Win-win negotiating urges parties to satisfy one another's needs by taking part in a process of generating options that increase the resources available to meet all interests. The idea is that you expand the pie by working with the basic fact that the parties probably value things differently. Thus one party will value the quantity of water more than anything else, another will value security of supply, a third will value money first. Increasing the pie may not mean adding to the supply of the one resource at the center of the dispute but may mean putting other valuable considerations on the table.[11]

The trouble with this theory is that no matter how big you make the pie, you have to cut it at some point. So a more accurate description of what happens is that parties move back and forth, alternately making suggestions on how to meet interests and putting in their claims for how much they have to get.[12]

What complicates this process, however, is that the parties may never stop threatening each other. That is, they remind each other that they are, in fact, powerful enough to wreak havoc if they do not get what they need. This is often a necessary and painful part of the negotiation process that can even cause a temporary breakdown of the talks. Parties remain at the table only as long as they believe they have to. As soon as the situation changes to permit them to think that some other process—such as political pressure, congressional action, or litigation—will get them what they want without the need to compromise with others, they will start to move in that direction. Other parties will respond in kind and threaten punitive action in return, and the negotiation may fall apart completely unless the parties, in examining their strategic choices, again come to the conclusion that the negotiation forum will in fact meet their needs in ways that other processes cannot.

In other words, there seems to be a centrifugal force tending to sweep the parties away from the table, and that is countered by the force (or cost of alternatives) that pushes them back. If the cost of alternatives falls lower than the cost of staying at the table, the parties will likely go for those options. One of the most difficult tasks facing the mediator is to remind the parties of his or her assessment of the power balance and the costs and benefits of different strategic options. In other words, he or she may have to offer an opinion about the limits of the power of a party. Or he or she may have to concede that for the moment it may make more sense for the parties to return to an adversarial process and reassess at a later time whether negotiation will still serve their purposes.

These parallel processes of creating/claiming value and testing the limits of power are what make negotiation so difficult and so vulnerable to breakdown. Understanding something about the dynamics of the process can help the parties make sense out of a situation that may otherwise simply seem to be blowing up on them because of a lack of good faith on the part of certain negotiators.

The final resolution of a dispute through negotiation occurs when all the various interests are satisfied. This is the most difficult moment in the entire process because a final commitment must be made. The parties must be willing to live up to the terms of the agreement and face the consequences with their clients and constituents. Reputations are on the line. Property interests of great value are at risk. Usually, it takes the force of a deadline to bring about the final commitment. A deadline is a point in time after which the real costs or at least the risks to the parties will greatly increase. Artificial deadlines are often set in these processes, but the parties are aware of the real time frame and will usually negotiate to that limit.[13]

The Parties and Their Interests in the Context of Indian Water Rights Cases

Having reviewed some of the general principles of dispute resolution, we can focus on a few key elements of Indian water settlements to see how these principles translate into practice. In the last three decades there have been numerous negotiated agreements regarding Indian rights to water. These include the Navajo Indian Irrigation Project Agreement of 1962 (relating to the San Juan–Chama Diversion Project), the Ute Deferral Agreement of 1965 (relating to the Central Utah Project), the Navajo Colorado River Agreement of 1966 (facilitating construction of a power plant), the Ak-Chin agreements of 1978 and 1984, the Southern Arizona Water Rights Settlement Act of 1982 (Tohono O'odham Nation), the Fort Peck–Montana Compact of 1985, the Florida Seminole agreement and act of 1987, the Colorado Ute agreement and act of 1988, the San Luis Rey settlement act of 1988, and the Salt River Pima-Maricopa Indian Community agreement and act of 1988.[14] More recently, agreements have been reached regarding the Pyramid Lake Paiute, Fort McDowell Indian Community, Northern Ute, San Carlos Apache, Northern Cheyenne, Fort Hall Shoshone Bannock, and Jicarilla Apache claims. Others are still under negotiation.

It is safe to say in these cases that all parties made a strategic decision that satisfying their basic interests of security and access to supply, financial remuneration, or other benefits was more important than establishing their rights or power. Negotiation was thus the logical choice of forum, within the framework of the paradigm of dispute resolution strategic choices discussed above.

On behalf of the Navajo Nation, for example, the Tribal Council negotiated two limited agreements rather than comprehensive settlements. In one case, the council accepted arrangements that gave them numerous benefits for postponing their use of Colorado River rights; non-Indians, in turn, satisfied their basic need to secure water for construction of a major power plant.[15] In a second Navajo case, New Mexico interests needed to resolve certain issues surrounding tribal water rights in the San Juan basin to construct a major transbasin water diversion facility. Arizona cities and irrigators likewise found it essential to negotiate settlements to the water claims of three Indian communities in the 1980s and two more thus far in the 1990s, and are working on even more complex settlements at present. Each of these is based on supplying the tribes' needs for firm supply and construction of appropriate water distribution facilities as well as for the provision of funds for economic development.

A typical settlement agreement is essentially a contract among the parties signing it by which each agrees to provide certain things and in return to receive certain things. For example, the Fort Peck–Montana Compact is a form of contract under which the state of Montana and the tribes of the Fort Peck Reservation agree not to challenge each other legally in return for confirming the rights and arrangements spelled out in the agreement. Since most Indian water agreements grow out of litigation or take place under the threat of litigation, the parties are essentially offering each other the waiver of litigation in order to get on with the management and use of water. This is a basic quid pro quo of most water agreements.

In such agreements, the definition of rights has been carefully crafted to meet the interests of the federal government, the state, and non-Indian water users as well as those of the tribes. Because the definition meets the interests of all the parties, they are willing to forgo a definitive judicial ruling on their respective rights, but they are willing to do this only if obtaining such a ruling about their rights is less compelling to them than the goal of satisfying basic interests, i.e., actually obtaining or removing uncertainty surrounding water supplies.

The key parties in most Indian water cases are the tribes, the states (or political subdivisions of a state), the water user entities, and the federal government. Each governmental party plays multiple roles, and this complicates the process of distinguishing the underlying objectives of each and also makes more difficult the dynamics of a negotiation process once it is under way.[16] Each of these parties is, in fact, many parties. There is usually a complicated process of internal negotiation that must go on among all the communities of interest within each tribe, state, and federal team. John Dunlap has said that for every two-party negotiation,

153

there are three agreements: one between the parties and one each representing the internal agreement of the different interests represented by each party.[17] In Indian water cases, the Indian community, the state, the federal government, and other groups (such as cities, irrigation districts, or private corporations) each represents a multiplicity of interests. Even if each is clear about its goals at the outset of the process, each will be confronted with new information and unexpected choices that require constant internal discussion and negotiation to arrive at a coherent and attainable set of objectives. Such internal negotiation is usually the key to the success of any negotiation process.

Achieving Stability through Negotiation

There are three expected achievements of negotiated agreements in Indian water cases: (1) interests are satisfied through the specific provisions recognizing rights, promising benefits, and suspending litigation; (2) the framework for long-term relationships among the parties regarding water resources is defined; and (3) stability for the full enjoyment of resource benefits is achieved through resolution of the first two elements.

Satisfying Interests

Indian governments have built power in the field of water rights through litigation. It was through judicial decisions that Indian reserved water rights have been defined, and each tribe that has elected to negotiate has benefited from the cumulative force of Indian water decisions, even if it has not filed a suit of its own. Actual or potential lawsuits have created sufficient uncertainty for non-Indians that they have had strong incentive in many cases to agree to negotiate with tribes in order to clarify their own rights of access to water. Nor have non-Indian water users been the only ones to face uncertainty; the institutions of state government charged with managing water resources have also confronted this incentive to negotiate. Indian litigation has challenged state authority in many respects relating to jurisdiction and management authority as well. In addition, the federal government has published guidelines regarding Indian water settlements that make the removal of all potential claims a requirement for federal approval. The permanent elimination of the litigation threat, then, has been defined as a principal interest in the settlements of the present era for non-Indian water users as well as for state and federal governmental entities. The agreements of the 1960s were much more limited in scope and seemed aimed instead at facilitating specific non-Indian needs for water use that were immediately foreseeable.

For non-Indians, their major interests have been satisfied through the following categories of benefits:

1. Waiver or deferral of claims. The bedrock of each agreement has been the removal of the threat of Indian claims to water supplies that would disturb present or planned non-Indian uses. This has been achieved in some cases by a long-term deferral of the assertion of Indian claims to facilitate a project utilizing a water supply to which the Indians have a right. The Ute Deferral Agreement of 1965 and the Navajo agreements of the 1960s assured construction of major water and energy projects. In more recent cases of comprehensive settlement, this has been achieved by a permanent waiver of all claims—past, present, and future—that an Indian community might assert with respect to water, except those claims relating to performance of the agreement.

2. Protection of non-Indian uses. Of equivalent importance have been provisions assuring that the use of Indian water protected by the agreement will not interfere with existing non-Indian uses. This is achieved by varied means, including the subordination of Indian priority dates, the sharing of shortages, conformance of Indian water uses to standards equivalent to those of state law, review of changes in Indian uses by state agencies, and confirmation of water supply arrangements that might have been subject to legal challenge.

3. State jurisdiction. Several agreements have elaborate provisions to remove controversy about the relative limits of state and tribal jurisdiction to manage water. Agreements have been especially attentive to off-reservation uses of Indian water supplies and have generally either banned these altogether, defined in the agreement precisely what was permitted, or made them subject to requirements of state law. This area is discussed further in the next section on long-term relationships.

In return for removing legal threats to the above, Indian communities have used agreements to secure benefits in one of several ways.

1. Definition of water rights. Although the agreements of the 1960s were not concerned with final definitions of Indian water rights, the settlements of more recent years generally specify the quantity, source, and other terms of use of the Indian right to use water. This definition is thus achieved by the tribes without the cost and risk of the lengthy water adjudication process.

2. Financial benefits. In some cases, the tribes defer or waive rights beyond those defined in the agreement to secure either immediate financial benefits (such as trust funds, lease payments, and development grants) or the potential for future benefits through a definition of the right to lease or make other marketing arrangements.

155

3. Construction of facilities. Since historically one of the great barriers to tribal water use has been the lack of water delivery and water use facilities, several agreements have provided these to tribes. Such benefits are often cited as exemplifying an advantage of negotiated as opposed to litigated settlement since they provide "wet" or delivered water instead of "paper" rights defined through a decree but not realized through engineering systems.[18]
4. Guarantee of water delivery. The five Arizona agreements, the Colorado Ute settlement, and the San Luis Rey agreement all focus on the delivery to the Indian communities of specific quantities of water. Failure to deliver creates a cause for damages or other penalties, usually borne by the federal government.

Framework for Future Relationships Regarding Water

The management of water, especially of water sources that cross boundaries, requires continuing relationships over time, if only for the purpose of later dispute resolution.

Negotiated agreements establish the legal framework within which the parties must develop working relationships about water management. The implementation process for Indian water agreements is lengthy and complex, frequently requiring the parties to test each other's understanding of and commitment to the language and spirit of the settlement. In addition, the parties will continue to be neighbors permanently and will inevitably encounter further differences, often relating to the interpretation of specific settlement provisions.

The process of implementation, then, can be as important as the immediate outcome to the long-term stability of the pattern of resource use the parties are trying to establish. Provisions relating to this area address issues of water management and dispute resolution. In effect, the agreements are the new law under which relations among the water users will be conducted.

An extremely important part of each agreement is the penalties imposed for failure to implement terms. These provisions are the only ones tribes and other parties can turn to should execution falter. Since almost every agreement requires implementation steps, including passage of legislation by Congress, ratification by parties, construction of facilities by the federal government, and appropriation of funds, such provisions are extremely important. In addition, each agreement must provide for potential future amendment.

The most basic penalty for the tribes, should they fail to execute the waivers discussed above, is the loss of payments and other benefits. Similarly, if the federal and state parties fail to provide their shares, the tribes may generally continue litigation or may simply remain free to press any and all claims against the other parties. Often, a specific basis for a legal claim by a tribe against the federal government for failure to comply with water delivery terms is included. This provides compensation to the tribe without upsetting the entire agreement.

Provisions about water management also define long-term relationships. Both the states and the tribes have strong interests in how the administration and management of waters are handled, and several agreements have complex arrangements for dividing authority between the two jurisdictions. In general, the agreements provide for tribal jurisdiction of the tribal water right within the reservations from the point at which water enters the Indian distribution system. State laws generally prevail up to that point. The Fort Peck Compact has the most elaborate administrative regime and links the tribes and the state closely, for example, in the area of off-reservation marketing.

The Salt River Pima-Maricopa agreement generally does not address the allocation of jurisdictional authority between the state and the tribe. Rather, it is concerned with the detailed restrictions on water use under the control of local water management districts and generally confirms existing management practices. The Colorado Ute agreement originally left to future litigation the question of out-of-state leasing, but this provision was modified as regional and national interests worked out their differences on this issue in Congress during debates on the bill implementing the agreement.

Stability

There is a great distance separating the assertion of permanent resolution in the language of an agreement and the achievement of actual stability. As we have seen, agreements resolving disputes about Indian water rights typically contain provisions forever waiving the rights of tribes to press claims to water in the courts. Through sweeping language, all legal rights are waived except for those defined in the agreement and except for recourse to claims should the provisions of the agreement not be implemented. So fundamental are these provisions to negotiations of the past fifteen years that it may be said that the chief, perhaps only, bargaining chip of the tribes consists of their ability to press their claims in court, thus frustrating the quest for permanent removal of the threat that these claims pose to non-Indians and to state and federal government agencies.

Non-Indian communities and state agencies, for their part, must permanently recognize a certain entitlement of the tribes to water, one that has been carefully quantified or otherwise conditioned to pose the least disturbance to the present and future water needs of non-Indian communities. The conditioning of the quantification may be just as important as a numerical limitation on Indian rights. For example, Montana negotiated with the Fort Peck tribes a substantial water right but then as a trade-off secured the agreement of the tribes under certain circumstances to follow state law or equivalent provisions specified in the agreement

157

regarding certain uses, especially at off-reservation locations, that protected the state's interests. The tribes also agreed not to cause adverse impacts on non-Indian water uses in Montana without the consent of the affected water rights holders.

Do these provisions really achieve stability for the parties? It is in the long-term interest of the parties to ensure that all sides, after careful reflection, believe their future as well as present needs are met. If one party secures the agreement of another to a settlement that will reveal numerous restrictions on closer examination at a later time, the stage is set for future conflict. Although in business negotiations it is often thought to be a clever strategy to convince a negotiating partner to accept something less than what he or she might have achieved with different advice, the history of Indian/non-Indian agreements regarding natural resources demonstrates that inequities revealed after the point of agreement create instability.

For example, the Ute Tribe of Utah, after having accepted a deferral agreement in 1965, reopened water issues in the 1970s and only recently concluded a final agreement with Utah on a comprehensive water compact. Although the original agreement was intended to facilitate Utah's access to Colorado River water, the water rights necessary for the completion of the Central Utah Project have remained in question almost to the conclusion of the physical construction of the project.[19] Recently, the tribal business council suspended the 1965 agreement.[20] In the energy area, leases accepted by the Northern Cheyenne Tribe for coal exploration in the 1960s and 1970s were later considered unconscionable, and the tribe persisted in efforts to break the leases until finally succeeding through a congressional enactment. No coal was ever mined under those leases.[21] Numerous other cases can be cited relating to Indian land claims, economic development, and many other areas pointing to the reality that an agreement giving what may come to be perceived as inequitable access to resources will ultimately perpetuate conflict and uncertainty about the resource rights in question. Similarly, an agreement that gives advantages to Indians that non-Indians later discover and feel are unfair will also lead to instability. If the outcry is strong enough, Congress or the courts can alter "final" agreements in many ways. All parties, then, have an interest in seeing to it that each party fully understands the implications and long-term consequences of an agreement if that agreement is to stand the test of time and allow the parties access to the rights and resources they need.

It is in this context that the paradigm of negotiations offered above takes on meaning. The parties have an interest in seeing that one another's needs, both long term and short term, are satisfied. If they allow one party to accept something that will cause trouble later, they are not meeting their own needs for security of access to the resource. An agreement containing the seeds of instability helps no one, even if the instability and its causes take years to emerge during the implementation process.

158

The Future of Indian Water Negotiations

If the language of permanence does not always guarantee stability, is it possible to imagine agreements creating stability that do not include such language? In other words, is it always necessary to require Indian communities to waive forever certain claims and rights, the future value of which cannot be established at the present time?

Negotiated agreements containing such permanent waivers are extremely rare. Labor management contracts, for example, are in effect for specified terms, and the parties know that they will have future chances to alter terms they find onerous in the present contract. Commercial agreements relate to the achievement of specific business objectives. Even international treaties and conventions, while intended to last for very long terms, are rarely intended to be permanent. Many treaties have been decried as unjust in the decades following their adoption, and such pressure has formed the successful basis for revision of international agreements.[22]

Negotiated agreements about Indian water rights are handled more like claims for damages. In such cases, it is necessary for the claimant to forswear all further claims in exchange for the benefits of the settlement. The overriding goal for the defendant is to remove forever the uncertainties of unquantified claims. The federal government has made this the cornerstone of its policy with respect to Indian water settlements. There is a question, however, as to whether this approach is appropriate for dealing with the property rights of Indian communities. There is a damage claim implicit in every Indian water case because the federal government is accused by both Indian and non-Indian rights holders for having created the situation of conflict, either by its active involvement in building water projects for non-Indian use that depended on utilizing waters to which Indians had rights or by its passive acceptance of state water rights regimes that did not take implied Indian rights into account.

There is a distinction, however, between such a claim for past damage based on the action or inaction of a party and the definition and use of water rights per se. To treat the future use of such rights as equivalent to a potential claim for damages requires Indian communities to carry out in present terms an evaluation of a property right of great potential value. The likelihood that such an evaluation will appear accurate or just to future generations of tribal members is dubious, if the experience of the Ute Deferral Agreement or the Northern Cheyenne coal leases or tribal land claims based on treaties concluded in earlier centuries is any indication.

The trade-offs defined in Indian water settlements, though, can appear quite reasonable given the immediate pressures and problems apparent to the negotiators of these agreements. The achievements of these agreements are often

159

remarkable from the perspective of the present generation of parties. It is not the purpose of this article to second-guess the strategies and accomplishments of the negotiators of these agreements but only to raise the question of whether their reach into the future will in fact create problems that are now unforeseen, perhaps unforeseeable.

Is it possible to consider more flexible arrangements that attempt to achieve more limited goals? Clearly, in some cases the underlying needs of non-Indian water users may be achievable only by a final removal of future uncertainty about Indian water rights, but in other cases the real goals may have to do with confirmation of non-Indian access to water. Perhaps a standard for that degree of finality could be derived from the water adjudication process on which holders of water rights normally rely. Non-Indian rights are defined by a decree in such cases but are thereafter subject to challenges for many reasons, including due diligence in putting rights to use, forfeiture for lack of use, impairment of rights through change of use or point of diversion, abandonment, or future adjudication, with its attendant expense, even if the rights have been properly put to use. Perhaps the objectives of non-Indian water users and of state and federal governments may be achieved in periods of some decades, requiring "certainty" for forty or fifty years rather than forever.

The importance of negotiation is that it offers flexibility to meet the real needs of the parties as opposed to their publicly stated positions or their legal theories. While it is far too early to evaluate the ultimate significance of most agreements relating to Indian water rights, it is important to raise the question of whether the attempt to achieve permanence in settlement may itself not create instability in the future.

This analysis of some of the major components of agreements concerning Indian claims to water points out the common elements that induced the parties to agree to negotiate and the nature of the trade-offs that were made to achieve settlement. All of the agreements concluded in the past ten years include permanent waivers of legal rights by the Indians. Other elements of these agreements can be thought of as the price the Indians were able to exact in return for making this concession. The permanent waiver of a vital legal right to water can only be made if the terms are such as to promise long-term benefits, yet all parties must evaluate those benefits with the necessarily limited knowledge of the present.

There is no universal model for negotiated settlement of water issues. The above material is intended to help identify only the most basic elements of the process of conflict resolution and the nature of the agreement that is typically reached in water cases. The specific terms will vary widely depending on what the parties together can agree to. The final decision on what is acceptable can only be made by each party itself. That is one of the strengths of negotiated dispute resolution. While there is rarely equality of power among the parties, the process (when compared to other approaches) at least leaves them, as a group, more directly in control of the outcomes affecting their basic interests.

NOTES

1. Howard Raiffa, *The Art and Science of Negotiation* (Cambridge, Mass.: Harvard University Press, 1982); Thomas C. Schelling, *The Strategy of Conflict* (Cambridge, Mass.: Harvard University Press, 1960); Lawrence Susskind and Jeffrey Cruikshank, *Breaking the Impasse* (New York: Basic Books, 1987).

2. Gail Bingham, *Resolving Environmental Disputes* (Washington, D.C.: Conservation Foundation, 1986), pp. 13ff.

3. Lawrence S. Bacow and Michael Wheeler, *Environmental Dispute Resolution* (New York: Plenum Press), p. 157.

4. Dean Mann, "Institutional Framework for Agricultural Water Conservation and Reallocation in the West: A Policy Analysis," in *Water and Agriculture in the Western U.S.,* ed. Gary Weatherford (Boulder, Colo.: Westview Press, 1982), p. 41; Daniel McCool, *Command of the Waters* (Berkeley: University of California Press, 1987), p. 7.

5. William L. Ury, Jeanne M. Brett, and Stephen B. Goldberg, *Getting Disputes Resolved* (San Francisco: Jossey-Bass, 1988), pp. 3ff.

6. Schelling, *Strategy of Conflict,* p. 83.

7. Susskind and Cruikshank, *Breaking the Impasse,* p. 103.

8. *Congressional Record,* October 14, 1988, "Colorado Ute Indian Water Rights Settlement Act," p. S16244.

9. John A. Folk-Williams, *Western Water Flows to the Cities* (Santa Fe, N.M.: Western Network; and Washington, D.C.: Island Press, 1985), p. 44; House Interior and Insular Affairs Committee, *Water Rights of the Ak-Chin Indian Community,* 98th Cong., 2d sess., September 14, 1984, H.Rept. 98-1026, p. 6.

10. David A. Lax and James K. Sebenius, *The Manager as Negotiator* (New York: Free Press, 1986), pp. 88ff.

11. Roger Fisher and William Ury, *Getting to Yes: Negotiating Agreement Without Giving In* (Boston: Houghton Mifflin, 1981), pp. 17ff.

12. Lax and Sebenius, *Manager as Negotiator,* pp. 154ff.

13. Susskind and Cruikshank, *Breaking the Impasse,* p. 191.

14. John A. Folk-Williams, "The Use of Negotiated Agreements to Resolve Water Disputes Involving Indian Rights," *Natural Resources Journal* 28, no. 1 (1988): 74ff; Peter W. Sly, *Reserved Water Rights Settlement Manual* (Washington, D.C.: Island Press, 1988), pp. 25ff.

15. Monroe Price and Gary Weatherford, "Indian Water Rights in Theory and Practice: Navajo Experience in the Colorado River Basin," *Law and Contemporary Problems* 40 (1976): 97.

16. Sly, *Reserved Water Rights Settlement Manual,* pp. 44ff.

17. John T. Dunlap, *Dispute Resolution* (Dover, Mass.: Auburn House, 1984), p. 10.

18. Elizabeth Checchio and Bonnie G. Colby, *Indian Water Rights: Negotiating the Future* (Tucson: University of Arizona, Water Resources Research Center, forthcoming), p. 14.

19. Clark B. Fetzer, "The Ute Indian Water Compact," *Journal of Energy Law and Policy* 2 (1982): 190.

20. U.S. Bureau of Indian Affairs, *B.I.A. Tribal Newsletter,* September 30, 1989, Phoenix Area Office, p. 10.

21. Joseph G. Jorgensen, ed., *Native Americans and Energy Development,* vol. 2 (Boston: Anthropology Resource Center and Seventh Generation Fund, 1984), p. 15.

22. J. L. Brierly, *The Law of Nations,* 6th edition, ed. H. Waldock (Oxford: Oxford University Press, 1963), pp. 340ff.

PART IV   USE

12

CHEAP WATER IN INDIAN COUNTRY: A COST-EFFECTIVE RURAL DEVELOPMENT TOOL?

Robert A. Young and Roger Mann

The belief that the development of irrigation water supplies in the semiarid West is a wise public investment forms part of the basis for the continuing bitter struggles to control water rights in the region. A version of the conventional wisdom holds that irrigation development creates important economic and social benefits and is an assured path to rural economic development. Three related economic theses are frequently proposed. First, irrigation projects are said to provide numerous additional jobs on farms. Second, the agricultural intensification represented by irrigation is asserted to generate significant spinoffs of employment and business activity in nearby communities. Finally, with somewhat less assurance, it is claimed that irrigation provides a high return on invested public capital. These theses, combined with an assumption that irrigation can help create the small, self-sufficient local communities of the Jeffersonian vision, have served to justify public subsidies of irrigation.

An alternative hypothesis holds that although the above propositions may have once been accurate, they have been overtaken by the economic, organizational, and technological realities of contemporary agricultural production. This contrary thesis maintains that in the century or more since the federal government began its policy of encouraging western irrigation, agriculture has changed considerably. Most agricultural output occurs on relatively large, technologically advanced farms. With the advent of modern transportation and communications, agricultural producers must compete in national and world markets. Technological advances have made overproduction and low returns to resources the dominant policy problem of U.S. agriculture. Furthermore, the regional economic development benefits of agricultural production have declined as capital and technology have substituted for local labor and farm purchases and expenditures are conducted farther from the local community.[1]

The resolution of these competing hypotheses will have important economic consequences, not only for a number of Native American tribes, but also for the taxpaying public. Many western tribes have based their claims for federally reserved water rights on the practicably irrigable acreage (PIA) concept established in Arizona's suit against California over the right to use waters of the Colorado River. The PIA principle appears to grant entitlements to water simply upon demonstration of the economic feasibility of specific proposed irrigation developments. To an even greater extent than it has for non-Indian projects, the federal government is expected to finance most of the costs of capturing, storing, and transporting water that result from successful Indian claims.

We believe much of the impetus for irrigation development on Native American reservations is due to this federal policy of requiring no cost sharing by Indian beneficiaries on capital expenditures and only partial cost sharing on operating and maintenance expenditures. Under this policy, the major tribal expense for an irrigation water supply is for lobbyists, attorneys, and consultants to formulate and market a proposal and to demonstrate its economic feasibility. Since such costs are a small percent of perceived tribal economic returns, it would be irrational for tribes to respond other than as they have, petitioning the courts for entitlements and Congress for water project appropriations.

This policy of public subsidy to irrigation investments on Indian reservations deserves careful examination. Public subsidies to the private economic sector can be justified if the private economic activities generate noteworthy economic or social benefits to society that would not be forthcoming without the subsidy. But the claims for the economic desirability of new irrigation development as a tool for rural area development on Native American reservations also require justification, from the perspectives of both the public taxpayers and the Native American tribes. Perhaps enhancing the economic status of Native Americans can be better served by channeling scarce federal funds for Native Americans toward more productive activities. From this perspective, issues of irrigation-induced profitability, employment, and regional growth can be productively critiqued if placed within the current national agricultural situation and outlook. Moreover, the competing hypotheses relating to these issues can be tested by reviewing actual experience with irrigation development on several southwestern Indian reservations.

A Historic Perspective on the Economics of U.S. Agriculture

The Early Era: Emphasizing Productivity Growth

Since its very inception, the United States government has pursued policies that increase the productive capacity of the agricultural sector.[2] In accordance with the Jeffersonian vision of a nation of small independent land holders, and for the purposes of settling and securing the new territories, the first major tool of agricultural development policy was the distribution of publicly owned lands to settlers. This general policy of encouraging family farms was continued with the Homestead Act of 1862 and in related legislation as the tide of non-Indian settlement flowed westward throughout the nineteenth century.

A century and a quarter ago, a new instrument of this policy aimed at developing capacity for food and fiber production was introduced: public support of agricultural research and education. Many policies with respect to education and technology present parallels with the earlier land disbursement programs in that research, information, and credit facilities were provided free or at low cost to promote wide acceptance and application.

Water resource development in the arid West was another facet of federal agricultural development policies. Initiated primarily as an encouragement to settlement of the new territories, federal incentives to private irrigation development came with the Confirmation of Western Water Rights Act in 1866, the Desert Land Act of 1877, and the Carey Act of 1894. In 1902, direct federal participation in arid land reclamation was initiated with the adoption of the Reclamation Act. The sale of public lands was to provide a revolving fund to be used for construction of the major irrigation facilities. As with the Homestead Act, settlers were to receive land without cost but were to repay without interest the public investment in irrigation structures. This money in turn was expected to finance future projects. By providing capital and expertise for water development facilities on a scale larger than that which could be afforded by local interests, settlement of the public domain could continue, new communities could be developed, and farm output and income could be enhanced and stabilized.

Agricultural programs have greatly contributed to the nation's economic development by providing abundant food supplies at low prices and by freeing labor and other resources to be used to produce goods and services in other sectors of the economy. Just over two percent of our work force produces our basic food and fiber products to satisfy domestic and overseas commercial markets.

The Era of Food Abundance

More recently, this wealth for the nation has created problems for the agricultural sector. Until the early 1900s, a steady growth of food output was needed for a

167

rapidly expanding population. The increasing incomes of consumers led to increases in per capita food consumption, and world markets readily absorbed any excess agricultural production.

However, soon after World War I, both population and food exports ceased to grow at so rapid a rate. Also, living standards increased to where little of the additional per capita income was spent on food. These events combined with an unprecedented technological advance in agriculture, largely as a result of decades of public investment in research, education, and distribution of new technology.

Agricultural prices, after a brief postwar boom, had plummeted by 1921. This, from today's perspective, marked the beginning of excess capacity in the agricultural sector that has persisted, with the exception of wartime emergencies, through the ensuing decades. At the farm level, increases in food output tend to lead to proportionally larger decreases in price (i.e., demand for food is price-inelastic). Increased food production thus brings about significant decreases in farm income. Throughout the 1920s, agriculture was the laggard sector in an otherwise prosperous economy. The Great Depression turned an already serious problem into disastrous proportions, and the New Deal brought forth a whole set of federal policies aimed at controlling the output of basic commodities and raising and stabilizing farm income.

These policies, which persist today, insulate the production of certain basic commodities from the forces of the market, control the allocation of land devoted to these commodities, and replace market prices with supported or subsidized returns. Government measures to help balance supply with demand and to raise product prices include commodity purchases, marketing agreements and orders, and commodity storage.

Because of these factors, there is a chronic excess of cropland devoted to commodity production. Land diversion and retirement programs and acreage allotments have been adopted to reduce production by limiting the amount of land devoted to the cultivation of program commodities. Agricultural policy has also attempted to expand the demand for food to dispose of excess production through measures such as the food stamp program. In practice, these commodity programs in the United States support world prices and help other nations become more competitive in international agricultural trade.

Policies to encourage irrigation, centered in the Interior Department agencies (Bureaus of Reclamation and Indian Affairs) thus run counter to the Agriculture Department's policies that attempt to deal with the chronic overabundance of food and fiber. However, part of the problem lies with the farm program system, which sends false signals of food scarcity to the local interests promoting public irrigation as a regional development tool.

Changing Economic Features of U.S. Agriculture and Irrigated Crop Production

A number of general forces in the agricultural economy are likely to influence the long-term rural development potential of irrigation investments, including increased farm size, the cost-price squeeze, rising costs of new irrigation water supplies, a decline in the availability of productive new lands, and increased competition in markets for high-income specialty crops. Reviewing these forces will be helpful for understanding the expected future economic environment for irrigated agriculture.

Increased Size of Profitable and Viable Farms

Proponents of irrigation development seem to have in mind a modern version of Jefferson's vision of communities of small, independent and self-sufficient farms. In the current era, this conception confronts what some have called the "modern dilemma of agriculture"—the tension between the desire for smaller, traditional farms versus the reality of the larger size, managerial expertise, and up-to-date technology needed to compete effectively in the increasingly open, competitive, and technologically driven world markets for food and fiber.

Luther G. Tweeten notes that the farm sector in the United States has evolved into two distinct groups of producers.[3] The "commercial" sector (or as some prefer to call it, the "industrialized" sector) is conventionally defined as comprising those farms bringing in over $100,000 of annual sales. These units number only about 300,000 nationwide (14 percent of all farms) but account for the great majority (70 percent) of all farm revenues. The other group, the "noncommercial" farms, whose yearly sales fall below $100,000, are much more numerous, numbering 1.8 million units. In 1984, they represented some 85 percent of all farms but generated only 30 percent of national agricultural sales. Most of the income of families on noncommercial farms is from nonfarm sources (off-farm jobs, investments, pensions, transfer payments). Farms of this size tend to lose money from farming operations, their primary focus being nonmonetary benefits of the rural lifestyle.[4]

The profitable farms of the future, those that return a competitive rate on labor and capital, must be large enough to be recognized as significant small business enterprises. Tweeten has recently updated his estimates of the size of farm yielding a competitive return on capital and labor, reporting that only those farm businesses with annual sales exceeding $200,000 are likely to meet this standard.[5] Farm businesses at Tweeten's cutoff size, still mostly family-owned and operated, typically would command productive assets (real estate, machinery, buildings, and other production capital) approaching one million dollars in value.

169

The Cost-Price Squeeze

Agriculture is a highly competitive industry, on the average showing narrow profit margins. The forces accounting for the cost-price squeeze in the past are likely to continue in the future.

Technology has been one of the major driving forces in changing the American agricultural scene, and we expect it to continue to play this role. Genetic engineering, advances in electronics, and improved mechanical equipment can be expected to increase the productivity of resources and reduce the demand for farm labor.[6] As in the past, the early adopters (primarily on the larger farms) will tend to capture the majority of benefits of technical change.

Farm commodity prices have been an important aspect of change in agriculture. They can be expected to continue to decline in real or constant dollar terms (after adjusting for inflation). The long-term decline in farm product prices has been given impetus by the increasing self-sufficiency of food production in the Third World. Switching to incentive-based food policies in these nations has helped speed the adoption of more advanced production techniques and has reduced the need for food imports.[7] Although weather, policy changes, and other factors will from time to time contribute to temporary cyclical upswings in commodity prices, prudent planning for agricultural investments would include preparations to offset cyclical declines. Over the longer term, continued declines in real crop prices are the most likely scenario.

Farm production costs (measured in terms of the prices paid by farmers for production inputs) have, in the modern technological era, risen faster than have prices for farm products. One well-known measure, the parity ratio (a ratio of the index of prices received to an index of prices paid), has fallen by over 50 percent over the last seventy-five years. To use a more concrete example, forty years ago a bushel of corn sold for about $7 in 1988 price levels; in the past three years the same bushel has brought an average of somewhat over $2. To accommodate, farmers have been forced to increase farm size and to keep up with technological change.

Rising Costs of New Irrigation Water Supplies

The opportunity for inexpensively developing significant new water supplies has largely passed. Earlier irrigation developments were typically served by gravity delivery systems. Hydroelectric power sales could often pay the costs of water storage and delivery facilities. Now, most prospective irrigation systems are distant in both space and altitude from water sources. Hence, the capital costs for storage and conveyance structures are high. Many recent and proposed projects are heavy energy consumers rather than net energy producers.

170

Low Productivity and Expense of Developing Remaining Available Lands

Although there are some exceptions, as in central Arizona, sites with extensive tracts of level, deep, and productive soils are scarce. Those that are also near adequate water supplies are especially rare. Topography is often not level, requiring expensive pipeline networks and sprinkler systems to convey the water and apply it to fields. Potential new projects frequently are in climatic zones that do not enjoy the long growing seasons that permit high productivity from a wide range of crops. The shorter frost-free period limits production largely to lower-income crops.

Limited Potential for High-Income Specialty Crops

F. Lee Brown and Helen M. Ingram are prominent among those who advocate the production of perishable fruit and vegetable crops as a major component of agriculture-based regional development proposals, because such crops generate high net returns over operating costs and require relatively large amounts of labor per acre.[8]

In many parts of the western United States, however, the opportunities for profitable new specialty crop operations are limited by both production and marketing conditions. The most favorable conditions for the production and marketing of specialty crops are found in localities where harvest can take place at times when the rest of the country is experiencing adverse growing conditions and cannot produce these specialty crops (the "market window"). These favorable conditions occur most frequently in the desert Southwest. Also, even in the most favorable climatic zones, rarely do specialty crops account for more than 15 percent of the acreage of crops grown. There is little reason to assume a shortage of suitable locations for additional specialty crop production.

The high net returns to specialty crops are, on closer examination, necessary to recompense growers for the special management requirements for growing and marketing the crops, for the production and price risks involved, and to provide a normal return on the high capital investment. Three sources of risk must be recognized when considering specialty crops: (1) high price volatility is typical; (2) production may vary due to unpredictable and adverse changes in weather or pests; and (3) there is uncertainty about the extent of the demand. If the market is limited, as it frequently is for perishable crops, additional production can drive down the market price, reducing profitability. A small specialty crop development might find a ready local market, but expanded output must be sold into highly competitive regional and national markets.

There is little reason to believe that there are the true excess economic profits in specialty crop production that would signal a need for additional resources in the sector. To assert that new specialty crop production capacity would be especially profitable is to contend that the present decentralized production and marketing system is somehow failing to adequately do its economic tasks.

Potential Employment and Regional Economic Development Impacts from Irrigation Development

Prevailing wisdom seems to be that irrigation development can create relatively large on-farm and secondary employment impacts as well as secondary regional income effects. Our assessment of the evidence suggests that in this aspect of the issue, also, high expectations are not likely to be achieved because the demand for labor has become limited and highly seasonal, local secondary economic impacts are no longer very large, irrigation development is water intensive as well as capital intensive, new irrigation development will increasingly impose external costs on others in society, and federal project evaluation procedures are biased and overly optimistic.

Limited, Seasonal Demand for Labor

Most tasks on U.S. farms are now highly mechanized and need relatively little labor. Field crops such as corn, wheat, and hay require only five to ten worker-hours per acre per year, so that two to three hundred acres or more are required to generate one full-time equivalent worker-year of employment (conventionally measured as 2,000 working hours). Moreover, those working hours on irrigated crop farms largely fall within a short four- to six-month season with peak demands occurring for a few weeks at planting and harvest.

Our own early experiences in the farm labor force suggest that the reality of farm work more often than not departs from the idyllic mountain meadow horse roundups or happy crews of grape-pickers so often portrayed in television advertisements. Field work tends to be physically demanding and repetitive and must often be performed under hot, dusty, or otherwise less-than-ideal conditions. Wages from farm work tend to be low, erratic, and seasonal.

Experience in the United States and elsewhere demonstrates that the most productive organization of agricultural production is for capital and labor to be combined into a privately owned business, so that the necessary field tasks are performed as recompense for the advantages of independence and the opportunity for owners to capture the fruits of their own skills and efforts. It is this group, largely "family farmers," who have made our agriculture the productive success it has become.

Decreased Local Secondary Economic Impacts of Irrigated Farming

The conventional wisdom in farming communities has maintained that high local spinoffs are achieved from irrigated farming enterprises. A favorite example quotes the "multiplier of seven," meaning that each $1 of farm sales creates $7 of further sales in the local economy. However, as we show below, no evidence can be found in support of a local multiplier that large. Technological change, increasing farm size, and capital intensification are reducing the impact of the farm sector on the local economy. Increasingly, the production inputs used by farmers are produced elsewhere and may be purchased through wholesale outlets from regional centers, limiting the local economic impact. (Mechanical equipment, fertilizers, and pesticides to substitute for labor are examples.)

Employment and job creation are useful measures of regional economic growth impacts. Taking Colorado as an example, we find the agribusiness sector employs statewide only about 70 percent as many workers as does the farm production sector itself. The backward-linked input suppliers (supplying items such as machinery, fertilizer, and pesticides, which are necessary for the production of agricultural commodities) are the smaller agribusiness component, employing only 20 percent as many workers as do farming and ranching. The forward-linked sectors (i.e., processing, storage, transportation, and marketing services) account for about half as many as does the farm production sector. Moreover, many of the agribusiness jobs are located in metropolitan centers, far from the local farm communities.[9]

Agricultural producers, of course, also purchase consumption goods and services locally, and this represents an important contribution to the immediate region's economy. It is difficult to isolate the regional effects of consumption purchases from those from production. We have elsewhere attempted to estimate the total effect. Using census data, we and a colleague found that in 1980, in the groundwater-irrigated counties of the northern High Plains, 1.6 local off-farm jobs were created for every farm job in the county.[10] However, comparisons with similar measurements for earlier decades show a long-term declining trend. As on-farm worker numbers have declined, the corresponding secondary employment impacts have also declined. Secondary jobs created per thousand irrigated acres fell by almost one-half between 1950 and 1980, from about 11 to 5.5. Direct farm jobs per thousand acres fell even more during the same period, from 16 to 3.4 per thousand acres, a decline of nearly 80 percent.

Our conclusion on this point is that a very large irrigation development is required to make an appreciable impact on a regional economy. For example, a 20,000-acre development, which might cost more than $200 million under current conditions, might account for only 70 full-time equivalent farm jobs and another 110 secondary jobs in the surrounding area.

Water- and Capital-Intensive Nature of Irrigation Developments

The scarcest resources on Indian reservations are water and capital. However, irrigation developments require extensive use of these resources and yield low returns on both. Nonagricultural business activities can require less than one half acre-foot per year per job created, on the average (mostly for household use by the workers' families). In contrast, irrigation of field crops can consume over 400 acre-feet per job per year, up to 800 times as much water as nonagricultural business activities. The manufacturing sector in the United States requires an average investment of about $60,000 of capital per job. The combined public and private investment on irrigation in recent and proposed federal projects in the upper Colorado River basin imply 10 to 15 (or more) times as much capital investment per job created.

Economic development will take place when resources are channeled into activities yielding the highest returns. Market allocation of resources is more likely to effectively perform this function than will the central government planning and facilities ownership characteristic of federal irrigation programs.

External Costs of New Irrigation Development

Many otherwise beneficial irrigation projects carry with them costs or transfers of value from other U.S. citizens. For example, increased water use in most regions of the West must be at the expense of existing water users. External costs may also appear in the form of increasing salinity damages and reduced in-stream flows and hydroelectric power generation. Income from added specialty crops is often transferred from other producers, and farm commodities programs represent transfers from taxpayers and consumers to the beneficiaries of the irrigation project.

Bias in Federal Irrigation Project Evaluations

Support for irrigation development projects frequently is based on favorable economic evaluations performed by federal agencies. However, academic economists have long contended that Interior Department procedures for preconstruction economic appraisal (commonly called "cost-benefit analysis") are highly biased in favor of irrigation project approval and present an overly optimistic view of the economic possibilities.[11] Generally speaking, federal cost-benefit methods systematically understate costs and overstate benefits to more readily justify public expenditures to build irrigation systems.

It is clear that construction costs are typically underestimated in preproject planning. Actual expenditures necessary to construct projects completed or under construction in the Colorado River basin (e.g., the Central Arizona Project, the Central Utah Project, and the Dallas Creek, Dolores, and Navajo Indian irrigation projects) are three to four times (or more) larger than the amounts projected in the documents originally submitted to Congress with requests for approval to appropriate funds. Some of these overruns can be attributed to inflationary forces, which are not real economic costs. However, even allowing for inflation, it appears that actual outlays for the above projects will generally amount to more than twice the original forecasts.

The estimated costs of energy and capital are also understated. Irrigation projects that have been recently completed or are currently planned typically involve substantial pumping lifts, but electricity is incorrectly priced at the low historical cost of hydropower generation rather than the actual cost to the economy of developing new energy supplies. The opportunity cost of capital (as represented by the planning interest rate) has also been understated, inadequately accounting for the real opportunity costs of federal funds in today's integrated financial markets. Federal interest rate procedures, moreover, have failed to incorporate a premium to reflect the high risks inherent in investments in expensive irrigation projects. (Such a premium would be comparable to the higher interest rates necessary to market risky "junk bond" loans in the private sector.)

The economic benefits of irrigation projects are conventionally measured by the profits to water-using farmers. One way that benefits have been overstated is by not adequately accounting for family labor and management costs, thereby inflating forecasted profits. Crop revenues are often overstated, typically by assuming unrealistically high proportions of high-revenue specialty crops and by overestimating future crop prices and yields. Regional secondary economic (multiplier) impacts have sometimes been incorrectly added to direct economic benefits, while the offsetting (probably larger) secondary costs are ignored.

The pressure for biased appraisals can be traced to the government's cheap water policy and, further, to the "double subsidies" inherent in the federal farm commodities programs. Local water development interests perceive water, capital, and energy to be more plentiful than they really are, and food and fiber to be scarcer. When receipt of the public largesse is conditioned upon a showing of a favorable benefit-to-cost ratio, excessive pressure is placed on government analysts to accommodate the perceptions of client groups.

Support of these criticisms for federal planning procedures is found in the increasingly large subsidies required to enable farmers to use the water profitably. Further evidence is seen in the inability of users to repay even a small fraction of the actual costs of federal irrigation projects.[12]

Case Studies in the Southwest

In this section, we review the experience with irrigation on four southwestern Indian irrigation systems to test the above analysis. Published literature was supplemented by interviews with project and tribal officials where possible. "Traditional" developments on the Navajo and Ute reservations in the Four Corners area represent one general case. In sharp contrast are two distinctly modern developments: the Navajo Indian Irrigation Project (NIIP) in northwestern New Mexico and the Colorado River Indian Reservation in western Arizona.

The Traditional Way

The Navajo Reservation / Extending across a vast area on the Colorado Plateau, the Navajo Reservation lies primarily in Arizona and New Mexico. Because of the arid climate, little nonirrigated crop production is observed. A relatively limited frost-free season occurs over much of the reservation.

Steve M. Jones reports that about 46,000 acres have been developed for irrigation (in addition to the NIIP acreage) on about 80 separate sites; but only about 17,000 acres are still actively irrigated.[13] Jones indicates considerable deterioration in water delivery works, and because of leaky canals, losses of water regularly exceed 50 percent. John W. Leeper attributes the abandonment of some lands to inadequate water delivery, citing financial limitations and lack of effective maintenance.[14] The crops under cultivation are primarily hay and pasture. Corn is also important, and some vegetables and fruits can be observed. The yield per acre of hay is less than half that observed on NIIP or on non-Indian lands in the region.

The tribe assigns farming permits to the traditional lands according to historic use. The average allotment of irrigated land was less than seven acres in 1986. According to a survey by James K. McNeley, about 72 percent of output was used at home, while only 12 percent found its way to off-reservation markets.[15] The total market value of production from these small plots could rarely exceed a few thousand dollars per year per farmer, and the production and profits could hardly be expected to provide even a subsistence income.

The Southern Ute Reservation / Located nearby in southwestern Colorado, the Southern Ute irrigation situation in many ways is similar to the historic Navajo lands. Tribal members have first priority water rights from the Pine River, sufficient for about 10,000 acres. Also, some small parcels are supplied from the San Juan and Florida rivers.

Practically all of the Southern Ute lands are used to grow pasture or hay, mostly for cattle and horse feed. Production practices are similar to those on the historic Navajo lands, there being little use of fertilizer or chemicals. Most of the acreage is in old stands of native hay or grass alfalfa mix, yielding two to three tons per acre.

Farm size is larger than on the Navajo Reservation, averaging 70 acres. Few Utes, however, make their entire living from farming. About 60 percent of the Pine River lands are leased to non-Indians. The tribe itself previously leased much of the Utes' land directly to non-Indian farmers. This practice has largely been discontinued; however, the Indian assignees frequently lease directly to non-Indians.

The "traditional way" is characterized by small farm holdings, a limited use of modern farming techniques, low-efficiency surface irrigation methods, relatively high labor use per acre, and on-farm or local disposition of production. Much of the significance of farming is linked to personal, traditional, and rural lifestyle values. Because of the small size of the typical unit, very few of those farmers with irrigated land assignments obtain significant income from these operations. The agricultural activities might be classified as noncommercial or subsistence in nature. Employment is limited and seasonal. It is very difficult to determine the economic merits of irrigation under these conditions.

The New Way

The Navajo Indian Irrigation Project / The Navajo Indian Irrigation Project (NIIP) stands in sharp contrast to the traditional lands described above. The NIIP can use water from the San Juan River to irrigate nearly 50,000 acres just south of Farmington, New Mexico. The project lands are part of an elevated plain ranging from 4,400 to 6,400 feet above sea level at an elevation of 200 to 1,000 feet above the river, according to 1984 data from the Interior Department. The growing season averages about 160 days, and the average annual precipitation is about 8 inches.

The project received federal approval in 1962, after protracted negotiations regarding the distribution of Upper Basin water rights specified by the Colorado River Compact. The federal legislation provided for 508,000 acre-feet annually to irrigate 110,000 acres. Initial appropriations for construction soon followed, but progress was much slower than had been planned. The first water applied to crops occurred in 1976, fourteen years after authorization. The costs of construction far exceeded the initial forecasts, in part due to funding delays and to inflation.

The original concept was for numerous small, family-owned and operated farms, using surface irrigation technology that was the standard at the time. In 1970, the organizational concept was shifted to a centralized, corporate management system under the Navajo Agricultural Products Industry (NAPI). All workers are hired by the farming organization, which also maintains control of the lands. In 1972, partly because of a recognition that water supplies were limited, plans were revised so that all water would be applied by sprinklers. This change resulted in substantially reduced labor requirements but also required much higher capital outlays by the Navajo Nation. Initially, the sprinklers were mostly of the semiautomated side-roll type, but by 1988, all but about 2,000 acres used fully automated center-pivot sprinklers.

177

The principal crops grown using NIIP water are corn, dry beans, and alfalfa, each accounting for about one-sixth of the acreage in 1988. Small grains (wheat, barley) occupied another 10 percent, and potatoes and onions over 8 percent. (The latter crops are estimated to provide over one-quarter of the revenue but also account for a similar portion of the costs.) Another 6 percent are scattered among annual vine crops (e.g., watermelons), pasture, grass, and sod. Finally, another 23 percent was in fallow or federal set-aside programs.

Yields have probably reached economically attainable levels. For example, corn yields were 178 bushels per acre in 1988, while alfalfa hay yielded 5.7 tons, and potatoes 422 hundredweight per acre. By aggressive marketing, NAPI has been able to establish markets for its products. About half the hay and corn produced are used in the NAPI feedlot. Most of the potato and bean crops are marketed to major food processors.

As is typical of the optimistic projections supporting publicly financed irrigation projects, Congress was originally told that the project would provide the Navajos with 1,120 family farms and 9,000 jobs. As recently as 1984, it was claimed that "the project will provide a substantial part of the livelihood for about 17,000 people." [16]

The current reality differs from the projections. There are no family farms; rather, the operation—with its large size, centralized ownership and control, and cadre of seasonal hired labor—more closely resembles the plantation farms of the tropics. With the project half completed, about 770 workers, not all of whom are Navajos, find work on the project and associated NAPI enterprises. This amount of labor is substantially higher than could be afforded by family farms whose resource costs are not subsidized to the degree enjoyed by NIIP.

The project might well be counted an engineering and an agronomic success, but the economic returns are less impressive. In fact, from either the federal or the Navajo perspective, the project operates substantially at a deficit. Federal planning procedures define an irrigation project as profitable if annual crop revenues exceed the total of (1) annual farm operating costs (labor, chemicals, seed, etc.); (2) annual depreciation and interest on the irrigation delivery system, machinery, and other durable capital; (3) annual project operating costs (energy, maintenance, labor), and (4) annual depreciation and interest on project water storage and delivery facilities. This is, of course, the same definition that would apply to a similar private sector investment. Another way of expressing the same formula is to require farm profits (farm revenues minus farm operating and overhead costs) to exceed the annual operating and capital costs for the project. Federal repayment procedures for irrigation projects require little or no reimbursement of capital costs and only partial reimbursement of project operating costs, thereby creating strong local incentives to seek federal funding as a mechanism for economic development.

178

Originally, the enabling legislation provided for $135 million for construction for the NIIP. A recent Interior Department auditor's report estimated that $339 million of federal funds had been expended for project construction, and the lands were less than half developed.[17] In addition, the report indicated that the Navajo Nation's agricultural enterprise itself had not had a single profitable year by 1987. (However, profits to the Navajo Nation totaling $5 million were reported in 1988 and 1989, years of relatively favorable crop prices due to drought and government supply control programs). The audit further stated, "Total cumulative losses were $64 million through 1986, even though the Bureau of Indian Affairs subsidized at least $83 million of the farming operation for such items as operation and maintenance, energy and on-farm development. We estimate that these subsidies could amount to at least $8.7 million annually after Project completion." Our own estimates imply that depreciation and interest on public funds already expended would amount to over $25 million per year. It appears that farming profits are unlikely in the long run to exceed actual project operating costs, let alone provide a return on the original capital invested. The combined federal and tribal investment approaches one-half million dollars per job created. The annual capital subsidy of $37,000 per job created undeniably places a very high price tag on this development initiative.

The auditor's report indicated that to complete the entire 110,000 acres, another $476 million would be required. The report concluded with the recommendation that the project not be completed and that other methods be sought to satisfy the federal government's obligation to help the Navajos achieve their development objectives.

Those conversant with the economics of irrigation in the Four Corners region should not be surprised that economic difficulties have emerged, given the market and the soils and climatic conditions on the project site. A team of New Mexico State economists estimated in 1979 that NIIP water returned $21 per acre-foot per year.[18] Another New Mexico study reported on market values of water rights as an indicator of economic returns.[19] For the San Juan basin, the market value of water in 1972 (converted to annualized terms) was less than $10 per acre-foot. The annual operating costs per acre-foot of the NIIP greatly exceeds either of these values, not counting the annualized capital costs exceeding $200 per acre-foot.

Let us be clear that we are not laying the blame for these financial results on the Navajo Nation and its managers. The cost overrun can, in part, be attributed to inflation and an inefficiently slow construction schedule. More important, the large cumulative losses can mostly be assessed against highly unrealistic expectations in the original planning documents about the costs of developing and operating a capital-intensive and energy-intensive irrigation system and overly optimistic expectations regarding potential commodity prices and marketing opportunities, labor needs, and secondary employment impacts.

179

The Colorado River Indian Tribes / About 72,000 acres can be irrigated with water from the Colorado River on the Colorado River Indian Reservation, mainly in La Paz County, on the southwestern edge of Arizona. With relatively level lands, a benign climate, and a gravity system for delivering water, irrigation has been developed at a relatively low capital and operating cost per acre.

The Colorado River Indian Tribes use a centralized organization to manage their lands. Some are farmed by individual Indians, some by the tribal organization, but the majority are leased out to non-Indian farmers. In 1986, 64,000 acres (85 percent of the total) were leased for farming by non-Indians. Lessees must follow strict guidelines. Long-term development leases are made available at low rents in return for the development of an on-farm irrigation system by the lessee. However, the annual rents are relatively high when compared with rents or profits in the Four Corners sites. The proportion of leasing to non-Indians may be expected to fall in the future as the initial development leases expire.

The potential choice of crops is much larger than is available in the Four Corners region. Here again, however (as indicated by Bureau of Indian Affairs annual reports), alfalfa hay was the leading crop, accounting for about 43 percent of the cropped acres in 1984–86, the last years for which we have data. Cotton was close behind, at about 30 percent. Ten percent was in wheat, and some of the acres were committed to the Agricultural Conservation Reserve. The remaining 15 percent was in specialty vegetables, mainly melons and lettuce.

This irrigation development benefits from favorable climate, soils, and location with respect to urban markets, plus an inexpensive gravity-fed water supply. Even so, specialty crop production represents only a small fraction of the project lands, and the crops produced have relatively little value to the nation for the water utilized. Participation in management and the farm labor force by tribal members is limited.

Conclusions

A realistic examination of the economics of agriculture in the late twentieth century suggests the following: profitable farms, and ones that can provide a standard of family living comparable to that from the nonfarm economy, are likely to be farms with larger resource endowments, larger sales, and up-to-date technology. Families on smaller farms and temporary hired farm workers will continue to require nonfarm sources of revenue if they are to approach a reasonable standard of living. Continued technological advances and increasing world competition are likely to perpetuate the historical decline in inflation-adjusted crop prices and the cost-price squeeze. Modern large farms generate relatively little employment for the amount of capital investment required. Irrigated specialty crops (perishable fruits and vegetables), which generate higher income and employment per acre than standard commodities, have limited potential, because of specific climatic, soil, management, financial, and marketing requirements. Local economic multiplier effects from farming activities, whether measured in employment or income creation, are no longer very large and continue to decline with the increasing capital-intensive nature of commercial farming and easier access to regional input and processing markets. Finally, sites that have the necessary combination of inexpensive water, favorable soil, and climatic resources, along with accessible markets—which together can make new irrigation developments profitable and self-sustaining—are increasingly scarce. The capital costs of job creation through irrigation are several times higher than those of investments in the manufacturing or service industries.

The implications of this overview of present-day U.S. agriculture are not contradicted by actual experience with irrigation on southwestern Indian reservations. The contrast between the "traditional" and the "new" ways to develop irrigation on southwestern Indian reservations illustrates what some have called the "modern dilemma of agriculture." The dilemma refers to the apparent incompatibility of desires for small-scale, sustainable, low-input farming with the demands for a reasonable standard of living in a technology-driven, internationalized market agriculture where production becomes more economical with large size. Traditional irrigation systems, delivering to smallholder plots, yield what many regard as important community values and the promise of sustainability. However, small plots provide limited and seasonal employment opportunities and below-subsistence incomes. Other income sources must be drawn upon to provide a satisfactory standard of living. Modern, large-scale irrigation investments can be highly productive in agronomic terms but require large federal and perhaps tribal subsidies in most instances. Specialty crops can typically account for only a small portion of irrigated acreage, similar to the situation observed on non-Indian areas. For the capital expended, relatively little employment and local-area development can be observed in either the traditional or the new ways of utilizing irrigation water on Indian reservations.

We have been accused, when making these criticisms in other forums, of being biased against irrigation and biased against Native Americans. We reject both charges.[20] We do favor a realistic recognition of the high costs and limited employment-creating capacity of agricultural investments to achieve employment, poverty reduction, and rural development goals as we approach the twenty-first century. We also admit to a policy preference for cost-effective solutions to rural development in Indian country, ones that can demonstrate real economic returns to federal and tribal investments. Cheap irrigation water for Native Americans does not satisfy these criteria. We suspect that we and our critics differ more on the means than on the ends of economic policy for Native Americans. If the distorting incentives of the cost-sharing policy chosen by Congress were removed, we would probably find little to disagree on.

Several tribes have shown a keen interest in provisions permitting them to resell water rights created from federally funded projects. Seeking federal construction monies to obtain firm water rights ("wet water") against an uncertain economic and political future has, of course, been successfully practiced in the non-Indian western community. However, creating wet water with federal funds will come at a cost to the nation that promises to be several times greater than the probable market value of the water developed. From the federal taxpayer's perspective, the same financial benefits to Native Americans can be achieved much less expensively by addressing tribal development needs more directly. Much more rural development "bang" is likely to be achieved for the public "buck" if programs are aimed at supplying the real and emerging needs of the economy and the tribes rather than clinging to outmoded policies. As it has done with non-Indian projects, a small (perhaps 25 percent) tribal cost share imposed on proposed irrigation investments would do much to reorient the efforts presently devoted to obtaining money for water toward more appropriate and cost-effective policies.

Our analysis is directed to those public and tribal officials who may be called upon to decide on policies designed to further Native American aspirations for improved standards of living. Public subsidy policies are sometimes an appropriate means of providing economic benefits to the society that are not otherwise available from the market economy. A public subsidy policy for irrigation made sense in an era when food supplies were often inadequate, when the agricultural economy was such that agricultural development was an effective mechanism for regional economic growth, and when settling empty spaces was an important policy goal.

At the end of the twentieth century, however, events and technology have made obsolete these benefits of the irrigation subsidy policy. Public funds would be much more effectively spent for "people" rather than for "places."[21] In particular, resources should be directed toward increased training and education to help Native Americans enter the work force in the twenty-first century and toward institutions designed to encourage employment opportunities in industrial and service industries.[22] In view of the escalating costs and limited returns of the irrigation approach, tribal governments, Congress, and the Supreme Court would do well to rethink the whole issue of how to assure future Native American access to a fair share of scarce western water and to an acceptable standard of living without premature and wasteful expenditure on irrigation water projects.

NOTES

The research underlying this chapter was supported by a grant from the Western Rural Development Center at Oregon State University and by Colorado State University's Agricultural Experiment Station. This chapter was adapted from the project completion report submitted to the Western Rural Development Center in 1990. The findings and policy views expressed here are our own, and neither of the aforementioned agencies should necessarily be assumed to endorse the above analysis or its conclusions. Without implicating them for the findings, the authors also wish to thank Warren Trock of Colorado State University and William B. Lord and Harry W. Ayer of the University of Arizona for their comments and suggestions on earlier drafts.

1. The contrary hypothesis has been developed elsewhere by, among others, Maurice M. Kelso, William E. Martin, and Lawrence E. Mack, *Water Supplies and Economic Growth: An Arizona Case Study* (Tucson: University of Arizona Press, 1972); and Robert A. Young, "Water Scarcity: Local and Regional Impacts," in *Water Scarcity: Impacts on Western Agriculture,* ed. Ernest A. Englebert and Ann F. Sheuring (Berkeley: University of California Press, 1984), pp. 244–65.

2. Luther G. Tweeten, *Farm Policy Analysis* (Boulder, Colo.: Westview Press, 1989).

3. Luther G. Tweeten, "Adjustments in Agriculture and Its Infrastructure in the 1990s," in *Positioning Agriculture for the 1990s: A New Decade of Change,* ed. Mark Drabenstott, Report No. 238 (Washington, D.C.: National Planning Association, 1989), pp. 85–112.

4. Marvin R. Duncan, "U.S. Agriculture: Hard Realities and New Opportunities," in Drabenstott, *Positioning Agriculture for the 1990s,* pp. 3–28.

5. Tweeten, "Adjustments in Agriculture," p. 93.

6. Glenn L. Johnson, "Technological Innovations: Implications for Agricultural Economics," in *Agriculture and Rural Areas Approaching the Twenty-first Century,* ed. R. James Hildreth, Kathryn L. Lipton, and Kenneth C. Clayton (Ames: Iowa State University Press, 1988), pp. 82–108.

7. John M. Antle, *World Agricultural Development and the Future of U.S. Agriculture* (Washington, D.C.: American Enterprise Institute, 1988).

8. F. Lee Brown and Helen M. Ingram, *Water and Poverty in the Southwest* (Tucson: University of Arizona Press, 1987).

9. Thomas A. Miller, S. Lee Gray, and Warren L. Trock, *Colorado's Farm and Food System: Economic Contributions to Rural and Metropolitan Counties,* Research Report AR87-5 (Fort Collins: Colorado State University, Department of Agricultural and Resource Economics, 1987).

10. Roger Mann, Edward W. Sparling, and Robert A. Young, "Irrigation Development and Regional Economic Growth: Evidence from the High Plains," *Water Resources Research* 23, no. 9 (1987): 1711–16.

11. Robert A. Young, "Economic Analysis and Federal Irrigation Policy: A Reappraisal," *Western Journal of Agricultural Economics* 3, no. 2 (1978): 257–68.

183

12. Douglas R. Franklin and Ronda K. Hageman, "Cost Sharing with Irrigated Agriculture: Promise Versus Performance," *Water Resources Research* 20, no. 8 (1984): 1047–51.

13. Steve M. Jones, *Inventory of Navajo Indian Irrigation Projects* (Flagstaff, Ariz.: U.S. Department of Agriculture, Soil Conservation Service, 1985).

14. John W. Leeper, "The Impact of Water Control on Navajo Irrigation Projects," chapter 13, this volume.

15. James K. McNeley, *The San Juan Agricultural Inventory and Planning Survey: A Summary and Analysis* (Shiprock, N.M.: Navajo Community College, 1988).

16. Bureau of Reclamation, *Navajo Indian Irrigation Project: A Promise Fulfilled* (Farmington, N.M.: U.S. Department of the Interior, Bureau of Reclamation, 1984).

17. Office of the Inspector General, *Audit Report: Navajo Indian Irrigation Project* Report No. 88-43 (Washington, D.C.: U.S. Department of the Interior, Office of the Inspector General, 1988).

18. Noel R. Gollehon, Robert R. Lansford, Bobby J. Creel, and Fred Roach, "Impacts on Irrigated Agriculture from Energy Development in the Rocky Mountain Region," *Southwestern Review of Management and Economics* 1, no. 1 (1981): 61–88.

19. F. Lee Brown, "Conflicting Claims to Southwestern Water: The Equity and Management Issues," *Southwestern Review of Management and Economics* 1, no. 1 (1981): 35–60.

20. Criticism of a policy favored by some Native Americans should not be equated with "bias" against all Native Americans. See James A. Clifton, ed., *The Invented Indian: Cultural Fictions and Government Policies* (New Brunswick, N.J.: Transaction Publishers, 1990).

21. Jim Hite, "Places versus People in Rural Development Policy," *Choices: The Magazine of Food, Farm and Resource Issues* 7, no. 1 (1992): 36–37.

22. Terry L. Anderson, ed., *Property Rights and Indian Economies* (Lanham, Md.: Rowman and Littlefield, 1992).

13

THE IMPACT OF WATER CONTROL ON NAVAJO IRRIGATION PROJECTS

John W. Leeper

The performance of Navajo irrigation systems lags far behind the performance of non-Indian systems in the western United States. The aggregate cropping intensity on U.S. Bureau of Reclamation projects is over 85 percent, while the average cropping intensity on the Navajo projects is approximately 33 percent. Over the last fifty years, the Navajo systems have been trapped in a cycle of rehabilitation, deterioration, abandonment, and rehabilitation. Numerous theories have been proposed to explain this poor performance, including (1) small, economically nonviable farm size; (2) lack of maintenance; (3) lack of funding; (4) institutional conflict; (5) lack of extension efforts and technology; (6) lack of credit; (7) lack of education; and (8) the possibility that irrigated agriculture is culturally unacceptable.

Many tribal and nontribal authorities believe that recent irrigation efforts on the Navajo Nation are unsuccessful. These authorities suggest that small-scale, irrigated agriculture is neither culturally nor economically viable and cannot play a role in Navajo development. This chapter questions such conventional wisdom.

On certain projects, under certain circumstances, Navajos find irrigated agriculture viable. A more precise diagnosis of the problems and opportunities facing these farmers is essential if the cycle of rehabilitation and deterioration is to be broken.

The principal hypothesis of this chapter is that one of the fundamental constraints facing Navajo farmers, and by implication farmers elsewhere in the world, is a lack of physical and organizational control over their water resources. The role of water control, however, has rarely been explicitly recognized in the literature on Native American irrigation. If this hypothesis is correct, increasing system performance will require providing or returning the control of water to the water users.

A Historical Overview

Although the traditional Navajo economy has been depicted as one based primarily on nomadic stock raising, prior to the 1930s sedentary agriculture occupied a position of importance. But in the arid Navajo countryside the natural resources needed for survival are widely scattered. Consequently, the Navajos were neither completely sedentary nor completely nomadic. Instead, they lived near their farms and moved their sheep according to the season. If the cultivated land deteriorated and yields declined, a new farm was established nearby. In areas with assured water supplies, Navajos intercepted water at the mouths of ravines, diked flat areas to catch spring floods, and built small dams to divert river water onto their fields.[1]

In the early 1900s, Indian agents reported that Navajos dug thirty-seven miles of ditches and developed more than 270 irrigated fields along the San Juan River. Other irrigated fields were located on the Carrizo Wash, at Two Grey Hills, Wheatfields, Red Lake, Rock Point, and Fort Defiance. These developments were almost exclusively initiated by Indians.[2]

In 1939, the U.S. Indian Service reported sixty-seven irrigation projects on the reservation, subjugating 22,000 acres, of which 13,800 were cultivated. Twenty-five of those projects were considered Indian systems, and about eight were built by Mormon settlers or trading post operators. By 1948 the U.S. Department of the Interior reported seventy-eight projects subjugating 34,000 acres, of which 17,000 were cultivated. But by 1960 the irrigated acreage declined to about 10,000 acres, roughly the same amount reported in 1881.

During this period the character of the Navajo economy changed dramatically. In the 1940s, agriculture contributed about 60 percent of all Navajo income, and wage work contributed about 30 percent. By 1958 agriculture only contributed about 10 percent of earned income. At that time a Navajo working in the coal mines could make twelve times as much income as could one working on the family's small farm. By 1988 agriculture contributed less than 3 percent of earned income.[3]

Water Control on Irrigation Systems

The irrigation management literature defines water control on an irrigation system in terms of the water's adequacy, reliability, and equity of distribution. Each of these elements in turn has a physical and an organizational component. One of the most serious problems facing many irrigation systems throughout the world is articulation between the requirements of individual water users and the requirements of the irrigation bureaucracy.[4] One reason for this gap is that irrigation systems bring together two groups with very different and frequently conflicting objectives.

The meaning of water control shifts as one moves down the system. For main system managers, water control means moving large quantities of water that must be kept within relatively narrow and stable parameters. In theory, main system managers are rewarded for operating the system based on the aggregate need of the entire system.

For farmers, however, water control means reliably delivering relatively small volumes of water to the unique conditions of a particular field at a particular time. The farmer is optimizing water use based on the needs of his or her own fields and family. Farmers will pay a premium for water that they control but will not invest time and labor in a irrigation system that they do not control or one that fails to deliver adequate and reliable water.[5]

The resulting behavior exhibited by the farmers may be suboptimal for the overall system and may appear irrational to the main system operators. For instance, the first few farmers on a system may overirrigate. Their reduced irrigation efficiency might be a very rational strategy of substituting water for labor and other capital inputs or it may be in response to uncertainty over the future availability of water. In either case it may occur at the expense of other farmers on the system.

Similarly, lack of maintenance is frequently cited as a primary cause for the poor performance of Indian systems.[6] Based on this chapter's hypothesis, however, poor maintenance is a symptom of other, more fundamental problems. For instance, in some organizational climates it is rational for the main system managers to defer maintenance. The immediate consequences of delaying maintenance are not felt at the main system level, and the scarce resources that are diverted can be used in ways that provide more visible and immediate benefits for the manager. In many situations the supporting agencies will only provide assistance if the situation has deteriorated to the point of an emergency.[7]

Analysis of System-Wide Parameters

Data drawn from the 1986 San Juan Agricultural Inventory and Planning Survey conducted by the Navajo Division of Water Resources may be used to evaluate system performance on Navajo irrigation projects. The objective of the survey was to determine the attitudes of Navajo residents on the Hogback, Fruitland, and Cudei irrigation systems toward farming in general and to determine what specific changes the farming community would like to see.

187

TABLE 13.1. Stratification by System Cropping Intensity, 1985

Factors	Low 0–19% (*N* = 32)	Medium 20–49% (*N* = 31)	High 50–100% (*N* = 16)
Available water supply (AF/acre)	2.3	3.2	7.0
Number of people benefited	84.0	120.0	230.0
Maximum irrigable acreage 1948	573	557	1,499
Subjugated acreage 1985	535	447	981
Farm size (acres)	26.9	13.0	13.9
% of irrigable land subjugated	93%	80%	65%
Subjugated acres per person	10.5	7.0	5.5
% of respondents judging supply as dependable	54%	47%	75%

ABBREVIATIONS: AF = acre-feet; *N* = number of respondents
SOURCES: Steve Jones, *Inventory of Navajo Indian Irrigation Projects* (Flagstaff, Ariz.: U.S. Department of the Interior, Soil Conservation Service, 1985); J. A. Krug, *The Navajo: A Long Range Program for Navajo Rehabilitation* (Washington, D.C.: U.S. Department of the Interior, Bureau of Indian Affairs, 1948).

Navajo-speaking enumerators from the local chapter houses distributed the questionnaire to holders of farm permits. The enumerators visited each house two or three times. Out of about 800 permit holders, 600 surveys were completed. The nonrespondents do not represent a systematic bias in sampling; due to the rushed nature of the survey the absence of contact resulted largely from an accident of timing. There is nothing unusual about the nonrespondents' farm size or location. Moreover, about half of the nonresponse was the result of farm permits belonging to families that had already filled out a questionnaire.

The principal dependent variable used for evaluating the performance of these irrigation systems is cropping intensity. More sensitive parameters on cropping patterns, crop yields, and farm budgets are generally not available for the reservation systems.

In Table 13.1, the irrigation systems are stratified into three groups based on the system cropping intensity. This table demonstrates, first, that the systems with high cropping intensity have significantly more water available: seven acre-feet of water available per subjugated acre. Two or three acre-feet per acre at the head gates is simply not adequate for the farms to succeed. The amount of water available for the system was estimated as the lesser of either the seasonal water volume or the water capacity of the diversion structure listed in the 1985 Soil Conservation Service inventory.[8]

TABLE 13.2. Aggregate Cropping Intensity of Respondents, 1986

Land Use	Cudei		Hogback		Fruitland	
	Number of Acres	% of Total	Number of Acres	% of Total	Number of Acres	% of Total
Forage	179	34%	1,063	41%	1,640	53%
Corn	60	12%	282	11%	355	12%
Horticulture	17	3%	115	4%	125	4%
Small grains	6	1%	70	2%	54	2%
Subjugated acres	670		8,860		3,718	
Surveyed acres	503		2,550		3,061	
Irrigated acres	262	52%	1,530	60%	2,174	71%

Second, Table 13.1 shows that systems with higher cropping intensities are more likely to have a dependable water supply. The systems with lower cropping intensity may have been developed beyond their hydrologic capacity. By 1985, the systems with lower cropping intensities were developed, on average, to over 90 percent of the ultimate irrigable size reported in 1948. The systems with higher cropping intensity were only developed to about 65 percent of their ultimate size.

The Indian Service was under political pressure to present viable irrigation projects to Washington. No doubt there was also a sincere desire to develop as much project land as possible to improve the economic conditions on the reservation. A 1948 report noted that the systems with assured water supplies had already been developed.[9] If water control is defined in terms of adequacy and reliability, then lack of water control is a significant variable for these systems.

Finally, the Navajo systems with higher cropping intensities have larger populations. It is possible that the projects with larger populations are able to acquire more resources for their systems. The Hogback and Fruitland systems, for instance, serve hundreds of farmers who presumably have a major impact on their respective chapters and on tribal politics. It is also appears that labor is more readily available. Systems with high cropping intensity have one person per five acres and smaller average farm sizes. The systems in the low intensity group have one person per ten acres.

Table 13.2 shows the aggregate cropping intensity of the survey respondents, demonstrating that the Fruitland system has the highest overall cropping intensity. Fruitland farmers also reported the fewest problems in receiving water. Moreover, the percentages of corn, horticulture crops, and small grains were about the same

TABLE 13.3. Destination of Farm Products

Destination of Crop	Cudei	Hogback	Fruitland
Used by family	80%	82%	90%
Sold on the reservation	18%	12%	6%
Sold off the reservation	1%	6%	3%

on all three systems. The additional irrigated acreage on the Fruitland system is devoted largely to hay and forage crops.

If water is available, alfalfa is the preferred crop. The percentage of corn does not vary greatly from system to system. Alfalfa requires less labor and is easy to store and easy to sell. It also requires less precise water application. Crop budgets published by New Mexico State University show that alfalfa also has one of the best economic returns for part-time farmers.[10]

Table 13.3 shows the destination of the production from the three Navajo systems along the San Juan River. This table demonstrates that the bulk of the production is consumed by family members or relatives who may not have access to irrigated fields. In return for this produce, the farmer may receive meat from the livestock or wood for lumber or fuel. Surpluses are sold at local events or out of pickup trucks parked along the highway. Marketing surpluses is not a major concern.

Moreover, only a small fraction of the production ends up in the wider Anglo economy. The Hogback system, which is close to the reservation's border and two major state highways, has the highest off-reservation sales. The Cudei system, farthest from a paved highway, has the lowest percentage of off-reservation sales.

Based on classical economic principles, the small farms are not economically viable units. A part-time twenty-acre farm produces about $330 in total net operating profits. When interest charges are included on operating capital and equipment, the total farm return is a $59 loss.[11] Many of the farms are subsidized by off-reservation income. Yet Navajo farmers continue farming in an environment that is challenging at best and discouraging at worst. Few of these flexible resource farmers are optimizing economic returns.

The farming system is closely linked to the livestock grazing system. Because of small herds, low reproduction rates, and poor range conditions, raising livestock does not provide a positive economic rate of return. Instead, it represents a highly valued way of life and is a subsidized source of income for family members who would have little else to live on.

Of equal importance is the value of reciprocal social exchanges in traditional Navajo culture. Although this is less important today than it was in the past, exchanging produce is a sign of respect and friendship. Social exchanges of this nature are not unique to Navajos but are practiced by all societies. Driving a truck loaded with melons to a flea market might represent a hardship if one is only calculating economic efficiency. But the opportunity to visit with neighbors and distant relatives is highly valued. Programs designed to increase the off-reservation sales or establish corporate farms need to take into account the additional costs of disrupting the internal and almost invisible social and monetary economy.

Irrigation development may represent an opportunity to stimulate and strengthen the internal reservation economy. Resources designed to increase the system-wide performance of these irrigation projects may produce greater economic multipliers on the reservation than do other development activities.

Analysis of Organizational Parameters

Figure 13.1 is an organizational chart based on a 1987 draft by the management plan of the Irrigation branch of the former Navajo Division of Water Resources. Although this exact plan was never adopted, the existing organization is very similar. The figure shows that the Navajo farmers are institutionally disenfranchised on their own systems. The ditch rider (who is called a canal patrolman), his supervisor, and his assistants work for the central bureaucracy, not the farmers. On paper, the irrigation employees are rewarded for carrying out the bureaucracy's agenda, not the farmer's agenda. The employees look to the tribal capital in Window Rock for advancement and job security.

The assessments collected by the Navajo Irrigation Office end up in a revolving fund administered by the Navajo Nation. The perception exists among farmers that the assessment does not benefit the system. In this environment it is impossible for the farmers to directly invest in their own systems.

The only formal link between the farmers and the irrigation bureaucracy is the Farm Board. According to the San Juan Survey, only 20 percent of the farmers on the Fruitland system feel that they received services from the Farm Board. This result is not an indication of poor leadership skills or a lack of dedication on the part of the Farm Board members; instead, it reflects a 100-year legacy of poorly designed organizations. To succeed, a water users' organization needs to be accountable to the farmers it serves and have responsibility for the system it operates.

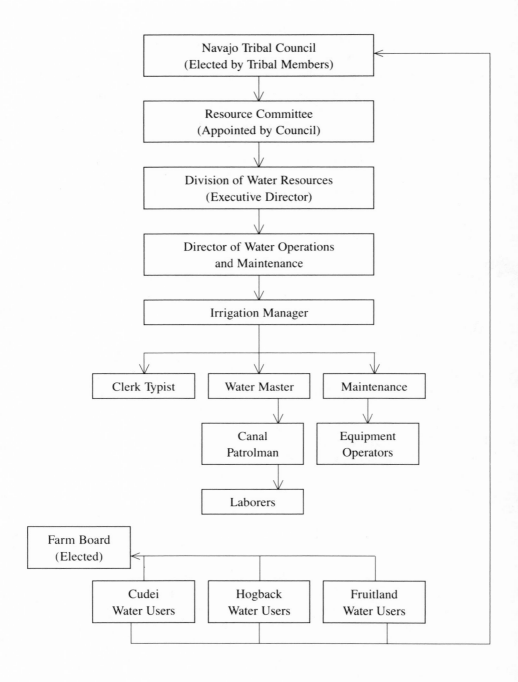

Figure 13.1 Irrigation Organization on the Navajo Reservation

Conclusions

On the Navajo Reservation, in spite of small farm size, no access to financing, and insufficient extension services, farmers who have control of their water are using it. The farms at the head of the Fruitland system, for instance, have a cropping intensity of almost 80 percent. Yet even on the Fruitland system, although the water supply is adequate, it is not reliable, nor is it distributed equitably. Without water control most of the farms experience crop-threatening water shortages sometime during the growing season.

No organization provides control of the water beyond the main system. The organizational vacuum has been filled by water anarchy. Past water users' organizations were little more than appendages of the central bureaucracy designed to collect assessments. Water anarchy is not a culturally predetermined condition. On the Navajo systems it is the result of fifty years of institutional mismanagement, which has created irrigation systems that are currently unmanageable.

Expending resources on education, extension, or exotic crops will have little impact if water control is lacking. Therefore, increasing farm performance on these systems requires increasing the farmers' physical and organizational control over the systems' water resources.

NOTES

1. Tom Sasaki, *Fruitland, New Mexico: A Navajo Community in Transition* (Ithaca, N.Y.: Cornell University Press, 1960).

2. Sam Bingham, "Navajo Farming" (Logan: Utah State University, 1979, unpublished manuscript).

3. Jerry Eckert, "Employment and Incomes in the Navajo Nation: 1987–1988 Estimates and Historical Trends" (Fort Collins: Colorado State University, 1989, unpublished manuscript); Clyde Kluckhohn, *The Navajo* (New York: Doubleday and Company, 1960).

4. Walter Coward, "Irrigation Development: Institutional and Organizational Issues" in *Irrigation and Agricultural Development in Asia: Perspectives from the Social Sciences,* ed. W. Coward (Ithaca, N.Y.: Cornell University Press, 1980), pp. 15–27.

5. David Freeman, *Notes on Water Users' Associations* (Fort Collins: Colorado State University, Colorado Institute of Irrigation Management, 1988).

6. Steve Jones, *Inventory of Navajo Indian Irrigation Projects* (Flagstaff, Ariz.: U.S. Department of the Interior, Soil Conservation Service, 1985).

7. Gilbert Levine, *The Challenge of Rehabilitation and Betterment* (Washington, D.C.: International Conference on Irrigation System Rehabilitation, 1987).

8. Jones, *Inventory of Navajo Indian Irrigation Projects.*

9. J. A. Krug, *The Navajo: A Long Range Program for Navajo Rehabilitation* (Washington, D.C.: U.S. Department of the Interior, Bureau of Indian Affairs, 1948).

10. Robert Lansford, *Costs and Returns for Producing Selected Irrigated Crops on Farms in San Juan County* (Las Cruces: New Mexico State University, 1981).

11. Ibid.

14

WATER TRANSFERS, PAPER RIGHTS, AND THE TRUCKEE-CARSON SETTLEMENT

David Yardas

High in the Sierra Nevada of California, the Truckee and Carson rivers begin their long eastward journey into Nevada's evaporative lakes and playas in the western Great Basin. The combined runoff from these rivers is normally sufficient to meet a total of about 750,000 acre-feet of decreed diversion demands, more than three-fourths of those for agricultural purposes.[1] Under current conditions, nondiverted runoff, usable spills, and conveyance and irrigation returns average less than 500,000 acre-feet. Such residuals serve as the predominant source of inflow to Pyramid Lake, a unique high-desert lake at the terminus of the Truckee River, and to the Lahontan Valley wetlands (a critical inland link in the Pacific Flyway at the end of the Carson River). Combined resource needs exceed available supplies by an average of 50,000–150,000 acre-feet.[2]

Nearly two-thirds of the agricultural water demands in the two basins involve the irrigation of about 60,000 acres of alfalfa, grains, and pasture at the Newlands Irrigation Project. Since 1905, transbasin diversions from the Truckee River to the Carson River's Lahontan Reservoir have helped to satisfy this project's irrigation demands. For decades, year-round Truckee River diversions also helped to sustain more than 44,000 acres of Carson basin wetlands, supported in part by freshwater inflows from single-purpose wintertime hydropower releases at Lahontan Dam.

Unfortunately, such year-round sustenance did not come without cost. Diversion of more than half of the Truckee's flow led to the permanent loss of wetlands at the now-vanished Winnemucca Lake National Wildlife Refuge adjacent to Pyramid Lake. Extinction of the lake's indigenous Lahontan cutthroat trout—

once a world-renowned trophy fish—followed, as did the near-extinction of the cui-ui, an endemic fish species found nowhere else in the world.[3]

By the mid 1960s, these and other losses prompted a series of lawsuits by the Pyramid Lake Paiute Tribe, whose ancestral home and present-day reservation entirely surround the lake. Under the predominant authority of the federal Endangered Species Act, a series of administrative and court-imposed regulatory actions has since reduced diversions from the Truckee River by eliminating wintertime hydropower releases, modifying diversion criteria, and improving the project's efficiency in the conveyance and distribution of irrigation supplies. The culmination of these efforts—known as the final Operating Criteria and Procedures (OCAP) for the Newlands Project—is expected to reduce the quantity and timing of diversions from the Truckee River to levels that "are not likely to jeopardize the continued existence of the cui-ui."[4]

Under the OCAP, however, the lake's recapture of Truckee River water comes largely at the expense of the wetlands. Among other factors, the near-elimination of freshwater inflows is expected to result in the permanent loss of up to 18,000 acres of wetland habitat, including the basins' second national wildlife refuge at Fallon.[5] The remaining "primary" Lahontan Valley wetlands, including the Stillwater National Wildlife Refuge and the Carson Lake Wildlife Management Area, are thus increasingly dependent on a meager soup of irrigation seepage and drainage that has contributed to a spate of disease outbreaks and bird die-offs in recent years and all but disappears during years of drought.

What has been characterized as a "painful environmental choice" between the wetlands and the lake is further complicated by the interests of the Fallon Paiute-Shoshone Tribes, whose culture, homeland, and present-day reservation are intimately linked to the Stillwater marsh and whose irrigated lands depend upon the delivery of Newlands Project water.[6]

Water Rights Acquisitions

Voluntary water rights acquisitions have become a leading alternative in efforts to avoid alleged trade-offs between Pyramid Lake and the Lahontan Valley wetlands. Such acquisitions, financed through a combination of federal, state, and private-sector funds, provide a means of increasing wetlands inflows, reducing project demands, and protecting both the Pyramid Lake ecosystem and the endangered cui-ui against increased diversions from the Truckee River. Water rights purchases also allow for the selective fallowing of lands that pose drainage problems, thus reducing the inflow of potentially toxic constituents to the marsh. Acquisitions can also help Newlands Project farmers (the nominal owners of project water rights) and the Truckee-Carson Irrigation District (TCID, the manager and fiscal agent of the Newlands Project under contract with the United States) to meet diversion and efficiency limits imposed by the OCAP.

During the past five years, a "water rights marketplace" for the Lahontan Valley wetlands has evolved from concept to reality. As early as 1988, the approach gained the qualified support of the TCID board due to the tireless advocacy of groups such as the Nevada Waterfowl Association and the Lahontan Valley Wetlands Coalition.[7] The Nature Conservancy has also played a major role, working with the U.S. Fish and Wildlife Service and the Nevada Department of Wildlife to acquire and transfer more than 11,000 acre-feet per year of perpetual irrigation rights to the Lahontan Valley wetlands. Five separate congressional appropriations and a state-sponsored parks and wildlife initiative have together provided nearly $14 million in acquisition capital since 1988.[8] Perhaps most important, the early success of the acquisition program helped to secure enactment of Public Law 101-618 in 1990, the Fallon Paiute–Shoshone and Truckee-Carson–Pyramid Lake water rights settlement acts, as discussed in more detail below.[9]

Water rights acquisitions will continue to play a fundamentally important role in meeting the long-term needs of the Lahontan Valley wetlands and Pyramid Lake alike. However, the specter of acquisitions involving "inactive" water rights—decreed entitlements that have never been perfected or have gone unused for extended periods of time—has threatened to perpetuate the allegedly "painful choice" first revealed under the OCAP. The manner in which this issue has been resolved offers hope for the successful resolution of many other issues that surround the development and implementation of viable, long-term, acquisition programs for the Lahontan Valley wetlands and Pyramid Lake alike.

Inactive Water Rights

Inactive water rights account for nearly a quarter of the decreed irrigation total in the lower reaches of the Truckee and Carson basins. More than half of these rights—almost 50,000 acre-feet—are appurtenant to lands within the Newlands Project. Because diversions from the Truckee under the OCAP are undertaken to supplement Carson River runoff, unused Newlands Project entitlements act as unexercised claims on Truckee River flows. The activation of inactive Newlands Project rights through purchase and transfer to the Lahontan Valley wetlands will therefore result in increased Truckee River diversions, perpetuating the very trade-offs that acquisitions were meant to resolve.

In spite of such impacts, inactive water rights have been viewed by many as a preferred source of acquired wetlands entitlements. In April of 1988, for example, the Nevada Department of Wildlife applied to the Nevada state engineer for transfer to the Stillwater National Wildlife Refuge of approximately 100 acre-feet per year of undisputedly inactive Newlands Project water rights. The actions of the Department of Wildlife were the result of years of frustrated efforts to gain "standing" under the OCAP and were designed primarily to bring wetland impacts into clear legal focus. But the department's applications were immediately protested by the Pyramid Lake tribe, and an approach that offered hope in the region's protracted water wars suddenly looked like just another source of trouble and conflict.[10]

In response to the Pyramid Lake tribe's protest of the Department of Wildlife transfers, the U.S. Department of the Interior concluded initially that "any potential increased demands on Truckee River water arising from these transfers would not pose a significant new effect to the cui-ui."[11] But the real issue was not the consequence of any single transfer involving inactive water rights, but the cumulative impact of many such transfers. If water rights acquisitions for the Lahontan Valley wetlands were to succeed in helping to resolve the basin's environmental conflicts, a standard of acceptability beyond the nominal legality or significance of any individual transfer would have to be found. What follows is a brief review of the issues that surrounded the development of such a standard.

Issues and Conflicts

Forfeiture and Abandonment

Nevada water law states that an appropriated right to use water "shall be deemed as having been abandoned" following any period of five successive years of nonuse.[12] Although explicit, this standard may not apply to the bulk of the rights in question. First, the majority of the basins' appropriated surface water rights (including those of the Newlands Project) enjoy priorities that predate the applicable statutory provisions of Nevada water law (1913). These rights may be excused from the statutory presumption of abandonment (i.e., forfeiture) through nonuse, in which case their loss would require a showing of common law abandonment with intent. That the owners of unused Newlands Project entitlements continue to make annual operations and maintenance (O&M) payments to TCID would seem to argue against such intentions. However, a recent decision by the federal Court of Appeals for the Ninth Circuit suggests that what matters with respect to applicability of the 1913 forfeiture statute may not be the Newlands Project's decreed, inchoate priority of 1902, but instead the year in which individual water rights were first put to use to irrigate the parcel specified in the original water right application or contract (in many cases substantially later than 1913).[13]

Also at issue is the alleged lack of perfection of at least certain inactive Newlands Project rights, which would be barred from transfer under existing state law. Finally, a large number of in-project transfers involving inactive water rights have been undertaken to "legitimize" several thousand acres of land that have long been irrigated without water rights. Deliveries to these now-contested parcels were historically justified on the basis of the "inchoate" nature of project water rights and a general lack of concern over the specific appurtenance of any particular water right. All of these issues are the subject of ongoing litigation.[14]

Acquisition-oriented activity restrictions could also affect upstream, urban interests. In the Reno-Sparks (Truckee Meadows) area, for example, acquired irrigation rights have been a major component of increased urban-sector water supplies for more than a decade and will continue in that role over the next decade and beyond.[15] But because more than half of the remaining Truckee Meadows irrigation entitlements are currently inactive, their purchase and exercise will inevitably result in some reduction in downstream flows. Unlike Newlands Project rights, however, there is apparently little question as to the "perfection" of each decreed Truckee Meadows irrigation right; moreover, all enjoy priorities senior to 1913 and are thus not subject to forfeiture. In any case, concerns over the potential forfeiture of unused groundwater rights (and an officially stated preference for the acquisition of inactive surface water rights, to avoid the fallowing of irrigated lands) have also been expressed in the upper Carson basin.[16]

Tribal Entitlements

Under the *Winters* decision, water rights sufficient to fulfill the "present and future" purposes of Indian and other federal reservations were reserved by implication when the reservations were created.[17] Although these rights conform with appropriated rights in the assignment of priorities, they differ in at least one important respect: they are subject neither to abandonment nor to forfeiture as a consequence of nonuse. Such distinctions are important, both legally and emotionally, in efforts to resolve questions over water rights activity and transferability throughout the basins.

Pyramid Lake Paiute / For the Pyramid Lake Paiute Tribe, an annual total of approximately 24,000 acre-feet of decreed irrigation rights was first asserted by the United States in 1913. No independent claims were made for the lake or its fishery, however, which for thousands of years have been the focus of tribal sustenance and culture.[18] Subsequent efforts to assert such rights—to recognize something other than irrigated agriculture as a basis for the tribe's water claims—were finally rejected by the U.S. Supreme Court in 1983.[19] Recent attempts to convert the tribe's unused irrigation rights into dual-purpose irrigation/fishery entitlements were also opposed by the state of Nevada and TCID.[20] At present, diversions at Derby Dam are constrained, as needed, to meet 8,000–15,000 acre-feet of active on-reservation irrigation demands; anywhere from 15,000 to 22,000 acre-feet of decreed irrigation rights remain unused.

DAVID YARDAS

Fallon Paiute-Shoshone / The Fallon Paiute-Shoshone Tribes assert that the full contours of their water rights have never been adjudicated.[21] In 1906, most of the 31,360 acres of allotted Indian lands in and around the once-bountiful marshes at Stillwater and Carson Lake were exchanged, by agreement with the United States, for what eventually amounted to 5,400 acres of land with "paid-in-full" Newlands Project irrigation rights—nearly 20,000 acre-feet in all.[22] No provision was made for the needs of adjacent or on-reservation wetlands, however, and a variety of soil and drainage problems with the original exchange lands precluded cultivation of even half of the tribes' water-righted acreage. In 1978, Congress recognized its unfulfilled exchange obligations in Public Law 95-337, adding 2,420 acres to the Fallon Reservation and directing the secretary of the interior to make as his first priority the improvement of such lands and irrigation works as would be necessary to deliver sufficient water to irrigate the practicably irrigable acres included therein.

To date, the major investment undertaken pursuant to Public Law 95-337—a deep cross-reservation ditch known as the T-J Drain—contributes inflows to the adjacent Stillwater marsh that have been classified as "acutely toxic" in laboratory bioassay analyses.[23] Utilization of the Fallon tribes' inactive irrigation rights as contemplated under Public Law 95-337 could also result in an annual increase in Truckee River diversions of more than 20,000 acre-feet—a result once characterized by the U.S. Bureau of Indian Affairs as a "distasteful" necessity (in terms of impacts on Pyramid Lake) if the Fallon tribes' claims were to be finally resolved.[24] One way or another, the legal and equitable distinctions between appropriated and tribal rights makes little difference in terms of the impacts on the Truckee River that are associated with their potential activation.

Toward Resolution

In light of its responsibilities at both ends of the Truckee and Carson rivers, the U.S. Fish and Wildlife Service sought to temper the Department of the Interior's initial response to the transfers requested by the Nevada Department of Wildlife and initiated multiparty discussions toward the development of an "activity" or "eligibility" standard for acquisition and transfer of Newlands Project water rights. Initial commitments to a qualitative acquisition standard (e.g., limiting transfers of acquired water rights to those that were "currently active" or "fully active") provided an important starting point but proved of little help in verifying the activity status of any particular water right acquired or offered for sale. For those purposes, a more precise quantitative definition was needed. Early discussions focused on the use of recorded irrigation deliveries over a recent five-year period (1983–1987) to provide a verifiable standard consistent with the nonuse period contained in Nevada's forfeiture statute, and to accommodate the reality of year-to-year changes in the activity status of individual parcels due to crop rotations, intermittent land fallowing, and other factors. But it soon became apparent that delivery-based criteria would not suffice because irrigation delivery records were not maintained at the required level of detail or accuracy.

Fortunately, the U.S. Bureau of Reclamation had made considerable progress in developing a geographic information system (GIS) for the Newlands Project, primarily for the purpose of determining legally irrigated acreage under the OCAP.[25] The GIS data base soon provided the platform for creation of a "provisional" water rights eligibility map depicting project lands that were irrigated and water-righted in one or more years between 1984 and 1989, but excluding irrigated lands involving contested water rights, groundwater rights, and, by request, water rights appurtenant to lands within the Fallon Indian Reservation. Ultimately, the U.S. Fish and Wildlife Service and the Nevada Department of Wildlife agreed to limit the transfer of acquired rights to just under 3.0 acre-feet per acre (the assumed annual rate of net consumptive use) for those lands identified on the provisional eligibility map. The Pyramid Lake tribe agreed not to protest any such transfer, and the purchase program was finally back on track.

The Truckee-Carson Settlement

The GIS-based eligibility map and associated transfer agreements helped pave the way for enactment of the Truckee-Carson settlement act by demonstrating that voluntary acquisitions could, in fact, be structured to avoid trade-offs between Pyramid Lake and the Lahontan Valley wetlands. Indeed, section 206 of the act, which contemplates a large-scale water rights purchase program as the core mechanism for restoring the Lahontan Valley wetlands, prescribes the development of certain "acquisition, selection, transfer, and application criteria" by the secretary of the interior to avoid the transfer of inactive rights, reflecting the existing GIS-based maps and agreements "in procedure, substance, and spirit."[26] A comparable approach was taken in section 207(c), which requires that water rights acquired to benefit the Pyramid Lake fishery "must satisfy eligibility criteria adopted by the Secretary."

Successful resolution of the activity issue also provided a model for resolving potentially conflicting federal trust responsibilities toward the Pyramid Lake and Fallon tribes. In particular, Title I of the act provides for settlement of the Fallon tribes' water rights claims through creation of a $43 million settlement fund (section 102) that was established in part to provide for acquisition of "active Newlands Reclamation Project water rights" (section 103). Like the asserted "painful choice" between Pyramid Lake and the Lahontan Valley wetlands, the approach adopted by the Fallon tribes ensured that long-standing federal commitments could be fulfilled without the "distasteful" increase in Truckee River diversions previously considered necessary by the Bureau of Indian Affairs. Indeed, the willingness and ability of both tribes to deal creatively with this long-festering tension proved critical to the final passage of the settlement act itself.

Lingering Concerns

Acquisition-oriented activity limitations will do little to resolve the ultimate status of inactive project rights, including their potential activation by other means. These uncertainties might be resolved in part through a program of "conditional" water rights purchases, under which the owners of inactive rights would be partially compensated for prior O&M payments to TCID in exchange for the express abandonment of the inactive rights. (The income stability of TCID would also need to be secured under any such plan.) As noted above, urban or municipal and industrial (M&I) purchases of inactive water rights pose related concerns, though agreements developed under the Truckee-Carson settlement (section 205) ensure that at least part of any such purchase will benefit the Pyramid Lake fishery through the automatic conversion of M&I storage credits to fishery credits during non-drought years (and through associated payments for the use of federal reservoirs, which will help to finance the purchase of environmental water rights). Ideally, the use of federal facilities for M&I credits and water-bank operations involving Newlands Project rights should be conditioned upon the kind of eligibility criteria outlined above, or upon comparable assurances of environmental protection and benefit.

At Pyramid Lake, unused irrigation rights continue to represent the tribe's single quantified claim to Truckee River water and will undoubtedly engender controversy should they be "activated" for any purpose other than cui-ui recovery. But realizing the full economic potential of their decreed water rights is no less important to the tribe than is the recovery of the Pyramid Lake ecosystem. With luck, a combination of river management changes, riparian habitat restoration efforts, and market-based water acquisitions will prove sufficient to meet both of these important objectives.

Conclusions

Environmental and tribal water problems in the Truckee and Carson river basins involve a number of common themes. The needs of Pyramid Lake were entirely ignored when irrigation claims were first asserted for the Pyramid Lake tribe, whose decreed entitlements amount to but a fraction of the lake's total need. Federal reclamation efforts also ignored the needs of the Lahontan Valley wetlands, while unfulfilled promises reduced the rights of the Fallon tribes by more than a factor of ten. Mandates and authorities under the Truckee-Carson settlement seek to redress these wrongs through combined programs of water rights acquisitions, increased efficiency, improved water management, and habitat restoration that require neither "painful" nor "distasteful" choices. A focus on active water rights remains fundamental to the long-term success of those efforts.

NOTES

The original work supporting this paper was made possible by a grant from the Ford Foundation to the Environmental Defense Fund's Rural Economy and Environment Program.

1. Throughout this chapter, hydrologic totals are given as long-term annual averages; water rights totals are given as perpetual annual entitlements.

2. Kennedy/Jenks/Chilton, Inc., *Carson River Management Program*. Prepared for the Carson Water Subconservancy District, Minden, Nevada, 1988. On file with the Carson Water Subconservancy District. See also U.S. District Court, Nevada, *Annual Diversion Report 1987* (Reno, Nev.: Federal Watermaster's Office, 1988).

3. U.S. Department of the Interior, *Newlands Project, Nevada-California, Operating Criteria and Procedures, Record of Decision* (Washington, D.C.: U.S. Department of the Interior, Office of the Secretary, 1988); Nevada Board of Wildlife Commissioners, "Position Statement: Lahontan Valley Wetlands" (1989). On file with the Nevada Department of Wildlife, Reno.

4. U.S. Department of the Interior, *Newlands Project Operating Criteria and Procedures* (Sacramento, Calif.: U.S. Department of the Interior, Bureau of Reclamation, 1987).

5. U.S. Department of the Interior, "Newlands Project Operating Criteria and Procedures, Record of Decision, Wetland Analysis," Memorandum Report (Reno, Nev.: U.S. Department of the Interior, Fish and Wildlife Service, 1988). On file with the U.S. Fish and Wildlife Service, Reno.

6. Lyndsey Gruson, "Painful Environmental Choice: Save a Fish or Preserve a Wetland?" *New York Times,* April 26, 1988; Inter-Tribal Council of Nevada, *Numa: A Northern Paiute History* (Salt Lake City: University of Utah Printing Service, 1976).

7. Truckee-Carson Irrigation District, "Position Statement Regarding the Purchase/Transfer of Newlands Project Water Right Lahontan Valley Wetlands" (1988). On file with the Truckee-Carson Irrigation District, Reno, Nevada.

8. U.S. Department of the Interior, *Environmental Assessment: Acquisition of Water Rights for Stillwater National Wildlife Refuge, Fiscal Years 1991–1993* (Portland, Oreg.: U.S. Department of the Interior, Fish and Wildlife Service, Region 1, 1991).

9. State of Nevada, S.B. 189, March 14, 1989; P.L. 101-618, the Fallon Paiute Shoshone Indian Tribes Water Rights Settlement Act of 1990 (Title I) and the Truckee-Carson–Pyramid Lake Water Rights Settlement Act (Title II), 104 Stat. 3289, November 16, 1990. For a detailed description, see David Yardas, "Restoring Endangered

Ecosystems: The Truckee-Carson Water Rights Settlement," *Resource Law Notes,* January 1992. (Newsletter published in Boulder by the University of Colorado School of Law.)

10. Pyramid Lake Paiute Tribe of Indians, "Protest to the Nevada State Engineer in the Matter of Applications 52039 and 52040 filed by the Nevada Department of Wildlife" (1988). On file with the Nevada State Engineer, Carson City.

11. U.S. Department of the Interior, "Letter to the Attorney for the Pyramid Lake Paiute Tribe of Indians" (Washington, D.C.: U.S. Department of the Interior, Fish and Wildlife Service, July 28, 1988). On file with the Environmental Defense Fund, Oakland, Calif.

12. Nevada Department of Conservation and Natural Resources, *Nevada Water Laws* (1982).

13. *U.S. v. Alpine,* Order and Opinion, Ninth Circuit Court of Appeals No. 90-16460, May 26, 1992.

14. *U.S. v. Alpine,* Brief of Appellant on Appeal from the United States District Court, Nevada, 1987; *U.S. v. Alpine Land and Reservoir Company et al.,* Brief of Respondents on Appeal from the United States District Court, Nevada, Nos. 87-1746 and 87-1747, 1987; *U.S. v. Alpine,* Order and Opinion, Ninth Circuit Court of Appeals No. 90-16460, May 26, 1992.

15. Westpac Utilities, *Water Resources Plan 1988–2008* (Reno, Nev.: Westpac Utilities, 1989). On file with Sierra Pacific Power Company, Reno.

16. Carson Water Subconservancy District, letter to Senator Harry Reid re "Draft bill to authorize water rights purchases for wildlife areas in Nevada," December 7, 1988. On file with the Environmental Defense Fund, Oakland, Calif. See also Kennedy/Jenks/Chilton, *Carson River Management Program.*

17. John A. Folk-Williams, *What Indian Water Means to the West* (Santa Fe, N.M.: Western Network, 1982).

18. Catherine S. Fowler and Sven Liljebland, "Northern Paiute," in *Great Basin,* ed. W. L. D'Azevedo, vol. 11 of *Handbook of North American Indians,* ed. W. C. Sturtevant (Washington, D.C.: Smithsonian Institution, 1986), pp. 435–65.

19. *Nevada v. United States et al.,* 103 S.Ct. 2906 (1983).

20. Nevada Office of the Attorney General, "Memorandum in Support of Response to Petition for Change in Place and Purpose of Use: *U.S. v. Orr Water Ditch Company et al.,* in Equity No. A-3" (1979); Truckee-Carson Irrigation District, "Answer in Opposition to Petition for Change in Place and Purpose of Use: *U.S. v. Orr Water Ditch Company et al.,* in Equity No. A-3" (1979).

21. Fallon Paiute-Shoshone Tribes, "Objections to Final OCAP and Preliminary Supporting Legal Contentions: *Pyramid Lake Tribe v. Hodel* No. CV-R-85-197 BRT" (1988).

22. University of Nevada–Reno, *Economic Evaluation of Potential Benefits of Public Law 95-337 to the Fallon Indian Reservation* (Reno: University of Nevada, Department of Agricultural Economics).

23. S. E. Finger, S. J. Olson, and A. C. Livingstone, *On-Site Toxicity of Irrigation Drainwater from Stillwater* (Columbia, Md.: U.S. Fish and Wildlife Service, 1989).

24. U.S. Department of the Interior, "Water Problems: Fallon Indian Reservation," Bureau of Indian Affairs Memorandum, Phoenix Area Office (October 27, 1970). On file with the Environmental Defense Fund, Oakland, Calif.

25. David W. Eckhardt, James P. Verdin, and Gordon R. Lyford, "Automated Update of an Irrigated Lands GIS Using SPOT HRV Imagery," *Photogrammetric Engineering and Remote Sensing* 56, no. 11 (1990).

26. Senate Select Committee on Indian Affairs, *Providing for the Settlement of Water Rights Claims of the Fallon Paiute-Shoshone Indian Tribes, and for Other Purposes,* 101st Cong., 2d sess., October 25, 1990, S.Rept. 101-555, p. 25.

PART V   REFLECTIONS

15

THE BIG HORNS OF A DILEMMA

Teno Roncalio

On June 26, 1989, the United States Supreme Court affirmed, by a tie vote, the Wyoming Supreme Court judgment in the adjudication of Indian water rights in the Big Horn basin. In this case, *Wyoming v. United States,* the high court had denied review of the *Winters* doctrine of federal water rights and heard argument only on the quantification formula of practicably irrigable acreage (PIA), first approved in 1963 in *Arizona v. California.* An equally divided Court decision has no value in establishing a precedent, but it has full force and effect in Wyoming. Nevertheless, a realistic national assessment suggests that the PIA concept as it applies to other reservations with differing soil qualities, agricultural economics, terrain, and purposes of establishment, may soon again be under attack by non-Indian water entities of other western states.

In January of 1977—just two days after Wyoming lawmakers enacted special enabling legislation—the state of Wyoming brought suit against the tribes of the only Indian reservation in the state and (since it was a general adjudication) against some 20,000 water rights holders who irrigate over 653,000 acres of ceded and other privately owned land on, near, or around the Wind River Indian Reservation and other areas of the Big Horn basin.

In April of 1989 the Indian water rights portion of this massive lawsuit was argued before the United States Supreme Court, with Wyoming bringing suit against the United States in an appeal from a judgment of the Wyoming Supreme Court. Nine western states, and a host of other water entities, filed *amicus* briefs supporting the Wyoming effort, a cause celebre to many water users in the West.

Why? What interest did this coalition have in a water squabble between the leaders of Wyoming's Indian reservation and nearby irrigators? This chapter will reflect on the reason, in as few words as possible for one who served as special master and whose recommended decree—though fine-tuned by three reviewing courts—was still the basic judgment under attack by so many divergent groups in the West's never-ending war for water.

The Wind River begins in the high country of northwestern Wyoming, meanders southeasterly through the Wind River Indian Reservation, thence to the environs of Riverton, in central Wyoming, where it begins a sweeping northerly course. As it leaves the geologically famous Wind River Canyon north of Boysen Reservoir through a calm stretch known as the Wedding of the Waters, it is no longer the Wind River. It has become the Big Horn, and as the Big Horn River it continues northward into Montana.

In 1868, twenty-one years before Wyoming statehood, the United States agreed to "cede and grant" 3,054,000 acres to the Shoshone and other tribes for a permanent homeland. In exchange the Shoshone agreed to relinquish all title, claims, or rights to 44,672,000 acres of land in what are now the states of Wyoming, Colorado, and Utah. In 1878 the Northern Arapaho were permanently settled by the United States on the reservation, and it has since been a homeland for both tribes.

Subsequently, the tribes ceded back to the United States large areas of land that are now the environs of Lander, Riverton, and Thermopolis, Wyoming, and received modest cash payments. Conversion to an agricultural life proved to be difficult, and by the turn of the century the Indians were dependent upon the federal government for food, clothing, and shelter. In 1905 the tribes again ceded lands, this time a huge area, essentially the northern two-thirds of what remained of their land. This was the famed 1905 Act, which threw the reservation open to settlers. But unlike earlier cessions, the federal government acted only as an agent and conveyed to the tribes whatever was received for the sale of land. Sales were slow and were discontinued altogether in 1934.

Over the decades, the United States built projects for the settlers, while little was spent for Indian irrigation. An example of this is the Riverton Reclamation Project, largely non-Indian, which to date has received $70 million of federal funding during the same period that $4.4 million was spent on Indian systems.

Except for two landmark United States Supreme Court decisions, this historic pattern might well have survived to the present. Each set of citizens would have enjoyed state-issued water rights, most of which carried a 1905 priority date for the tribes and a 1906 date for settlers, the year the land sales began. The famed *Winters* case of 1908, however, said simply that Congress, when it created an Indian reservation in Montana, intended to grant a water right at that time also, since it was untenable that Congress intended to leave Indians without the water needed to sustain life, particularly in the arid West. In Wyoming, first in time is first in right, and the 1868 priority date became a beacon to Indians.

In 1963 in an equally significant case now referred to as *Arizona I* (*Arizona v. California*), the Supreme Court accepted the decree of Special Master Simon Rifkind, which held that the only fair and feasible way to determine the measure of an Indian reservation water right was to determine its practicably irrigable acreage. This was precisely what was under attack in Wyoming's 1989 appeal to the Supreme Court.

I faced this reality when appointed special master to the Big Horn case in 1979. It was apparent that *Winters* was very much the law of the land. It had survived several appeals, though it was the subject of many law review articles pointing up the difficulty of its effect on western states. Nor was it possible to escape the force of *Arizona I,* since it also had been sustained. While it applied to Colorado River drainage areas, I could see no difference in its applicability to the headwaters of the Missouri River, particularly the Wind River.

The burdens of trial preparation—the discovery proceedings and resulting mounds of depositions, the scientific inquiry of acreage to be proven arable, thence irrigable, and finally practicably irrigable with economic tests of costs and benefits—consumed the first year of effort. There was total agreement with Master Rifkind who observed in his 1963 report that "discovery proceeds today without serious regulation, thus turning many areas of the law into sporting matches and endurance contests."

This contest produced a trial nearly two years in length, a transcript of over 15,000 pages, over 2,300 exhibits admitted into evidence, and a 450-page report. To that one can sadly observe that a dozen more years have passed, with a platoon of lawyers at work, committed to either sustaining or destroying its result. The state of Wyoming, as of a recent count, has spent nearly $9 million to bring and to maintain this action. The United States was charged with paying half the trial costs, about $325,000. To include the costs of attorneys of the Departments of Justice and the Interior, of the tribes, and of many private parties, plus attorneys and consultants added to the state payroll at work on the case, would surely run the total costs of litigation to well over $20 million. Another ordeal by litigation has evolved (as of 1993, this is still ongoing), and none who were or are now its key players can be proud of that. Even before the affirmance, many Wyoming lawmakers and officials regretted the day the lawsuit was filed.

The Zeal

Richard A. Simms is an eminent attorney for counties, municipalities, and twenty-two community acequias (ditch companies) in New Mexico. The interest of his clients in this case stems from being "similarly situated" with regard to federal reserved water rights of the Mescalero Apache Tribe. His summary of argument in the New Mexico *amicus* brief to the United States Supreme Court was that the long-established cost-benefit ratio, used to aid courts in determining feasibility, becomes contrived when used as an advocacy tool.

Here is a taste of his advocacy talent, in which contrivance is hardly absent: "Typically, the United States manufactures idealized projects and skews each of the elements of the analysis in order to arrive at a favorable cost-benefit ratio." He said it was "common knowledge that these projects will never be constructed" and that "they represent nothing more than a pretext to create large paper water rights as a form of wealth," all of which "belies any . . . need for water to satisfy the purposes for which an agricultural reservation was withdrawn from the public domain."

Michael D. White is a well-known litigator and was counsel of record for Wyoming. He was also fierce in his brief, in which he said the special master knew he was about to commit an injustice to certain non-Indian water users but did so anyway. "Hardship" might have been a more accurate term. White had run-ins with several lawyers but received high marks from associates and adversaries. As lead attorneys in the trial, he and his colleagues deserve much credit for a totally competent, difficult, and effective presentation of every conceivable ground supporting Wyoming's case.

But pushing became shoving on appeal. His argument that Indians enjoyed "an infusion of massive amounts of congressionally mandated expenditures for construction of water projects" brought a jolting response from the defending attorneys, who identified his statement in their reply briefs as "an unsupported, and indeed shameful" bit of advocacy talent. The $4.4 million mentioned above was cited in contrast to over $70 million spent for one of several largely non-Indian irrigation and reclamation projects.

Others riveted to this approach included John B. Weldon, Jr., counsel of record for the Salt River Project. In Arizona's *amicus* brief, he faulted PIA as an inappropriate standard of quantification, stressed that agriculture does little for general employment, and used a puzzling quote that 400 to 12,000 nonagricultural workers could be supported by the amount of water needed to generate one agricultural job. And six states signed on with Idaho in *amicus* briefs urging the Court to consider that "clarification of the implied reserve water right quantification would actually reduce conflicts between Indian and non-Indian." By this rationale, so would conquest.

If these examples of advocacy had prevailed, and the Supreme Court had reversed the Big Horn judgment, overturned the future PIA formula, and limited reservation water only to current volumes and uses, then deeply disturbing questions would have begotten a new round of turbulence and litigation. Among these questions are the following:

1. If the cost-benefit ratio was valid in establishing irrigation and reclamation projects in the West—allowing great population settlements and productivity—why should it now fail as a measure to mete out justice to Indians?
2. We are in a new age in water management, transfers, leasing, and marketing. Are Indians now to be stripped of a property right because future PIA calculations are not being developed immediately, and thus excluded from this economic activity of the new West?
3. For the last three decades, future PIA calculations have been the law of the land and a part of the inventory of tribal assets. Is not their "taking" now in fact a "condemnation" or a confiscation of property without due process of law?

The PIA concept of *Arizona I* underwent an unprecedented attack in the Wyoming Supreme Court. Most critics sought outright reversal; none called for a pragmatic limitation to its use, such as Wyoming Justice Richard V. Thomas suggested in his detailed dissent. He would apply the PIA measure only to future acreage that did not require taxpayer funding to be irrigated. Ultimately, the nation's high court affirmed the Wyoming court's support for PIA. The irony remains, however. Wyoming—whose motto is the Equality State—spent millions of dollars and twelve years to try to prove how unequally it could treat some of its citizens. We have not heard the last of PIA tests in the courts of our land.

Meanwhile, because of problems in distribution management and the need for structural improvements in delivery systems, the tribes and Wyoming entered into an agreement. Indians would abstain from exercising their new priority date, and in return, the state agreed to spend $3.3 million for improvements to the distribution system on which both Indians and non-Indians relied. But the plan was sadly short-lived. After one growing season, matters again became hostile, with virtually no communication between the parties.

The tribes announced that they were changing the use of a portion of their agricultural reserved water right to in-stream flows to protect their fisheries and that they were substituting their own tribal water agency for the State Engineer's Office as administrator of both reserved-right and state-permitted water on the reservation. Wyoming returned to the courts seeking to overturn this latest action, and a district court held for the tribes. Wyoming then appealed, and on June 5, 1992, the Wyoming Supreme Court reversed and found generally for the state on both issues. Has the litigation ended? Who knows. How long are the big horns of this dilemma!

The Future

Given the new age of water matters in the new West, the goal for Indians and for other water rights holders will be to wring the last possible dollar from every drop of water at their disposal—or, as David Getches more formally observed in *Water and the American West,* to get "optimum beneficial use" for their water, a task that "challenges the vision and the will of everyone concerned with western water law and policy." In the new West, will Upper Basin states soon exchange for cash a portion of their unutilized Colorado River Compact flows to interests in Nevada or Arizona or California? Will the Las Vegas plan to purchase water from shale oil firms on Colorado's Western Slope become a reality? Will Indians obtain the right to lease or sell their water for use off their reservations? Will massive desalination plants in Baja and southern California come on line to relieve the growing dependency on imported water?

Will the polarization of the past half-century give way to a new era of accord and understanding? I believe so. Creative solutions to common problems will be found. The potential is limitless, needing only—as has always been the case in the West—the people to match the challenges: a society to match the scenery, as Wallace Stegner expressed it.

16

DEALING WITH THE FEDERAL SOVEREIGN

Michael J. Clinton

In June 1989, the House Interior Appropriation subcommittee marked up a bill that had $32.1 million in it, which is the full funding for the San Luis Rey settlement. The administration fully supported the settlement, and it came through on target—on the budget numbers to which the U.S. Office of Management and Budget, the U.S. Department of Justice, and my clients had agreed. The administration also fully funded the requests for the Colorado Ute and the Salt River settlements. Also, the same day, the House Energy and Water Appropriations subcommittee marked up the construction bill and mandated in their report that the U.S. Bureau of Reclamation begin construction on the Animas–La Plata Project, which is integral to the Colorado Ute settlement.

Fallon

I had a lot of fun in my last job at Interior. I worked for a marvelous lady named Ann McLaughlin. She came to the Interior Department from the Treasury Department to be undersecretary, under William Clark. She brought a philosophy for settlements that I thought was unique and special and conformed to my western roots.

I grew up in Idaho, Montana, and Utah, and worked in Arizona and Nevada and almost all of the western states over my career. I grew up knowing that old saw: "You can mess with my wife and you can mess with my wallet, but don't touch my headgate." Indian water rights disputes in my mind and in Ms. McLaughlin's mind are disputes among neighbors. They are disputes, not with the

United States as a sovereign, nor with the state government in an adjudication process, but instead among people who live next to each other and have not found ways to live with each other.

In the mid 1980s, Ross Swimmer (the assistant secretary for Indian affairs) and I went to Fallon, Nevada. The Fallon Indian Reservation sits right in the middle of the Truckee-Carson Irrigation District, which is the old Newlands Project that some say stole the water from Pyramid Lake. The Fallon tribes used to own the Newlands Project but ceded it away so that they could get a small reservation with water on it. As happens in most deals that we look back on, the tribes never got their part of the deal, the water. In 1978, legislation was passed that committed the United States to go ahead and build that irrigation project on the Fallon Reservation. Again, it has never been built.

We sat down with the Fallon tribes, and we did a brainstorming process with them. We said, "Look: Uncle Sam, through the Congress, is committed to spend $20 or $30 million; you have a block of four or five thousand acres that you're going to irrigate with that money. You also want to build a homeland for your people. You have younger generations that want to come and live at home. The land you want to irrigate is underlain with selenium. That's a chemical we had a little problem with at Kesterson a few years ago. It's causing some problems in the Stillwater Wildlife Refuge. Now, it doesn't make much sense to irrigate that land you have. How about if you looked at this from a different approach? If I were a businessman in your situation, I would look at assets management. I would say, 'Here I have a block of money someone owes me. Here I have a block of land I'd rather put my people on than farm. Here's all of this land from the Newlands Project I used to own, which with that block of money I could buy. I also have some water rights for the land that's not farmed today that maybe I can trade to somebody. I would look at that mix and figure out what is best for my people. What's best for the Fallon Indian tribes? I would take my destiny in my own hands.'"

They were speechless. They said, "The Bureau of Indian Affairs does that for us. We can't do that." Well, three years later, the U.S. Bureau of Indian Affairs representative who has been working with them told me they heard what we said. They finally have decided not to wait for the Bureau of Indian Affairs but to start managing their own destiny. The bureau sent a man to Fallon in 1989 to figure out a way to help them do an assets management approach—to figure out what they want to do with their lives. For me, that's a lot of what settlements are about.

Risk

Some believe that the longer you procrastinate on settlements, the larger the doctrine of Indian reserved water rights will become. We will get precedents that say we can claim water rights for in-stream flows. We will get precedents that say we can transfer from one use to another. We will get precedents that say that permanent tribal homeland is the measure, not just practicably irrigable acreage. The courts historically have treated Indians very positively. We may have a conservative Supreme Court here that goes backwards for a while. But if a tribe is prepared and willing to allow the process to work through litigation, I am fully convinced that they will end up with more water then they could ever settle for today in negotiation.

But there is another side to that. You are not going to settle those litigations very quickly. My good friend John Weldon is not unlike many of his compatriots. I work for a consortium that includes the San Luis Rey tribes—five mission bands—and the cities of Escondido and Vista, California. They agreed to settle in 1988. Paul Engstrand, who is the attorney for Escondido, told me—and I believe him—that although that case has been to the Supreme Court once and the cities lost, Escondido and Vista would still prevent the tribes from obtaining any water from the system for another twenty years.

Other non-Indian attorneys across the western states are likewise pursuing litigation to allow their non-Indian water-user clients to continue the use of Indian water for at least another twenty years. And they can do that. This is something tribes have to look at. Are they willing to defer their gratification, to wait to receive a larger share? They also have to look at their risk. Sometimes they may lose. These are very important questions for tribes to ask as they go into the decision-making process: whether to litigate, to negotiate only on a water rights settlement, or to negotiate on an assets-management settlement as the Fallon people are doing.

Coexistence

I was at a celebration with my clients in San Diego County in December 1988. The San Luis Rey Settlement Act was signed by President Ronald Reagan on November 16. It took the Indian Water Authority only about a month to get a party together, but they did it marvelously. They had it on the La Jolla reservation with the Escondido City Council, the Vista Irrigation District Board of Directors, and all of their families—wives, husbands, children. The five tribal councils and their wives, husbands, and children also came to the celebration. They celebrated something that I'm not sure I understand yet. But it was a celebration, in my mind, of coexistence, that they had finally figured out that they could live together with each other. They could find ways to mutually solve their problems.

The next evening, the Escondido City Council invited the Indian Water Authority Board of Directors to the city council chambers for tea. As part of this litigation, Bob Pelcyger, the tribal attorney, had tied up twenty years ago an escrow fund to buy one of the local water companies. The settlement released that account. None of the other parties would receive its money for about six months, until the escrow cleared. That evening, the mayor of Escondido, to everybody's shock, signed a check for a quarter of a million dollars and handed it to the chairman of the Indian Water Authority Board of Directors. That partnership is growing continually. They are talking about ways to work together and to coexist.

That, I believe, is what this is all about. It is about coexistence. It is about lifestyles, standards of living. It is about getting things that you cannot get through litigation. That is what I found, and Ms. McLaughlin in my estimation was right. These are neighbors who have been fighting among themselves, and it is time that the United States be a facilitator and help them find ways to live with each other.

Washington

The evolution of thinking in Washington trails behind that of the rest of the country. Even so, since 1985, I have seen what I consider to be a radical evolution of thinking on Indian rights and Indian perspectives in Washington. I was fortunate enough to work with the Ad Hoc Group on Indian Reserved Water Rights (composed of western tribes, business, and government interests), which is trying to educate people in Washington as to how the rest of the world thinks they ought to consider Indian water rights settlements. They have run a couple of workshops. Let me walk through some of the things that have happened, from my perspective, over the last few years that demonstrate this change of thinking. The basic philosophical approach has changed radically.

In 1985, people thought that Indian water rights settlements were a fluke and a result only of a congressman named Morris Udall. They thought that the Ak-Chin and Tohono O'odham settlements were anomalies in the system, that there were no others coming. They have now come around to the point of agreeing that negotiated settlements are effective. Sometimes litigation has to go forward to prove a point of law or to decide when people will not look beyond their rights, or where the pie is not big enough to actually cut it in half.

But by and large the people in Congress and the people in the administration came to a conclusion that negotiated settlements are worthwhile and important. This has been long in coming. President Nixon put out a statement in his first term that said that was the way it ought to go; but it does not happen very quickly. I think the acceptance of negotiated settlements is quite a marvelous change of thinking. The settlements that have worked through Congress were very instrumental in doing that.

Another thing that has happened is that people have started thinking about what benefits the parties ought to receive from settlements. Generally people think it ought to be something less than the parties would have obtained through successful litigation if they had sustained their claims, but more than if they had lost that litigation. These are the kinds of changes in thinking that are starting to come through.

Who should bear the burden of the public interest in these settlements? Should it be solely the United States? Do states have a burden and a responsibility here? The thinking is starting to evolve that states do have a responsibility. Their citizens have benefited from the trespass on Indian water over the years. Communities that have had the benefit ought to bear some of the burden of these settlements. The states can also be catalysts for economic development on reservations. From that side they should participate in the settlements. These are also the kinds of changes in thinking that have come out of this dialogue in the last few years.

What is the role of the United States in these settlements? Does the federal government have an obligation to Indian tribes? The general thinking is yes. And that obligation does not involve just litigating and protecting tribal water rights. The government's obligation goes further, to bring Native Americans out of the poverty cycles that they have been in and to bring them up to a standard of living that is comparable to that of their neighbors. This again is an awakening that I think is tremendously important, and it has come through the consideration of the settlements in the last few years.

Congress is very sensitive to the use of federal assets because every federal asset has a constituency. Members of Congress are open to using federal assets, but they warn that if you're going to attach Bureau of Reclamation water, federal power, Forest Service trees, Bureau of Land Management land, or other federal assets and resources, you'd better get that agency into your negotiation and you'd better get their constituency into your negotiations right away. It is a very effective way to help finance, build, and enlarge the pie for water rights settlements. Everybody in Washington concurs with doing it, but you must bring in those interests who have a proprietary stake in the assets.

There is also the issue of the financial responsibility of the parties. Everyone has a risk, and everyone has an opportunity in a settlement. They would not be talking otherwise. Responsibility has to be decided on a case-by-case basis. Maybe a marvelous formula can be discovered, but I doubt it. These settlements are so locally unique and by necessity tailored to the local settings that I am not sure you can ever write a formula for how settlements get financed. However, the basic principle is that those who benefit from the settlement and those who are liable for litigation and have that liability resolved through the settlement ought to pay. Also, the United States has a trust responsibility and a fiduciary role that, as I mentioned earlier, can bring Indians out of the poverty cycles.

Congress has put some limitations on settlements. What should those limitations be? One of the most pernicious is something called "precedent." Every time

Congress acts, if you have enough votes, you create a precedent. If you do not have enough votes, the precedent that you are trying to create (or modify, if it exists already) does not work. That is the simplest way to look at precedent. What was done in the Ak-Chin settlement by fully developing every inch of farmland with cash from the federal treasury is a precedent that I do not think will ever happen again. I think everybody learned that that is not the appropriate way to develop settlements.

Equity

In 1987, during consideration of the Salt River settlement, Assistant Interior Secretary Jim Ziglar said something very important: "These people haven't been treated right." You cannot put that in a formula. The Western Governors' Association has estimated that settlement of the fifty lawsuits underway today may cost the federal treasury between $3 and $5 billion. Congress has been asked to consider making the first installment on that. The Bush administration's 1989–1990 budget had $15 million in it for three settlements. The House Interior Appropriation Committee, playing poker, upped that $15 million to $162 million. Senator Daniel Inouye of Hawaii, who is the second-ranking member of the Senate Appropriation Committee and is also the chairman of the Senate Select Committee on Indian Affairs, has made a public commitment that he will help sustain that kind of settlement money on the Senate side. Congress feels the obligation that Assistant Secretary Ziglar felt. It is fed up with promising settlements and not delivering. Senators Mark Hatfield of Oregon and James McClure of Idaho took Interior Secretary Manuel Lujan apart limb by limb in front of the appropriations subcommittee hearings in 1989 on this very subject. They asked: "Why can't the administration agree that these settlements are a national obligation now to be funded? They need to be funded not from the offsets of the Bureau of Indian Affairs program, which takes the money from other Indians, but from the national programs that will compete against everything else in the country." That is what Congress did in the ensuing budget allocation and appropriations process, by providing full funding for the San Luis Rey, Salt River, and Colorado Ute settlements when the administration had failed to do so. I think we have seen the beauty of the system of our federal government: Congress, when the administration starts to slack off, can pick up the ball and run with it to make sure these settlements come to fruition.

220

17

LESSONS AND DIRECTIONS

Charles F. Wilkinson

The future for new projects in irrigated agriculture is bleak. If new construction is required, irrigation normally can not pay for itself. Tribes ought to take note of that. Tribes are increasingly undertaking comprehensive planning efforts. They are moving beyond generalities about water being precious and valuable and taking a hard look at future irrigation projects.

Economics as well as history tells us in very sharp terms the advantage that water projects of all kinds have had over the past century and a quarter, particularly in not having to pay for the water itself. Unlike nearly every other public resource, water has been handed out freely, in marked contrast to rights to public timber, oil, gas, coal, even rangeland. It is for reasons of history, rather than economics or conscious public policy, that water has been free. Developers of water projects have never been required to make payments to the government even though the water is a public resource. They did not have to pay fair market value for the public lands that were flooded. They did not have to pay the real value of Hetch Hetchy, Glen Canyon, and all the other areas that have been lost. They also did not have to pay for the externalities, including the damage that the urban projects caused to rural communities; the damage to the commercial fishing runs, both Indian and non-Indian, or to the sports fisheries; and the damages to downstream users such as Mexico, for which we are paying now.

Project developers also did not have to go through normal financing channels. Rather, the state gave special water districts the power normally reserved for public bodies to tax people within the boundaries of the projects even though the water would ultimately go to private users. Project developers did not have to pay for most of the construction costs or for many other urban costs. If the projects had been required to bear those costs, things would have been very different. Nearly all of the projects, although publicly subsidized and often referred to as public projects, were in essence private. The water ultimately was put on private farmland and went into taps in private households. Developers received more benefit than anyone. They were the ones who pushed the projects and used city, state, and federal governing bodies to fund new land development. If we could turn back the clock and apply the historic and economic lessons we have learned, to recognize in advance that these projects were ultimately private, many of these projects would never have been built.

Today, these factors are taken into account. We do not have full computation of the costs, but we do try. In those areas where we can not adequately compute costs, we worry about the impacts. Today we are beginning to realize that if there had been no subsidies, fewer projects would have been built and they would have been built differently. Conservation efforts would be in place across the West, and it would be a very different society.

These forces will, however, be at work in the future. One of the realities for Indian water is that irrigation is not normally going to pay its way. That is just one reality, and it is only the beginning of the discussion, not the end. Many of the authors here have in different ways addressed other realities that are more abstract but are in fact driving Indian water policy.

Michael Clinton also has views on subsidies for irrigated agriculture. He believes in irrigated agriculture, in some of the abstract values inherent in it. He also believes there is a community value in water that is very hard to measure but is very important. Water projects can destroy community values, but they can also build them. Through irrigated agriculture, valuable societies, including farm and rural societies and societies in Indian Country, have been built and are a cornerstone of the West.

Clinton also argues that you cannot just look at the cost-benefit analysis, but that you also have to recognize that the United States is making an investment in a community when it builds water projects, that community value is a reason to support projects. However, he also argues, as do I, that our society is laced with subsidies at all levels and the real issue is to identify a subsidy, recognize it, analyze it, and decide upon it consciously. We have not done that historically in this field, although we are starting to do that now. Indian water policy is a classic example of the recognition that there is a community value and that subsidy can be an investment in the community. There are subsidies for which there are compelling reasons.

Other authors in this volume approach the subject of Indian water rights in different ways. John Weldon, for example, makes a point of separating out the goal of cooperation as a goal to be pursued in negotiations of Indian water rights.

And Indians speak of homelands, something they feel very passionately about. I think that word needs to be appraised carefully. A homeland, a community, is a principal reason for justifying a water project that may not be adequately accounted for in a cost-benefit analysis. These reasons are part of an "ethic of place," a sense of cooperation we have lacked in the West, but one that has been building.

Other authors demonstrate that the current settlements of Indian water rights (and, I believe, future settlements) look beyond economic analysis for another reason, which is again shown by history. David Getches calls it the period of disregard, when after *Winters* was handed down in 1908, the United States proceeded to build subsidized projects for non-Indians rather than Indians even though the Indians had the same interests and more rights. However, they had much less power during that period.

The real flesh to this book is the case studies. When examined together, several trends emerge clearly. One is surprising: the way government works. At the beginning of negotiations, earnest federal officials get on a plane in Washington, fly out West, and intone to all parties that there can be no more federal commitment, since it is Gramm-Rudman-Hollins time, and that whatever monetary commitment is asked of the federal government, it cannot be given. Parties have to figure out their own solutions, and they will have to do so without the federal government.

The western parties are polite, thank the federal official, and the official leaves. Then the western parties get on the phone to their senator or representative in Congress, who becomes very interested. Soon there is a conference call with the tribal chairperson, a head of a special irrigation district, and maybe a state representative. A water project with a federal component begins to develop. Whether it is construction funds as were provided in the Animas–La Plata Project, or substitute water, or buying out land, there is bound to be a federal component.

Peter Sly, in what I think is a very principled and interesting analysis of state interests, said that the Animas–La Plata Project was almost a miracle in Congress. That is an important point and that is one way, a perfectly accurate way, to describe it. Nevertheless, miracles seem to be very common these days in Indian water rights settlements. The case studies show that interested parties are finding federal dollars, acquiring federal commitments; and it seems to be a consensus projection that the federal commitments will continue.

They will continue for the structural reasons that these case studies illuminate. The tribes have important and well-positioned allies at the state and local levels. This new development in Indian Country has come about in part because of the politics of water and, ironically, the contentiousness over water. The tribes are building allies who out of their own self-interest support tribal projects.

Second, the tribes today, and again this is a dramatic change from past realities, have excellent technical support: engineers, lawyers, hydrologists, and econo-mists. In all these negotiations, it was clear that the tribes were at a level bar-gaining table with respect to data and representation. Tribal councilpeople have been superb negotiators, and they have more than held their own during the negotiations. The tribes, not just the representatives but the staff and council as well, do their homework. They put a lot into it. Tribal natural resources staffs are growing, and growing quickly.

Another reason Indian water rights settlements have been successful in secur-ing federal commitments is that the tribes align their congressional delegations behind the settlement. This is also a new development. Most tribes now have good day-to-day or weekly contacts with their congressional delegations over water and other issues.

Last (and this is central to the settlement process), the concept of equity favors tribal water rights. Nevertheless, the frustration and amount of time and energy it takes to work legislative settlements through Congress should not be under-stated. Tribes have a huge task ahead of them to put a settlement through, a task that is likely to take years and cause some heartache. But to be essentially opti-mistic, and assuming we will operate within the framework described above, the federal contribution will come in spite of that early conversation with the young federal official, and the states will probably contribute as well.

Indian water marketing is an important issue now and will be in the future. As a little bit of background, one of the first laws passed by the first Congress of the United States in 1790 was the Indian Non-Intercourse Act in which Congress regulated trade and intercourse with tribes. This act stated that no sale of Indian land or other real property would be valid unless Congress approved the trans-action. This was not an innovation; it had been the common law and policy of Great Britain. Since 1790, the tribes have not been able to sell real property without federal approval.

Over the ensuing years, and particularly in this century, through legislation, Congress has authorized leases and sometimes sales of tribal real property inter-ests of both specific tribal resources and allottee resources. In all of these statutes, Congress delegated authority to the Department of the Interior to monitor these leases and sales. For example, Congress has passed a tightly tailored land sale statute that allows some sales of allotment land, a much broader statute that permits leases of tribal lands and allotments, and timber sale, mineral leasing, and grazing statutes that allow alienation of these resources.

The one exception is water. Water is excepted not because of opposition to water marketing but because large-scale water marketing is a recent phenomenon in almost every part of the West. Indian water marketing is a particularly new development because the tribal water rights were not quantified, and there was also serious opposition within tribes. This opposition is dwindling, but there is still no general law that allows water marketing. Instead, water marketing is affirmed in some fashion in many water rights settlements. Water markets for Indian water are beginning to develop under individual settlement acts.

Daniel McCool draws a model for how things ought to be done. Congress has difficulty in doing anything the right way, but ideal models are valuable as a starting point or a benchmark. As I see it, the model for Indian water marketing should reflect the model set up for other Indian resources. Marketing should be allowed subject to the approval of the tribe and the Department of the Interior. Marketing agreements would also have to incorporate the principles of state law that apply, certainly the rule that no harm comes to other users of water.

There is vehement opposition now from some quarters to Indian water marketing, although this opposition has not been realized in laws that prohibit Indian water marketing. Western governors and Indian leaders have been talking about this issue and are beginning to move toward a consensus. Both sides are moving gingerly toward the idea that marketing should be subject to the concepts that underlie state water laws.

The climate of opinion on Indian water marketing will change, perhaps very rapidly, in favor of Indian marketing because of the tribes' allies at the state and local levels. These allies will be have-nots, people who are looking for water rights now. They will tend to support new supplies of water from tribes to have new sellers in the market. These potential allies are very powerful entities, including municipalities and energy companies. The consensus will build for reasons of self-interest as well as equity. It is hard to draw a principled rationale for denying tribes the right to market, for denying them the ability to treat their resource in the same manner as any other water users in the same basin. The climate will change, and at some point individual bills will be passed and Indians will be participating in water markets on their own terms. Of course, no one is going to direct them to market.

The Supreme Court's decision in the Wind River case has generated quite a bit of debate. David Getches believes the *Winters* doctrine has been preserved by the case, while John Weldon did a count of the Court and concluded that the times are changing. *Winters* and the practicably irrigable acreage test will evolve as they already have in this era of the McCarran Amendment, to the detriment of tribes. Basically, tribes are likely to lose acre-feet of water through upcoming constructions by the Court, but the *Winters* doctrine will remain substantially in place.

Lawyers and others following the development of Indian water law agree that while the ramifications of the Wind River decision have not yet been fully understood, negotiations should proceed on the basis of existing law. These settlements are some of the most progressive events in all of western public policy. They are historic for the West. They are historic for the communities in which they are

225

located. They resolve disputes and build cooperation between neighbors on water use, which provides a base for building cooperation on other levels not involving water. When negotiations result in a few agreements, the channels are established and agreements on other issues follow.

The larger context is also important here. The dream of making Indian home-lands cannot be realized unless neighbors can end their contentiousness. The case studies in this book are witness to what a good society can do when circumstances are right, because there really is justice and community building in every one of these settlements, and the West is a place that needs tight communities.

In sum, although no one can precisely determine what the Court intended when handing down the *Winters* decision, it is a decision that I feel comfortable with. Justice McKenna, a westerner, wrote evocatively in the *Winters* decision and therein set down some of the most important words ever written for the American West: that there are reasons of equity as well as real historical reasons requiring that those waters be reserved. These words evidenced a real sense of morality, built an ethic of keeping promises, and built an understanding of the ground conditions in Indian country. The *Winters* decision was intended to mean what was said in it.

In my twenty-five years of working in this field, it has been the role of morality that has touched my mind and my heart. It is a morality that comes from a sense of community, a sense of homeland, a sense of history, and a sense of promises. It is fascinating the way an abstraction such as morality can be so intensely practical. Without that morality, there would be no *Winters* doctrine and no water settlements, because it is a sense of morality that drives Indian policy. Tribal leaders are able to express this morality in an evocative and fair way, explaining the history, the promises, and the period of neglect, explaining the importance of homelands and other values that none of us fully comprehend. This morality has carried these Indian water settlements and other aspects of Indian policy.

Morality matters profoundly because it is the backdrop for all the technical matters contained in these settlements. My expectation is that this backdrop of morality will remain vivid and will remain in place and will continue to be the setting against which more fair, equitable, and community-oriented water settle-ments will be enacted.

INDEX

McClure, James, 90, 220
McLaughlin, Ann, 215, 218
Markets, agricultural, 171, 178, 180,
    190
Mescalero Apache Tribe, 212
Metropolitan Water District of Southern
    California, 76, 96
Mexico, 135, 221
Milk River, 9, 18, 79, 106
Miller, George, 91–92, 98, 99
Missouri River, 9, 104, 106, 109, 110
Missouri River basin, 67–68, 76, 108,
    110, 113 n. 17
Montana, 68, 73, 76, 103–4
Montana, state of, 73, 105, 108, 109, 112
    n. 14, 153, 157–58
Montana Attorney General's Office, 107
Montana Department of Natural Re-
    sources and Conservation, 74, 105,
    107, 109, 111
Montana Reserved Water Rights Compact
    Commission, 76, 103, 104–5, 107–9
Montana State Water Court, 76

NAPI, 177, 178–79
National forests, 15–16, 24 n. 18
National Water Commission, 13–14
National Wildlife Federation, 91
Native American Rights Fund, 73
Nature Conservancy, 197
Navajo Agricultural Products Industry,
    177, 178–79
Navajo Colorado River Agreement, 152
Navajo Division of Water Resources, 187,
    191, 192
Navajo Farm Board, 191
Navajo Indian Irrigation Project, 174,
    176, 177–79
Navajo Indian Irrigation Project Agree-
    ment, 29, 152
Navajo Irrigation Office, 191, 192
Navajo Nation, 100, 153, 155, 179, 185–
    86, 191

Navajo Reservation, 75, 176, 186, 191–
    93
Nebraska, 65, 68
Need, quantification and, 80, 81–82, 85
Negotiated settlements. *See also*
    Settlements
    benefits of, 49, 218–19
    characteristics of, 80, 84–85, 90
    federal role in, 20, 30–31, 76, 122
    goals of, 82, 94, 95–96, 154–58, 160–
        61
    implementation of, 95–96, 156–57
    influence of, 156, 225–26
    litigation and, 89, 219
    models of, 42, 115, 160–61
    participants in, 130
Negotiations
    drawbacks to, 34, 73, 100–101
    elements of, 27, 29, 33–34, 47, 90, 94,
        149, 151–52
    goals of, 31, 63–64, 90, 103, 147,
        148, 149, 158, 159–60, 222
    implementation of, 37, 158
    litigation and, 2, 3, 28, 35, 37, 96, 149
    participants in, 47, 49, 62, 76, 94, 136,
        148, 150, 153, 219, 224
    process of, 22, 151, 223
    purposes of, 19, 28–29, 30, 35, 77
    time required for, 103, 110
Nevada, 73
Nevada, state of, 22, 198, 199
Nevada Department of Wildlife, 197–98,
    200–201
Nevada Waterfowl Association, 197
Newlands Irrigation Project, 195
Newlands Reclamation Project, 16, 69 n.
    4, 196–98, 200–201
New Mexico, 73, 76, 211–12
New Mexico, state of, 77
NIIP, 29, 152, 174, 176, 177–79
1905 Act, 210
Ninth Circuit Court, 75–76
Nixon, Richard M., 218

CONTRIBUTORS

Editors

Thomas R. McGuire
  is Associate Research Anthropologist with the Bureau of Applied Research in
  Anthropology (BARA), University of Arizona. His publications include *Politics
  and Ethnicity on the Rio Yaqui: Potam Revisited* and articles on Native American resource use, which have appeared in *Human Organization, American
  Indian Culture and Research Journal, Journal of the Southwest,* and other
  journals. He was a principal investigator and coauthor of the socioeconomic
  impact assessment of the San Xavier Planned Community near Tucson, which
  has been issued as an occasional paper by BARA, entitled *A City on the Reservation*. His current research activities focus on the shrimp industry and
  endangered marine mammals in the Gulf of California. He received a Ph.D.
  in anthropology from the University of Arizona in 1979.

William B. Lord
  is Professor of Agricultural and Resource Economics, of Hydrology and Water
  Resources, and of Renewable Natural Resources at the University of Arizona.
  He is the former Director of the Water Resources Research Center at that
  university, as well as of the Center for Resource Policy Studies and Programs
  at the University of Wisconsin. His Ph.D. in natural resource economics is
  from the University of Michigan. He is the editor of the *Water Resources
  Bulletin*. His writings have appeared in the *Water Resources Bulletin, Natural*

Resources Journal, the *Journal of the American Agricultural Economics Association,* and others. Lord has two primary research interests, one in interdisciplinary collective choice theory, the other in multidisciplinary modeling as an aid to natural resource policy analysis and conflict resolution. He is currently leading a long-term, seven-state research program on institutional adaptation to severe drought in the Colorado River Basin.

Mary G. Wallace

is Senior Research Specialist with the Water Resources Research Center, University of Arizona. Her publications include book chapters, monographs, and other professional papers about various aspects of Indian water rights, including leasing and dispute resolution. Current research interests include improving the evaluation of natural resource policies, and ecosystem management approaches to natural resource management. She has a B.A. and an M.A. in Political Science from the University of Arizona and is currently enrolled in the Ph.D. program.

Contributors

Michael J. Clinton

is Senior Vice President, Bookman-Edmonston Engineering, Inc., Sacramento, California.

Harvey Doerksen

is a program analyst with the Office of Program Analysis, U.S. Department of the Interior, Washington, D.C.

John A. Folk-Williams

is a partner with Western Network, Santa Fe.

David H. Getches

is Professor of Law, University of Colorado.

John W. Leeper

is a senior engineer with Natural Resources Consulting Engineers, Inc., in Fort Collins, Colorado.

Daniel McCool

is Associate Dean of the College of Social and Behavioral Science and Associate Professor of Political Science, University of Utah.

Mary McNally

is Assistant Professor in the Department of Management and Economics, Eastern Montana College, Billings.

Roger Mann
  is a senior analyst with Biosystems Analysis, Inc., in Tiburon, California.

Kenneth G. Maxey
  is Assistant Administrator for Power, Operations and Maintenance, Western Area Power Administration.

Joseph R. Membrino
  is an attorney with the firm of Hall, Estill, Hardwick, Gable, Golden & Nelson, Washington.

Austin Nuñez
  is Chairman of the San Xavier District Council, Tohono O'odham Nation.

Teno Roncalio
  is an attorney in Cheyenne, Wyoming, and former Special Master for the Wind River adjudication.

Benjamin Simon
  is an economist with the Office of Program Analysis, U.S. Department of the Interior, Washington, D.C.

Peter W. Sly
  is an attorney with Payne, Thompson, Walker and Taaffe, San Francisco, and a former director of the Conference of Western Attorneys General.

Norman H. Starler
  is an analyst with the Water Resources Branch, Office of Management and Budget, Washington.

William H. Swan
  is an attorney for the Office of the Field Solicitor, U.S. Department of the Interior, Phoenix.

John B. Weldon, Jr.,
  is a partner in the law firm of Jennings, Strouss & Salmon, Phoenix.

Charles F. Wilkinson
  is the Moses Lasky Professor of Law, University of Colorado.

David Yardas
  is Water Resources Analyst with the Environmental Defense Fund, Oakland, California.

Robert A. Young
  is Professor Emeritus in the Department of Agricultural and Resource Economics, Colorado State University.